Inshore ~ Offshore

Inshore~ Offshore

Racing, Cruising & Design

Michael Pocock

NAUTICAL

Published in Great Britain 1986 by NAUTICAL BOOKS an imprint of Conway
Maritime Press Ltd., 24 Bride Lane, Fleet Street,
London EC4Y 8DR.

ISBN 0 85177 389 3

Typeset by Witwell Ltd, Liverpool
Printed in Great Britain by The Bath Press, Bath

Contents

ACKNOWLEDGEMENTS

The author and publisher wish to express their thanks to Peter Cook, editor of *Yachts and Yachting*, for permission to use the author's articles from that magazine, on which much of the material in this book is based.

Chapter 6 originally appeared in *Yachting Monthly* and thanks are due to the editor.

Illustrated by Ray Harvey MRINA, BSc, CEng.

Photographic credits:

Studio 77 (p 35); Patrick Roach (p 36, 143, 145, 147, 148, 179); Beken (p 158); William Payne (p 187, 193); Iain McLuckie (p 29); Brian Manby (p 12) and the Author.

Author's preface

Sailing has dominated my life since I first lived within reach of the water 35 years ago and I have seen many changes. One thing, however, has never changed and that is that magic feeling that one experiences when the sails fill and the boat comes to life. The quality of that magic is dependent on many things. It is spoiled by a poor hull shape or an overweight construction, by too much sail or too little, or by an unhappy crew. When all is as it should be in that small and immediate world that one occupies when at sea in a yacht, then one experiences Sailing with a Capital 'S'.

The sensation of everything falling into place is a marvellous feeling that lifts sailing from the commonplace of merely travelling across the water to the higher experience of a musician playing on a well-tuned and responsive instrument. This sense of rightness is to be found in every aspect of sailing from a sailboard to an 80-footer; from simple messing about in boats to world cruising and from the most modest attempts at racing to competing in 12 Metres for the America's Cup.

This coming to life has another aspect. One part of the magic is to have been involved in the building of a yacht, to have watched her grow as a lifeless shell in a shed, gradually acquiring more and more component parts, to see her launched and rigged and to hoist the sails for the first time. That collection of parts becomes a living whole. The unity of the total yacht becomes clear. Everything that was upright for so many months in a cradle moves together. Her movement can be felt through every part of her.

When a boat is building one can be excused for speaking of 'it' just as an unborn baby is an 'it' until its gender is known. Any man who speaks of his yacht as 'it', after he has sailed in her, has not felt that living quality that should be there.

The magic of sailing is to be found in so many ways and it would be quite wrong to assume that speed is an essential. Of course it is of paramount importance to the racing fraternity although, it is not necessarily out and out speed that provides the satisfaction. It is so often speed, attained in specific circumstances and within the limitations of a particular type, that is important. The racing sailor can gain equal satisfaction from $1\frac{1}{2}$ knots achieved in a near calm and on a glassy sea as he can from 8 knots in stronger conditions. To the cruising sailor satisfaction comes from a yacht that serves him well, from the confidence he has in her ability to withstand bad weather, and in the comforts that are built into the vessel, allowing the relaxation that is needed to complement the thrills and excitements that may be found upon the way. The cruising sailor needs to be proud of his yacht's performance, but only in the context of the limitations imposed by the standards of the living conditions that he wishes to take with him, and by the amount of physical effort that he and his crew are prepared to exert.

One of the great attractions of sailing is that it provides something for everybody, male and female, young and old alike. There are aspects of racing that require either physical strength or sheer weight such that few girls can attain. On the other hand, there are classes where all girls or mixed crews can compete on level terms. Clare Francis, Dame Naomi James and Cathy Foster have proved that there are few male bastions left that can not be entered by the fairer sex. There is unfortunately no singular pronoun available to apply to a sailor to accommodate both sexes so that when, within these pages, I speak of a sailing person as 'he' the 'he' or 'she' should please be understood. In my life it has been a source of constant delight that Pat and I sail together as a man and wife team. We have even been so fortunate as to have brought up a son and daughter both equally keen. We have enjoyed thousands of miles of cruising as a family and we are fully aware how fortunate we have been to have had this pleasure.

This question of a team effort is another of the intriguing aspects of sailing. This is, more so for some than others, and many find great delight in single handed sailing. Whether in a sailing dinghy or an ocean going yacht, the singlehander has a feeling of being at one with his machine. To the singlehander, probably more than any other, the boat takes on a personality complementary to his own. The great majority of sailors on the other hand enjoy the companionship and the sense of shared achievement that comes from sailing with others. The racing that takes place under the International Offshore Rule is very labour intensive, involving every member of the crew. This, to my mind, has been one of the greatest reasons for its success. Skippers and helmsmen tend to attract the limelight but they are nowhere without a good crew. This generates the 'esprit de corps' that binds a crew together so that they are proud to wear the yacht's name on their tee shirts and hunt as a group on their run ashore.

There are those for whom sailing has no delights to offer; obviously they are not attracted to the water in the same way. Some of them will attempt to mock the scene. Heaven knows, there are many, many aspects of sailing that just do not appear to make sense. It is clearly an anachronism in this supersonic day and age to travel in a vessel that for many of us never achieves much more than walking speed or, at best, a gentle trot. We are prepared to live in an oversize cocktail shaker, heeled to 20 degrees or more for long periods. We ignore the damp which, any other day of the week on shore, we would carp about very loudly.

We sometimes tell ourselves that the wind is free and we are getting something for nothing. This is nonsense. The fact that you are not burning fuel when under sail does little to compensate for the overspending that we are all of us prone to when it comes to equipping our boats. The old sayings that a yacht is a hole in the ocean into which we pour money, or, that ocean racing is like standing under a cold shower tearing up fivers are as true today as they ever were; with suitable adjustment for inflation!

It is probably because sailing is so opposite to our normal everyday routine, so devoid of mechanical noise, and so reliant on the forces of nature that it provides the escape and refreshment that we need.

To some the term 'yacht' has a certain ring of affluence. This is an understandable, though perhaps outdated attitude. It registers the same distinction as between a Yacht Club, with its echoes of a social elitism and a Sailing Club with a suggestion of a less status conscious way of doing things. One hopes that in the 1980s this division is a thing of the past. In the dictionary a yacht is a 'light sailing vessel for racing'; or 'a vessel other than a row boat or canoe kept for the owner's pleasure'. The second of these two definitions is to me the more acceptable allowing the owner the option of obtaining his pleasure from either racing or cruising, or a combination of the two.

When the media report on boat shows or major yachting events such as Cowes week, they love to drag the money side of the scene in front of the cameras. This is a natural tendency for a casual observer to take. If there were no rich men there would be no big yachts and how much poorer the scene would be if, in the great process of social levelling, we all ended up in a state of ghastly uniformity. I love the big yachts, their power and magnificence holds me spellbound, but I have not the least desire to own one. It should be remembered that an owner spending, say, £250,000 on a racing yacht probably carries a crew of 12 or more and many of these may be as poor as church mice. The rich owner very often provides a lot of enjoyment for the less well endowed and the sensation seeking commentators do not always recognize this view.

A love of boats will take different people down different paths. As a designer my activities afloat have inevitably been linked to my own designs. This, perhaps, is the principal reason why I have found myself racing as well as cruising.

To me racing is done on behalf of the boat, as a means of proving and developing my designs. Make no mistake, I have enjoyed my racing; particularly when we have won! I would not, on the other hand, find so much enjoyment from racing in a one-design class, where success depends less on the superiority of the boat and more on the skill of the helmsman and crew. I might never have won!

As a regular contributor to *Yachts and Yachting* magazine I have written about the things that I believe I know best. I have written about racing from the standpoint of an owner who wants his boat to have the best chance of success.

I have written about design in terms which I hope the layman will understand. As a layman myself for many years, I like to feel that I have a feeling for the aspects of design, that the ordinary mortal might have difficulty in digesting.

I have written about the International Offshore Rule, the IOR, because, whether you race or not, the rule has a vast influence on the yachts we sail today.

I have written about cruising because I love cruising. To me cruising under sail is the ultimate goal. Racing may be an excellent way of consuming an excess of adrenalin and packing some exciting sailing into limited available time. It could be because I am getting longer in the tooth, but to me, the time comes when I am no longer content with sailing round a course and I must seek further horizons, new anchorages and the satisfaction of efficient passage making.

This, therefore, is what this book is all about, a bit of racing, a bit of design, and a bit of cruising. If through these pages I help the readers to a greater enjoyment of their sailing then my object will have been achieved.

PART ONE

DESIGN

Starlight, *my first design, won the Class V RORC Points Championship in 1976.*

1

When lines are drawn

A certain amount is written in the yachting press today that features the latest computer-assisted design techniques, employed by some of the leading design offices. There is no doubt that, properly used, these facilities tremendously expand the scope of the designer and it would be understandably dismissed as sour grapes if I used these pages to snipe at such techniques.

What I feel should be remembered is that the computers still have to be programmed by humans employing the same basic precepts that are used in the humblest design offices.

I use a micro computer for the hydrostatic calculations, for the elementary disciplines of deck designs and for the calculation and analysis of IOR ratings. With regard to hull designs I am unlikely to become involved in computer techniques and, as I enjoy the traditional process of lines drawing, I am not particularly jealous of the more advanced methods that computerisation can make available.

In the pages that follow I refer entirely to the simple techniques which are to my mind the fundamentals.

To understand computer-assisted design one must first absorb the basic fundamentals that are the guide lines for the computer programme and for this reason alone I hope that these pages will be some use.

These elementary precepts are not outdated by the advent of the computer. The computer is a very powerful tool for exploring a multitude of options analytically. It can not, on the other hand, produce one single original thought and for this, thank God, a human brain is still required.

Starlight

Ten years on it seems that it must have been a particularly romantic notion that prompted me to take a clean sheet of paper and design my first boat. That piece of paper led to a winter of frantic boatbuilding culminating on April Fool's day, 1976, with the launch of *Starlight*. The season that followed included winning the RORC Class V Points Championship, and from that piece of paper I became a yacht designer.

Starlight was not revolutionary. She was basically the product of a study of contemporary designs at the forefront of the racing scene. I wrote two articles for *Yachts and Yachting* on the IOR based on three leading one tonners, *High Tension*, designed by Jac de Ridder, *Golden Apple*, designed by Ron Holland and *Gumboots*, designed by Doug Peterson. These articles appeared under the title of 'High Apple Boots'. Leading the reader through the main elements of the rule they created a hypothetical design based on an appreciation of the relevant values of the principal factors of the rule formula.

I still have that piece of paper, *Starlight's* lines drawing, today and it shows that I designed a boat first and learnt how I should have done it afterwards. In fact as designer, builder and owner, I was able to go to full size almost immediately and dispense with the need for particularly accurate drawing at a small scale.

The IOR has always placed great emphasis on particular measurement points so that, by comparison with the data which can be obtained from the certificates of leading boats, it is possible for the newcomer to identify any areas in which his design is far outside the norm. This gave me the confidence to go ahead and build *Starlight*.

The theme of the design was almost exactly as put forward in the 'High Apple Boots' articles. Thanks to an understanding of the rule which far exceeded my understanding of naval architecture in the wider sense, I was able to produce a winner which, in a more refined form, went into production the following winter and sold nearly 40 boats.

Two years in Laurent Giles' office, before once again becoming my own master, taught me those bits that I had dodged when drawing *Starlight*. The first thing that I did, under Peter Anstey's expert direction, was to redraw the *Starlight* lines plan to a professional standard. Since then lines drawing has become almost an obsession. Lines drawing always has been a most exacting ritual for most yacht designers and necessarily so. The nagging thought in the back of any designer's head is that, if the lines are not drawn meticulously and the

The Half Breadth Plan. The top half of the drawing is a contour map of the hull seen from above. The lines D1 to D7 are the 45° diagonals referred to in a later paragraph.

The Sheer Plan. This is in effect a contour map of the hull laid on its side. The grid lines have been marked so that the waterlines on the Half Breadth Plan are easily recognisable.

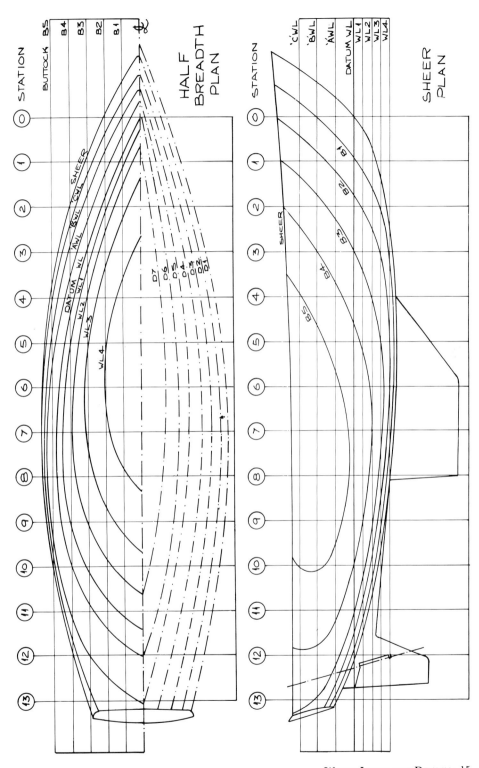

STATION

BUTTOCK BS
B4
B3
B2
B1
₵

HALF
BREADTH
PLAN

SHEER
BWL
CWL
AWL
DATUM WL
WL2 WL1
WL3
WL4

D7
D6
D5
D4
D3
D2
D1

STATION

'CWL
'BWL
'AWL
DATUM WL
WL1
WL2
WL3
WL4

SHEER
PLAN

B1
B2
B3
SHEER
B4
B5

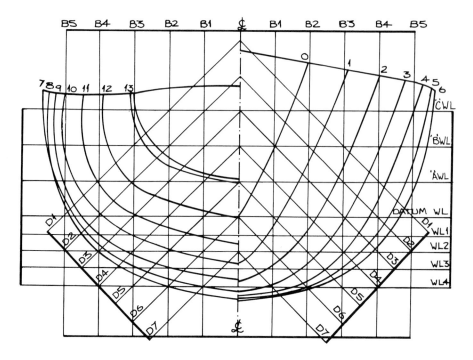

The Body Plan. The curved lines are the Stations 0—13. The grid lines have all been marked so that the relationship with the Half Breadth and Sheer Plans can be appreciated.

offsets very accurately taken off, then the builder will take over and build a compromise boat that is 'near enough' but may, in fact, differ radically from the original concept.

The hull of a yacht is an entirely three dimensional concept on the part of her designer, and the lines are a means of expressing that concept in a series of related two dimensional drawings. The mechanics of communicating the exact hull form, from the designer's drawing board to the boatbuilder, centre entirely round the lines. The basic procedure is that the designer draws an extremely accurate set of lines to a convenient scale. He then lifts with scale ruler and magnifying glass, the offsets, which are a series of coordinates related to a grid. These are then issued in the form of a schedule. They enable the builder to reproduce the designer's lines full size on the 'loft' floor and from that 'lofting' take a pattern or template of any fore and aft, or athwartships, section necessary to cut out the frames, bulkheads, stem sections, the transom and so on, depending on the form of construction.

The 'lines' are, in effect, a series of contour maps of the hull as seen from three separate angles. These are known as the half breadth plan, the sheer plan and the body plan.

If you imagine a hull upside down in a building shed and yourself as a fly on the ceiling looking down, then there below you is the half breadth plan. In order to be complete of course it is necessary for someone to have drawn lines on one half of the hull at specific levels parallel to the water line. Just as on an Ordnance Survey map, where the slope is steepest, as in the topsides, the contours are closest together and as the hull gets flatter underneath so they spread apart.

The sheer plan is a little more difficult to appreciate. It is easy enough to see that it is a view of the yacht from one side. The contours, in this case, are created by the imaginary application of a gigantic bacon slicer which has sliced the hull at regular intervals parallel to the centre line. They have then been glued together again leaving a line upon the surface of the hull. These lines are known as the bow and buttock lines, more simply referred to as the buttocks.

The body plan is the easiest to read. It shows the cross sections of the yacht at each station and sometimes as half stations. It is generally drawn with the forward half of the yacht on the right hand side of the plan and the aft sections on the left hand side.

Now it is not always fully understood how inter-related these three drawings really are. If you look at the body plan, you will see a grid of straight lines superimposed on the curves of the sections. The horizontal straight lines are the waterlines, which are the curved lines of the half breadth plan. The vertical straight lines are the buttocks which are the curved lines of the sheer plan. Now look at the sheer plan and you will see the grid again, waterlines running horizontally and sections, or stations as they should be called, drawn vertically. Look yet again at the half breadth plan and the stations are again the vertical straight lines and the horizontal straight lines are the buttocks.

For the designer's drawing to make sense, and to avoid embarrassment when his offsets reach the loft floor, all these intersections between curved 'hull lines' and straight 'grid lines' must exactly correspond in relation to the grid from one drawing to the other.

In addition to the waterlines, buttocks and sections, nearly all designers draw two or more diagonals, generally the development of slices cut at around 90°to the surface of the midsection). They act as an excellent guide to the three dimensional qualities of the lines when considered as a whole. Personally, having learnt my lines drawing in the Laurent Giles office, I draw all my diagonals at 45° to the centre line and waterlines.

From time to time this causes a few raised eyebrows and I am called upon to explain the merits of the system. With regard to their use in judging the quality of the lines, I have no reason to feel that they are any more or any less effective than diagonals laid out on any other basis. In this respect the most important fact is that I consistently lay them out in this way and so comparisons with previous lines are of the greatest value.

Where the 45° diagonals are most valuable in the development of the lines, is that their use means that fairness is almost guaranteed to a high standard straightaway. It should be explained that unlike the conventional diagonal, which is drawn as a projection of the slice of the boat laid flat, mine are in plan as they would be seen if they had been drawn in on the surface of the boat. The offsets that I lift from the lines plan are half breadths and Pythagoras must be employed to convert that to a measurement down the diagonal as is most useful when working on a body plan.

If you study the body plan you will appreciate that the grid is drawn in such a way that the 45° diagonals are passing through the intersections of the waterlines and the buttocks. This means that when on the half breadth plan a diagonal crosses a waterline it must do so where the waterline crosses the grid line of the relevant buttock. This presents the most powerful control so that, provided these interesections are carefully managed as the drawing develops, the results must be fair all the way from start to finish.

The easy way to explain the intricacies of lines drawing is to proceed, step by step, through the process and demonstrate the development of the lines.

Firstly I must stress that there is no such creature as a British Standard Yacht Designer and everybody's methods vary according to their original background. Various tricks of the trade have been developed to suit each designer's sense of priority and there is no laid down, hard and fast, procedure.

The first move is to draw the grid on a clean sheet of film. I use a polyester film. It is just like tracing paper except that it is demensionally stable; it does not shrink on a damp night; it does not stretch or wrinkle and it does not tear easily. It is not cheap.

My drawing board is 6ft long and flat and I choose the scale for each lines drawing to comfortably fit the grid for the half breadth and sheer plans, plus the body plan at the left hand end, on to the table.

In theory, at least, the larger the scale the greater the accuracy. I have never drawn lines to a larger scale that 1 : 8 and never smaller than 1 : 15. My opinion is that the beam of the yacht is more critical than the length and when drawing a 56ft yacht which had only 10ft 6in beam, I found it necessary to draw at 1 : 10 to obtain sufficient accuracy. At that scale the fore and aft drawing required the full length of the board and the body plan was consigned to a separate piece of film.

The grid should be drawn in ink with the thinnest practical line. A

This shows the construction of the master section of which the shaded, immersed, area is used to calculate a provisional displacement. The half breadth of the Datum Water Line is then transferred to the half breadth plan to create a controlling factor in the development of the Datum Water Line itself. The profile and sheer line are at this stage purely notional. (see page 23)

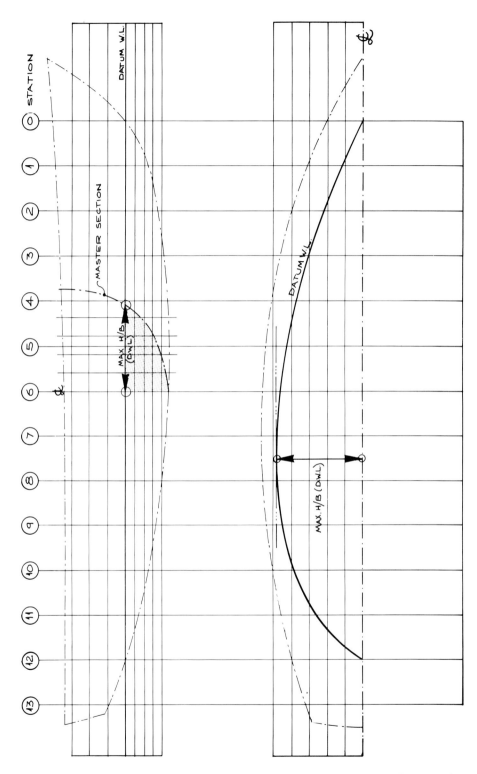

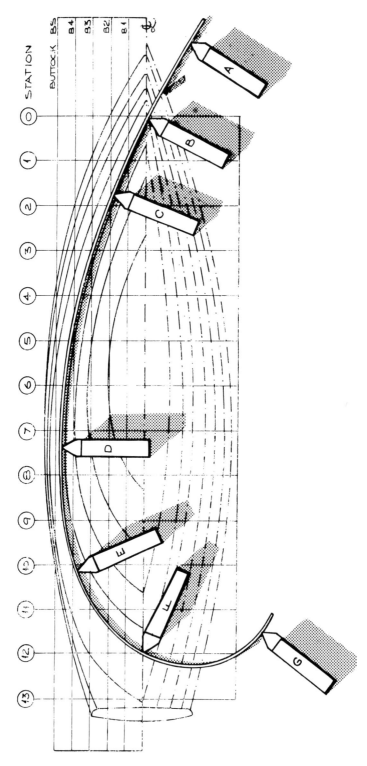

0.10 or 0.15mm nib is probably the ideal. It cannot be stressed too strongly that the accuracy of the grid is of paramount importance. There is no question of using a T square from the edge of the board. I have a first class steel straight edge, the length of the table and for verticals, I set the straight edge on a base line and use a good quality square.

Choosing the intervals for the waterlines and buttocks is a matter of personal choice. I like to have three or four waterlines (A–D) within the topsides and halve the spacing below Datum waterline.

Occasionally if I know that I am planning to make a half model from the lines, I choose an interval to suit available materials. If this is to be the case and the scale is 1 : 10 then waterlines at 240mm (120mm below DWL) will mean that 12mm ply will be ideal. The model can be made direct from the lines drawing and will be extremely accurate.

When I draw a lines drawing I superimpose the half breadth and sheer plans on each other. This makes the transfer of intersections from one to the other quicker and more accurate. What one is drawing is in fact exactly what the boatbuilder will draw full size on the loft floor.

Most designers divide the water line into ten equal intervals giving eleven stations; that is 0–10 inclusive. I prefer thirteen or, in other words 0–12 inclusive. The original reason for this was that in the days of imperial measurements a 30ft WL yacht had stations at 30in centres. However there is another reason which is related to Simpson's rule, by which displacement calculations are made. Simpson's relies on odd numbers of stations for which 0–10 or 0–12 are equally effective. However when developing lines in the early stages of design, it is useful to be able to take a quick displacement assessment off alternate stations. Taking the even numbers of 0–12 still gives an uneven number of stations, where 0–10 does not.

In addition to the principal stations it is usual to add stations in overhangs and intermediate stations in the forebody and skeg areas to provide greater accuracy when lifting offsets. When drawing a critical IOR design it is only sense to add stations in way of the measurement points in order to emphasise their importance to the builder. These supplementary stations are best added after the completion of the lines and before lifting offsets.

Using Station 6 as a centre line I draw in one side of the athwartships grid lightly in pencil and then I draw a 'master section'. This is not any particular station but a section drawn as though it passes through all the points of maximum beam at each level. It is in fact the outline of the yacht when seen from dead ahead. The significance of this will become clear as the drawing proceeds. (See diagram page 19)

If the curve is to be fair, it should be possible to move either weight C, D or E individually without the spline moving. (see page 23)

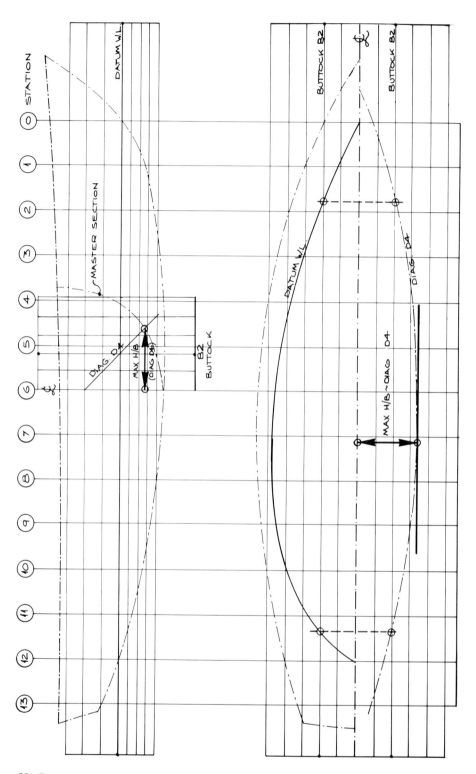

The master section is related to the canoe body only, the hull without appendages, and a measurement of the underwater area will give a reasonably accurate forecast of the ultimate volume of the whole canoe body. This is generally around about 56% of the product of the master section immersed area multiplied by the waterline length. This figure varies according to type and one learns from previous designs the most suitable factor.

Having drawn an acceptable master section, the next line to put in is the Datum Water Line. This must start from the centre line at Station 0 and terminate on the centre line at Station 12. We are not, at this stage, concerned with distortions and appendages which will come later. The other controlling factor which we know already is the maximum beam waterline which we can lift directly from the master section. By drawing a line parallel to the centre line at exactly the maximum beam I have a strict control knowing that the curve of Datum WL must be to that parallel line.

The character of the Datum WL is fundamental to the shape of the yacht and so it is a line which must be drawn with the utmost care and consideration. Each designer has very strong views on the creation of a DWL. It must be a line of impeccable quality or the whole of the rest of the design will be impaired.

This would seem to be a useful point to say something about the use splines and weights when drawing the lines of a fair hull. It has been said that only five weights should be needed to hold a spline when drawing a waterline and this is basically true. My own methods employ seven, of which any of the central three can be individually lifted without the spline moving. Of these seven, two of them are outside the boat. What is not always readily understood is that for a curve to be fair its continuation must be determined beyond the limit of direct interest. Consider the fig on p 20. The waterline is very nearly straight in the first few feet of the boat so that weight A has, in this case, little significance. However, in the run aft there is a great deal of curvature and this can not be achieved without weight G which is responsible for controlling the spline between F and E. It should be possible to lift either C, D or E in turn without any movement of the spline. Do not imagine, on the other hand, that you can draw an accurate line drawing with only seven weights. When the curve has been established and before running the pencil round the spline at least seven more weights should be added to guarantee that the spline does not deflect as the pencil passes. I have 18

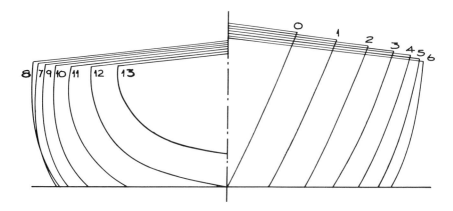

This diagram illustrates the discipline which is used to relate the sheer line to the deck outline. By drawing lines at a constant pitch from the centre line to cut the half breadth of the deck outline, a sheer line is created in profile. The vertical interval on the centre line controls the balance between forward and aft freeboard and the pitch controls the amount of hollow. Increase the angle and the sweep of the sheer will be more pronounced and vice versa. At 0° the sheer is straight.

weights most of which weigh 5lb, so my drawing table needs to be strong and stable.

The next line I draw is the diagonal which starts in the B waterline and crosses the DWL in buttock II. We already know the maximum beam of this diagonal and can once again draw a parallel line against which it must 'tan'. Putting in this diagonal forces me to consider the profile in the overhangs and this is necessarily related to the fore and aft position of the 'tan' point at its maximum beam. The nature of this diagonal and its fore and aft symmetry are to me fundamental to the balance characteristics of the hull.

My next move is to put in the deck and this requires a certain amount of what can best be described as judicious preconception. There is at this stage relatively little established with regard to the deck. The forward end can only be fixed by first deciding on the freeboard at the stem head and extending the profile of the stem, which is so far fixed at two points only. The maximum beam is only available from the master section if we first decide on the freeboard at the point of maximum beam. Finally, there is virtually no control over the aft end of the deck unless we draw a trial section on say Station 12. This can be done because the diagonal that we have drawn gives us a half breadth where the section crosses the diagonal and this limits the angle at which the curve rises from the centre line.

We have therefore, provisionally, a beam on deck at Station 12, a maximum beam on deck and a point on the centre line for the forward end of the deck. In choosing these points we have at the same time three provisional freeboard positions which will limit the character of the sheer line.

As we draw in our provisional deck outline we still have considerable option in choosing its characteristics. If we place the maximum beam position well forward we will tend to increase the flare of the bow sections and create a fullness in the deck outline forward. This may be good for a cruising boat but can obviously be rather overdone on a racing boat.

As soon as the deck outline is fixed I feel compelled to fix the sheer line at the same time. My sheer lines are fixed by a set formula related to the changing breadth of the deck. This is not my own invention but something that I learnt from Jack Giles long before I ever thought of being a designer myself. Unless the hollow of the sheer is very carefully related to the curve of the deck outline the effect, when seen in three dimensions, will be very disturbing. There are in existence yachts whose sheer lines have been considered in two dimensions only and when heeled their curve becomes totally unrelated to the original concept.

The principle I use is that the sheer line is created by a flat plane cutting the topsides at an angle, rather as though a pitch roof was set up over the deck. The ridge of that roof is falling from the bow to the stern and the greater the angle of the pitch, the greater the sweep or hollow of the sheer line. In Jack Giles days this effect was created on the drawing board graphically. Nowadays it is a simple matter to write a programme for a calculator or micro computer which, given the input of the half breadths of the deck, can print out the freeboards at each station to draw a perfect sheerline. The variables are the height at the stem, the pitch of the line that runs from the ridge to the deck edge, and the decrement by which the height of the ridge is reduced as it passes each station. I have a record of these figures for each yacht I have drawn and very easily adjust them to suit a new project. Some fiddling with the inputs is necessary to persuade the sheerline to correspond with the previously determined freeboard positions but this is not difficult.

Having fixed the deck outline, the datum waterline, and one diagonal we now have three fixed points on the rake curve. This is not a universally recognised feature of lines drawing but to me it is fundamental. If we consider the lines that we have already drawn (see page 27) and concentrate on the profile, we can transfer the points of maximum beam from the deck outline on to a point on the sheerline (A), from the datum waterline on to the relevant grid line (B) and from the diagonal and the master section to a point below the waterline (C) that corresponds when seen in profile.

Every time that we draw a new waterline or diagonal the point of maximum beam will generate another point somewhere between or below A, B and C and the line that is traced through them will be the Rake Curve. If the yacht is to have a fair hull body that Rake curve must be a smooth and logical curve.

Once one has experience of the use of the rake curve it will be found that, apart from being an aid to lines drawing, it is an instant signature of the character of the hull. Hull balance is essentially related to the character of the rake curve particularly in relation to the effects of heeling. When we come to put in the Buttocks their lowest point must occur on the rake curve at a height that can be transferred from the master section.

As a firm believer in the importance of the rake curve I invariably pencil it in at the earliest possible stage and use its existence as a major control point for each subsequent line that follows.

The truth about this system is that the design process centres round the creation of the master section, the datum waterline, the diagonal starting in the 'B' waterline, the development of the 12 station and the hardening in of the rake curve. Once these lines have been adopted the filling in of the remaining lines is a semi mechanical process over which a great deal of option has been surrendered by the adoption of those early lines.

All the above relates to the drawing of what may be described as the creation of a pure concept of totally fair lines. They will flow smoothly from one end to the other in any dimension that one may choose. Any influence of the IOR is going to cancel that purity instantly. In the first place the measurement of the Beam waterline and the rated Beam are both made in the same station as the Maximum Beam. As the designer wishes to obtain the maximum value in each case he is forced to draw a rake curve that is unnaturally steep, as near vertical as possible, from the waterline up to the deck and this is a very inhibiting factor. The flare of the aft sections necessary to obtain satisfactory values for Beam Aft and Beam Aft Inner is hardly conducive to a truly fair concept; to say nothing of the distortions at the aft end of the waterline to fudge the Aft Overhang Component. The mid depth station is often drawn with a curve not unlike the outline of a fifty pence piece so that purity of line is hardly likely.

What will she look like?

Sadly very few lines drawings are published these days. When they are it is sad to reflect how much stony ground the precious details fall upon. Lines drawings are not easily understood by the uninitiated but, given some study and consideration, they can be very rewarding.

Having introduced the reader to the language of the lines plan, the next stage is to try to suggest some means of translating the lines into understandable characteristics, so that faced with a lines drawing it will

Having drawn in the edge of deck and the sheer line it is possible to generate a Rake Curve through all the points of maximum beam transferred to the profile.

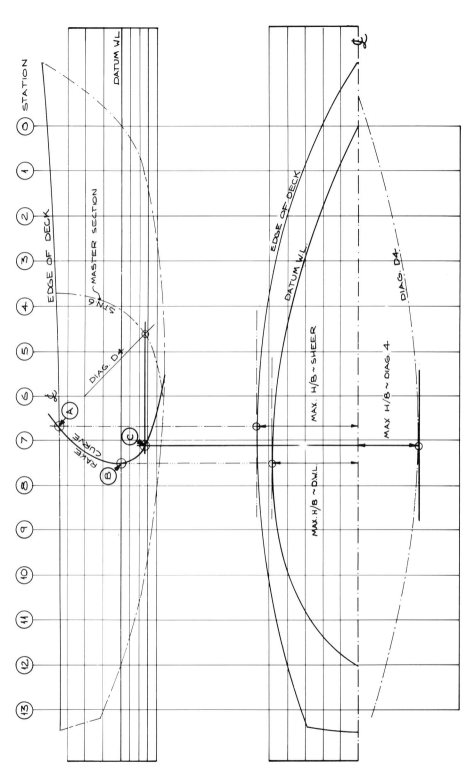

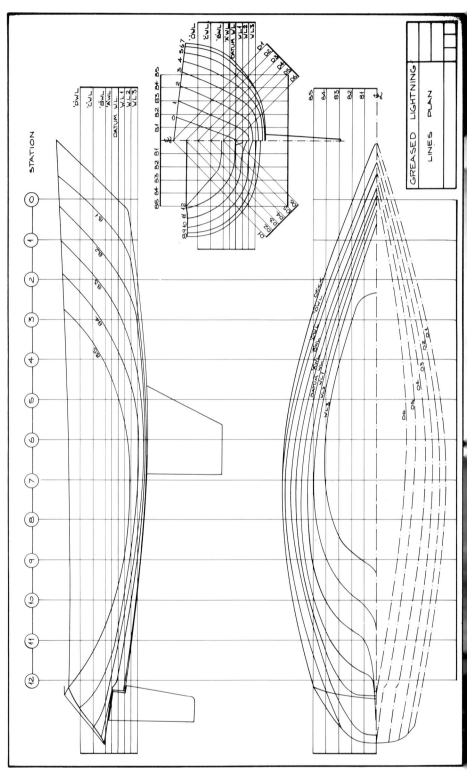

STATION

DWL
CWL
BWL
AWL
DATUM WL
WL 1
WL 2
WL 3

GREASED LIGHTNING

LINES PLAN

DOW DECK
DWL
CWL
BWL
AWL
DATUM WL
WL 1
WL 2
WL 3

Greased Lightning, *launched in 1982 has had a series of successful seasons racing in the Irish Sea.*

be possible to visualise the type of hull that the designer has drawn.

Pages 28 and 31 and show the lines of two of my designs which have been chosen principally because they provide a distinct contrast. *Greased Lightning* is an IOR design of 1982 vintage which enjoyed some success in the Irish sea in her first two seasons. She is 38ft loa, 30ft lwl, 12.07ft beam with a displacement of 6.2 tons. *Blackjack*, designed for the 1981 Two handed Transatlantic race, has total disregard of the IOR. Her length figures are identical to *Greased Lightning*, her beam, however, is only 11.08ft and her displacement is 7.6 tons. If you ignore the appendages *Blackjack* has a fair balanced hull with a well swept rake curve whereas *Greased Lightning*, though reasonably balanced for an IOR design, has a rake curve which is near vertical above the waterline and swept forward below. Distortions were the order of the day and purity of line was necessarily sacrificed.

The first and most obvious difference between the two drawings is the tight radius below the waterline, between the straight raked stem

Greased Lightning's *lines are fairly typical of IOR yachts of the early 80s. She has a distinct crease just aft of the Station 12 to reduce rated length. In this lines plan an additional waterline has been added above the DWL to ensure absolute accuracy in the critical areas.*

Blackjack *seen in profile showing the depth of the canoe body and the relatively large lateral area.*

and the forefoot on *Greased Lightning*, compared with the much more gentle transition on *Blackjack*. That tight radius is essentially related to the forward sections which are similarly straight above the waterline and tightly tucked into the underwater body. It will be seen that this radius becomes less tight at each station working aft and this is reflected in the buttocks, each one being progressively less tightly radiused as they come away from the centre line profile. On *Blackjack* the stations are again a reflection of the profile with a general absence of an abrupt angle between topsides and underwater form.

If it were not for the fullness of the deck outline on *Blackjack*, drawn to give a generous flare to the bow, both the stem and the forward sections would have had more curvature above the datum waterline. It should be noted that the greater beam on deck, coupled with the flare, generates a longer bow overhang with a stem angle closer to 45° more than *Greased Lightning*'s more upright stem which is related to a much harsher and more aggressive deck outline.

If the forward waterlines, sections and buttocks are compared it will

Blackjack's *lines make no concessions to any rule. Her hull form is moderate in all respects, relying on deep draft and a high ballast ratio to generate power, while her modest beam makes her easily driven and gives her a well balanced helm. In this lines plan an additional buttock has been added at half the normal interval to control the inflexions into the keel and bustle.*

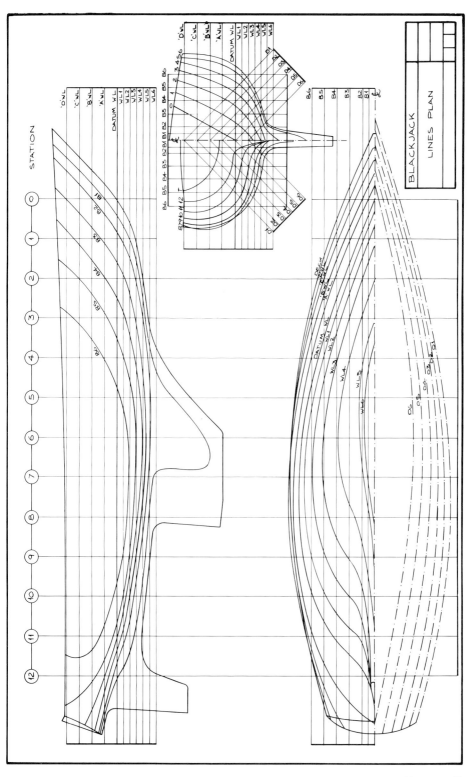

BLACKJACK
LINES PLAN

be seen that, in the case of *Greased Lightning*, there is quite a distinct area where straight lines predominate in all directions. This should be interpreted as indicating a genuinely flat panel, perfectly normal in her type. Although *Blackjack*'s lines forward have not got the fullness that a purely cruising design would have, it is not difficult to see that there is more curvature than on *Greased Lightning*.

At the risk of stating the obvious it is worth dwelling on this matter of the line of the stem a little longer and to consider the inverse situation. Where there is curvature in one dimension there must be curvature in at least one other.

A yacht with a curved stem and full buttocks can still have relatively straight waterlines but must have full sections. The International Dragon is an example of just such a bow. A yacht with a hollow in the stem will almost certainly have a flared bow with hollow bow sections.

The angle at which the waterlines join the centre line is another critical feature of lines plans. The angle indicates the amount of vee that exists in the relevant sections. Where a hull has a flat or fully rounded section passing through the centre line, then the waterlines at that point must be continuous from one side of the centre line to the other. The lowest waterline on *Greased Lightning* is meeting the centre line forward, by Station 2, almost at right angles and returns to the centre line just short of Station 9 at a definite angle. This highlights the characteristics of the sections which are giving a relatively flat underside to the forebody and a vee in the run forward of the skeg.

The buttocks, particularly those furthest from the centre line, give a picture of the topsides that is complementary to the sections. Any tumblehome that may exist will be highlighted by the buttocks that continue to curve until they are actually laying forward as they meet the rail. *Greased Lightning* has no tumblehome and, in fact, except amidships where the topsides are fairly close to perpendicular, there is a characteristic flare in the bow and stern which is confirmed by the slack angle of the buttocks as they meet the rail. *Blackjack*'s lines do include tumblehome, between Stations 6 and 12 and buttock B5 can be seen to end in a well rounded curve. It will also be seen how the upper waterlines cross over in the area of tumblehome.

The buttocks are also the clearest indicators of the nature of the run of the stern. The run is that part of the underbody aft of the midsection that influences the way in which the water leaves the back end when the yacht is underway. This is largely governed by the angle of the buttocks as they pass through the Datum Water line. In a fast reaching racing yacht or a full powered motor sailer the angle is generally very slight in order to offer the least resistance at high relative hull speeds. Where there is a steep rise of the buttocks aft, the resistance will be less at low speeds, but there will be a greater limit on all out performance. Parallel with this particular characteristic is the whole question of distortions in the lines, particularly in the stern. For these purposes the expression distortion is taken to indicate any departure from the natural curve that might be drawn on a simply planked canoe body. There are two reasons for distortion. Firstly, if the hull is faired into an appendage, such as the rudder and skeg, then the waterlines and buttocks closest to the appendage will be drawn out towards that appendage. Secondly, the dreaded IOR, which lays so much emphasis on certain measurement points, creates distortions away from fair curves in all three dimensions. *Greased Lightning* has both forms of distortion, particularly from Station 10 aft, where the vertical height of the hull has been artificially reduced by a dreadful device known as a Davidson crease, after the inventor, New Zealand designer, Laurie Davidson. Since 1982 the crease has gone out of fashion and distortions have generally grown less.

In the waterlines and buttocks forward of the rudder fairing the waterlines have a double inflection and the inside buttocks have a tendency to be pulled down where the hull body fairs into the skeg. *Blackjack*'s lines are only distorted as they turn into the skeg and the root of the keel and outside of buttock B1 are natural, fair curves.

The lines are the key to the good manners and sea kindliness of a yacht. Hidden within them are the secrets of balance, windward ability, roll characteristics, stability and so on. Many readers will probably have strong views on how their dream boat will look in reality. Only by study and careful thought is it possible to identify the lines drawing that corresponds to that dream.

It would be a sad day if it were possible to design the perfect yacht. The result would be a singularly tedious uniformity which would rob sailing of half its interest. It is not possible for even the most powerful computers to produce this phenomenom because the requirements differ so much and so many of these, such as speed and comfort, are contradictory, and a compromise solution is forced upon us.

Having considered the lines of a yacht, as a means of expressing a shape of hull, we now come to the much more difficult process of identifying the hull shape that will then provide the particular qualities needed to suit a particular purpose.

2

Displacement and shape

Thanks to the original thought of one, Archimedes and his bath water, we start our design process with the fixed and unalterable relationship between the weight, or displacement, of the yacht and the size of the hole it makes when floating in water. The volumetric capacity of that hole is such that the weight of water needed to fill it is exactly equal to the weight of the yacht. Reduce the weight and the hole must get smaller, increase it and vice versa.

Most designers will start their design process with an assumed displacement and an assumed waterline length. If you think of that displacement as a volume then the immediate question is how that volume should be distributed within the length of the waterline. Those readers, who are keen to adopt the jargon of design language, should take note of the expression, 'prismatic coefficient'. This is a factor that relates the area of a mid section to the volume of the whole hull. Mathematically the hull volume is the mid section × length waterline × prismatic coefficient. If the coefficient was 1.0, then the hull would have a constant section like a floating shoe box and the smaller the coefficient the finer the ends become and the greater the concentration of volume close to the mid section. I would advise against being involved in actual numbers because different designers calculate the coefficients in different ways and comparisons are not always reliable.

Having dealt with the jargon, what is the effect? Do you want your yacht to have a high or low prismatic. To consider this it is important to look at wave action on a moving hull. In the photo of *Double Trouble* you will see an example of a yacht moving at what is described as maximum hull speed. The bow wave and the stern wave have a single trough between them. The speed of waves is rigidly related to the length between crests and cannot vary. The only way that the yacht in the photograph could appreciably increase her speed is to increase the distance between the waves she is carrying with her. To do this the stern

The Ohlson 35 Double Trouble *sailing at 'full speed'.*

wave would have to become separated as in a planing condition. This is only possible with extremely light yachts in surfing conditions. So returning to *Double Trouble*, note how the effect of crest and trough has taken water away from the mid section and built it up around the bow and stern. This situation demands that the weight of the yacht is supported more by the water at the ends than was the case at rest in still water. If, as in the case of the yacht in the photograph, the ends are relatively fine and narrow, (a low prismatic), then she will have to sink lower into the water in order to be supported, with a consequent increase in resistance and steepening of the wave fronts.

So now you will be asking why is not every yacht drawn with a high

This shot of the Briand designed Local Hero III *racing in 1985 shows the extreme flair of the aft sections.*

prismatic? The answer is that it is only at high relative hull speeds that the wave making resistance is so critical. In terms of numbers, a conventional yacht reaches her peak of speed at around $1.4 \times \sqrt{\text{LWL}}$. In other words, a 24ft waterline yacht is running up against the speed barrier at around 6.9 knots. This is only attainable driven hard with a fair wind. For the greater part of the time underway the same yacht will be sailing at $1 \times \sqrt{\text{LWL}}$ or less. At these speeds other factors govern resistance and the finer-ended hull shape becomes more and more competitive at lower speeds.

To illustrate this you could consider the difference between a high powered sailing yacht and a genuine motor sailer. There are many sailing yachts with fairly average ends with large auxiliary engines. Under power they very quickly pick up speed, but after a certain speed further increases in power only serve to pull the stern wave up the transom and the extra fractions of a knot are not worth the effort. The genuine motor sailer is designed for the man who is not going to sail in light airs and so has a fuller hull shape designed to accept the power of a powerful engine without squatting. She will therefore motor much more smoothly at higher relative speeds.

So far we have looked only at the relationship between the ends of the yacht and the mid section. Equally important and far less understood is the relationship between the two ends. Because a sailing yacht has to sail efficiently at a range of heel angles, the designer must give special consideration to any changes in flotation that may occur. It is popularly thought that balance, as felt at the helm, is principally concerned with the relationship between the rig and the keel profile. While this is true in an upright condition it is only half the battle as the yacht begins to heel.

Because a yacht is symmetrical athwartships, when she is upright, the centre of buoyancy in each individual section is on the centre line. When she heels the centre of buoyancy of almost every section moves to leeward away from the centre of gravity, thus creating a righting moment, of which more later. If the centre of buoyancy moves further outboard at one end than the other, as in the case of a broad sterned, narrow bowed, scaled up dinghy type then the yacht will have a strong tendency to present its fin at an angle to the water. In the case of the full stern this means an increase in weather helm as the yacht tries to round up towards the wind.

It is in this area of design that the IOR and the yachts that are raced under its influence have a damaging effect on the cruising yacht, if the wrong characteristics are copied. The IOR is for fully crewed racing and among the lighter designs it is quite acceptable to draw a relatively unbalanced hull form. The disadvantages are overcome by constant crew activity continuously adjusting the rig, supplemented by the crew acting as movable ballast on the weather rail. By these means the heel angle can be limited to an acceptable minimum and speed maintained. This is no great joy to the cruising man with his family. The other rule factor which spoils the balance of the hull is that the handicap calculations place considerable emphasis on beam aft. In general this is measured across the deck at the transom and means that in the Figure below 'A' is more favoured than 'B'. It can be seen that when 'A' is heeled the centre of buoyancy of the aft sections is going to go on moving outboard long after 'B' has reached a limit. Transoms are unfortunately much governed by fashion and some cruising boats have been spoiled by aping the racing transom.

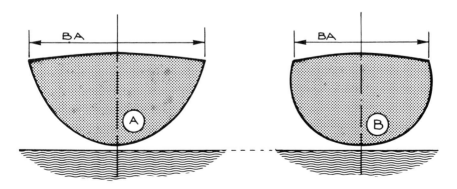

Section A and Section B have the same girth, but A has a much larger beam on deck (BA) and therefore a more favourable measurement of Rated length.

So when looking at the waterlines of a published design remember that the boat with a diamond shape may be superb in light airs, she may not however be so good as the more rounded outline at speed, running down wind in the northeast Trades. Equally you should be wary of buying a mixture of conical one end and lozenge shaped the other.

When you look at the body plan of a design and study the hull sections these should be your guide to the relative power or tenderness of the yacht. When a yacht is upright, the centre of gravity is in the same vertical plane, the fore and aft centre line, as the centre of buoyancy. Immediately the yacht begins to heel the centre of buoyancy moves away from the centre as the leeward side becomes more immersed than the windward side. Nothing has happened to alter the position of the centre of gravity within the yacht, so a righting moment is created by the natural tendency for the centre of gravity to want to get back under the centre of buoyancy. The further outboard the centre of buoyancy moves, the more powerful the righting moment becomes. Obviously the position of the centre of gravity is also an important factor because the lower this is, the greater tendency it has to move to windward away from the centre of buoyancy.

If we consider the mid section in isolation to begin with, we can begin to appreciate the different characteristics of each type. The Figure (right)

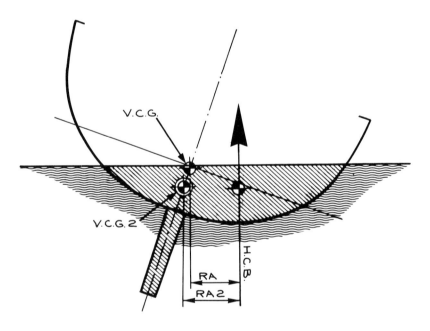

The righting arm is the horizontal distance between the VCG (Vertical Centre of Gravity) and the HCB (Heeled Centre of Buoyancy). Note how the Righting Arm increases when the VCG is lowered. The Righting Moment is the product of the Righting Arm multiplied by the Displacement.

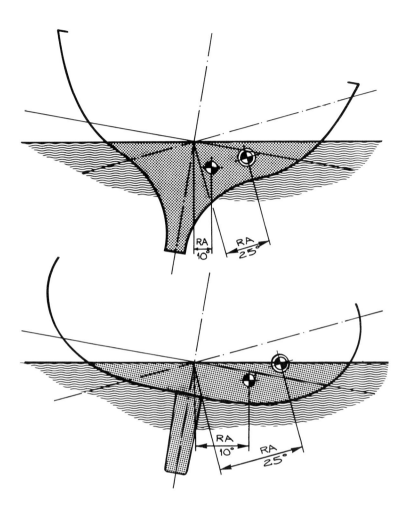

These diagrams illustrate how the flat-floored mid section will be initially stable but with only modest improvements as heel increases. The deep veed section will heel easily to begin with, but stiffness will steadily increase as the angle of heel becomes larger.

shows two exaggerated examples of a deeply veed and a flat floored mid section. The veed section will heel easily to begin with because the movement of the centre of buoyancy is relatively small. This movement will, on the other hand, progressively increase until the righting moment is greatest at the greatest heel angle. The flat floored section has the opposite effect. At small angles of heel the centre of buoyancy is moving outboard very rapidly. Beyond a certain angle, however, the increases are beginning to tail off. The conclusion to be drawn from this is that the veed section will be initially tender but may be ultimately quite stiff. The flat floored type will be initially stiff but may be ultimately quite tender. The latter is undoubtedly the more comfortable in average conditions, the former more reassuring in the ultimate storm. Stability is not quite so simple as this description would make it sound because, for simplicity, we looked at the mid section as though it were typical. In order to complete a full stability analysis of a design it is necessary to find the movement of the centre of buoyancy of the whole yacht, or all the sections, not just the midships area. So again we come back to the questions of the ends and realise that a fine ended design will have less power than one with relatively full sections in the bow and stern.

We have now considered the waterlines and sections, albeit very superficially, but there can be no conclusion without considering the sheer plan and how the buttocks can be seen to affect the characteristics of the design.

At the risk of being shot down by another designer, I will go so far as to say that these lines do not form an essential part of any of the normal design calculations. They do, however, give a useful visual indication, to those with an eye for a yacht, as to the possible behaviour of the design at sea. The placing of the fin, whether it is long or short, is a separate subject and, in the interests of concentrating on the 'hull lines', let us ignore the keel altogether. As we saw in the previous chapter the bow and buttock lines, to use their full title, illustrate the entry and the run of the bow and the stern. Any angle or knuckle in the sections is bound to be reflected in the buttocks but what the student of lines should look out for is an unnatural distortion particularly in the run aft. There is an unfortunate tendency to hold the buttocks down in the quarters with a consequent steepening of the rise through the aft end of the waterline. My antipathy to this particular trend is largely personal and relates to a wish to see the water pass under the yacht in a continuous smooth action.

For a buttock to indicate a length of relatively small rocker, combined with a deep chin forward and a steep rise aft, indicates a type that will be much more effective at moderate speeds in smooth water than at higher speeds in broken water. This characteristic is prompted by a desire to keep the centre of buoyancy as far aft as possible and is usually combined with a pronounced bustle. The result generally is a transom like an equilateral triangle and a yacht that pulls up a steep stern wave. Remembering the initial instability of a veed section, this sort of stern does not make for the most controlled downwind form.

The bustle is a feature of which much has been written in the past. It is probably the one underwater feature of a yacht that has gained the most from tank testing. There are three principal advantages to be gained from the development of the bustle. The first is the smoother water flow from the canoe body on to the blade of a skeg hung rudder. The second is the increase in buoyancy aft that helps to keep the centre of buoyancy as far aft as possible without upsetting a balanced form.

The third and perhaps more trivial is that it helps to lower the sole of an aft cabin and provides improved headroom.

If a rudder is hung on a skeg and the leading edge of that skeg has been given a reverse curve so that it leads into the canoe body profile at a shallow angle then a bustle is a natural form to develop. The designer will introduce an inflection between the sections and the sides of the skeg so that the hollow in the diagonals, which would otherwise produce a turbulence, in the heeled condition, is filled in. It does, of course, produce a distortion in the first buttock away from the centre line but this is, after all, only a transition between the pure canoe body buttocks and the centre line profile. Once the IOR influence is at work then the bustle is probably subordinated to the priority that the designer will give to the measurement points and the whole issue becomes fogged.

I think that the bustle should be limited to a drawing out of the lines into the skeg and rudder blade. It should be possible to visualise the canoe body running through to a fair shape, related to the remainder of the hull. It is when the designer has been so preoccupied with the bustle that he allows its shape to dominate the aft sections, that the yacht is spoiled and will develop a strange will of her own at speed.

In these few pages I have attempted to relate the lines plan to the behaviour of the yacht at sea. In many respects this has been necessarily an over simplification because a number of other factors will affect behaviour. Studying the lines in themselves will not, for instance, show the apparent distribution of weight. We have already seen that the lower the centre of gravity, the greater the righting moment. Why not go for the lowest possible centre of gravity in all boats? In lay terms, the pitfall of this characteristic is sometimes called the 'pendulum effect'. In more technical terms, the more you move concentrations of weight away from the centre of rotation the more the yacht will pitch and roll. So a tall heavy mast and a deep slung bulbed keel will result in a damaging pitching moment that will absorb a lot of energy as the hull attempts to damp it down.

One further thought that is worth considering when looking at the lines of a yacht, particularly a cruising yacht, is how she will behave in a head sea. Will she be wet? And will she slam? The wetness will depend on the character of the topsides forward. A hull with a lack of flare and overhang forward is likely to be wetter, although naturally liveliness is another factor. The moderate to heavy displacement yacht goes through the wave tops in a very satisfactory manner from the point of view of motion and sheer power. In doing so, however, there is a tendency to throw a good deal of water about. For this boat, flare is important to stop too much of that water coming over the deck. The lighter displacement types, given sufficient buoyancy, will lift over the wave tops giving a much quicker motion. They will, on the other hand, throw less water up in the air as they do so.

Slamming is an evil business and is as much a product of power and speed as hull form. The man who says his yacht never slams to windward should be careful to consider whether the performance potential is sufficient to generate slamming. In considering the lines, the aspect to look at is the shape of the sections that will hit the water first, when the yacht drops off the back of a wave. She is bound to be heeled going fast to windward so that a vee on the centre line is not a great deal of benefit. In theory at least, a U shape is kinder than a vee. Where the U shape is preferable to a vee is when going fast down wind. If the forebody is too veed there is a danger that it will dig in and encourage the rest of the yacht to sail round it, popularly known as griping. An ability for the forward sections to traverse easily is important.

Finally when looking at a set of lines look for harmony. This is something very difficult to describe in words. The old adage, 'handsome is as handsome does', is as true of a yacht's lines as of anything. So look for smooth curves, not too many sharp angles and an inter relationship that gives the lines drawing an appearance of complete harmony.

The reader will have detected an undertone in the previous pages that indicates that the author rather deplores some of the features of IOR designs. This is true in certain respects only. Firstly the lines of an IOR racing yacht do not satisfy a purist's eye from an aesthetic point of view, particularly if, as in my own case, one is conditioned to appreciate fair lines as should be the case if no rule factors were involved. Secondly there are features of IOR designs which are only justified on a basis of rule manipulation and to my mind these features have no place in a genuine crusing yacht that is never likely to be measured.

The other side of the coin must not be denied a mention. The IOR has produced some superb yachts with remarkable speed particularly up wind. Until recently the yachts built to the rule could be accepted as fitting the dual role, cruiser racer, concept intended to suit the needs of the majority.

It is significant that on Page 2 of the International Offshore Rule it says:

The council will act to discourage developments which lead to excessive costs, or reduce safety or the suitability of yachts for cruising.

Reading these words in the summer of 1985 and at the same time seeing the pattern of Grand Prix type racing yachts that are appearing on the scene, the concept that an out of date racing boat made a first class cruising boat is sadly an outdated and worn out suggestion.

For the large crews that sail IOR designs the racing is superb. The design trends have become reasonably stable but unfortunately, at the top level of competition, this has led to a technological armaments race that will have a serious down turn in enthusiasm amongst the less spendthrift, run-of-the-mill owner. Measurement fees have become far too costly and through a process of diminishing returns may well increase further. Ordinary mortals are turning to alternative handicap systems wherever they are available.

Maybe this attitude will be attributed to my advancing years, but my feeling is that unless some new injection of wisdom of Solomon quality is made soon, the IOR will become the Formula One of yacht racing which will only survive on a sponsored professional basis just as in motor racing.

3

Wide bodies

Every writer has his own pet themes and one of mine is an antipathy to excess beam, particularly when a design is being judged on its suitability for seakeeping in severe offshore conditions. On the other hand, not everyone is going to sail far from shelter and for them the advantage of a beamy yacht can outweigh the disadvantages. Recent comments on Boat Show exhibits have employed the term 'wide bodied' to embrace a new generation of cruising yachts. The inference of this term is plain enough. If aircraft designers can make 'widebodied' aircraft fly satisfactorily, supposedly the contemporary yacht designers must find a way to make widebodied yachts sail satisfactorily.

There can be no denying that in terms of comfort, harbour comfort particularly, generous beam well distributed over the greatest proportion of the length possible is a bonus all the way.

Is it right to treat the hull so unscientifically? After all the aircraft flies on its wings. Is the shape of the pod in the middle so vitally important? The performance of the yacht is entirely related to the shape of the hull. Once the bows are pointed out of the marina entrance and, even more so when we venture into the open sea, will the wide body be such an asset any longer?

Suitability for an intended purpose is the yardstick by which all products should be judged. The question is, is everyone's definition of the intended purpose identical? I dare say a statistician could tell you how many thousands of yachts are based in The Solent and, of those thousands, what percentage ever go beyond the Needles. That great majority whose sailing lives tend to be dominated by the relatively easy life of sailing in sheltered waters, with an easy refuge never far away, tend to have an influence on that definition of suitability that places other users in the category of specialists.

For the owner who keeps a yacht in some small harbour on the Atlantic coastline, where beyond the pierheads lies the mighty deep, the

The ultimate in wide bodied, shallow hulled, cruising design. Initial stability will be very high; ultimate stability will be less reassuring.

same values may not be quite so easily accepted. For him his day's sailing may take him straight into open water with considerably less protection and a big sea running. When he is at sea a change in conditions may make his home port dangerous to approach and he must be prepared to divert elsewhere. This may entail a hard flog to windward and he will be prepared for just such an eventuality. This owner's requirements are much more akin to the serious offshore cruising requirements of the deep sea sailor.

The theme which the writer is putting forward is that real weatherliness is in danger of becoming a specialist requirement, like four-wheel drive, and how is this to be identified by the purchasing public?

The salesman will tell you that the latest product has been out in Force 9 and behaved impeccably. Where? Probably off Calshot in a two-hour test sail. Has he tried to survive on board in the same conditions off the West coast of Scotland? Has he ever seen such conditions? This is the time that the wide-bodied floating home is going to be at its least attractive.

There are of course certain classics in the field of weatherliness and, as this is written, one can not help thinking of the S&S 34 of which a small number were built in this country and a much larger number in Australia. The most famous example is *Perie Banou* which, in addition to sailing twice round the world nonstop, took third place on corrected time in one of the roughest Sydney-Hobart races in history (15 years after Ted Heath's outright victory in the same race in his S&S 34, the first *Morning Cloud*.

By present-day standards the accommodation of an S&S 34 is positively cramped. The designers drew the hull first and put in the only layout that would fit. Their concern was with performance, those were the days when a good racing boat did make a good cruising boat as well.

What do we mean by wide body? In simple terms we mean above average beam without a corresponding increase in immersed depth; broad and shallow. Because the underwater volume is directly related to the displacement, the designer who wishes to push up the beam must keep the depth of his sections stricly under control, unless he is prepared for the displacement to increase. Displacement costs money and so to remain competitive in the market the designer can only achieve the extra beam at the expense of depth.

Broad and shallow hull shapes have many advantages. They provide nice stable platforms for happy family sailing on happy family sunny days. It is absolutely true that the broad shallow form provides excellent initial stability. When you step on board the yacht does not tip over towards you and, particularly for the beginner, this gives a feeling of confidence. In this respect the shape is fine, there should be no difficulty in drawing the lines so that the handling at moderate angles of heel is well up to standard. As the wind increases the sail area can be reduced and the angle of heel limited; so far so good.

There comes a time of course when, in order to limit heel, the sails have been reduced until there is insufficient power available to push the wide body through the increasing waves, assuming the course is to windward; no trouble if it isn't. Take down the jib, start up the diesel and we'll still be in Yarmouth for six o'clock drinks. Fine, but if the wide body creation is in different cicumstances, where the owners are faced with a long slog to windward which, because of a limited fuel reserve, must be tackled under sail, can it be achieved? What happens when the ultimate conditions are met and it is no longer possible to limit heel? How will she perform then? Knocked down to 30, 40 or even 50 degrees of heel, is the stability increasing or in danger of dropping? As the topsides become immersed is the yacht tending to ride up on her bilge bringing the keel and rudder, the all important control features, uncomfortably close to the surface?

The broad shallow yacht has, as a rule, a high centre of gravity

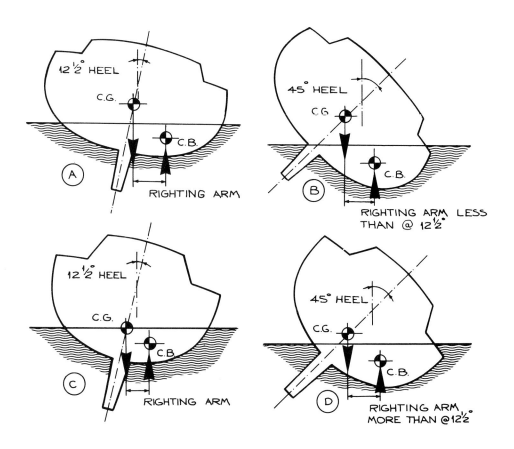

'A' and 'B' show a typical wide bodied hull heeled at 12½° and 45°. In 'A' the heeled centre of buoyancy has moved rapidly away from the centre line giving an excellent initial stability. In 'B' it can be seen that the centre of gravity (the position of which does not change) is closer in the horizontal dimension to the new heeled centre of buoyancy with a consequent reduction of righting moment. Ultimate stability is not so good.

'C' and 'D' show a more moderate concept at the same angles of heel, initial stability is less good but ultimate stability will be much better. It is a fundamental factor which is illustrated here that 'B' has risen up on the extra buoyancy of the wide beam to a greater extent than 'D', contributing to the loss of stability.

appreciably above the waterline. This can only be corrected by a high ballast ratio and a deep keel. As she rides on to the turn of the bilge the lever arm between the centre of buoyancy and the weight of the yacht acting through the centre of gravity will ultimately become shorter. As this happens the driving force of the sails becomes less and the ability to make ground to windward begins to fail. This in turn limits the skipper's choice of action and makes the whole task of survival a great deal more difficult.

If one is looking for a yacht with an above average ability to make ground to windward in severe conditions then ultimate stability, rather than initial stability, is of the greatest importance. Without being stupid and returning to the plank on edge concept of the Thirties, all that is needed is a sensible degree of moderation.

The centre of gravity must be as low as possible. This is much more easily obtained when the displacement is not too severely limited by cost. When the design has a greater depth to the underwater body it has correspondingly less superstructure for the same headroom and all weights are closer to, or even below, the waterline. A greater amount of vee in the hull sections will mean that the centre of buoyancy does not move athwartships so rapidly in the initial stages. The first ten or fifteen degrees of heel will be taken up quite early. The difference comes when the centre of buoyancy continues to move outboard as the heel increases. Without the wide body there is not the same tendency to ride up on the bilge and performance at extreme angles is not impaired.

The important thing for a prospective owner to appreciate is that there are horses for courses. There are many who dream of bashing to windward in all weathers and only a small percentage who actually achieve that dream; there are even less who find they enjoy the reality as much as the dream. The sensible owner is the one who recognises the type of sailing that his or her life style will require and buys accordingly. For at least two thirds the wide-bodied concept is ideal, but it is as well to realise that it may have limitations when taken outside its natural habitat.

NOTE: The writer has considered the wide bodied design as having an immersed hull body with a depth not more than 15% of the maximum beam and the moderate design as being at least 20% in the same dimension.

4

The right kind of deck

Many things in life are judged, at least initially, by the outward appearance of their upper parts. Yachts are certainly not the only feminine forms to be considered in this way. Largely because the lower parts are very often hidden from view, the superstructure is for many the make or break.

The aesthetics and the ergonomics of deck design go hand in hand, although in some respects the two requirements are contradictory. The best results are frequently those in which the happiest balance has been achieved.

For the pure racing yacht the influence of the interior arrangements on the geometry of the deck above has become very limited. In many cases it is a function of providing an adequate area below, which has sufficient headroom to satisfy the requirements of the Offshore Racing Council's accommodation standards. The contemporary One Ton Cup designs can achieve this with little more superstructure than the designer is seeking to provide as a table for halyard winches and to raise the hatchway sufficiently above the main deck for safety. It is at Half Ton level that the 'ORC coachroof' is most apparent with abruptly rising narrow boxlike excrescences that satisfy the ORC but do little to please the eye.

In more conventional craft and production cruiser racers the designer has to exercise the wisdom of Solomon. He must produce the maximum of interior volume while maintaining the sleek air of streamlining that is the proper expression of a performance yacht.

It is a give and take situation. The headroom requirements of the living part of the ship push the coachroof up and the needs of the cockpit extending downwards into the aft areas threaten to interfere with the aft cabin or quarter berth arrangements. This is never so complicated and difficult to resolve as in the centre cockpit layouts at around 36ft, when the possibility of a through passageway means that the cockpit is elevated until there is acceptable headroom under the cockpit seats. The idea should be banned in any boat less than 45ft. This is of course out of the question and, when the boatbuilder says we have to achieve a through passage in only 35ft, we are none of us so pure in heart that we do not sell our souls to the devil and draw the inevitable two-storey yacht. A look around at Earl's Court would soon show you what is meant.

Two major factors have to be resolved at an early stage. Firstly the temptation to increase the freeboard thereby reducing the relative height of the superstructure must be viewed in its true perspective. It is an easy solution – the GK29, drawn by the writer, is an obvious example. In her day the freeboard was above average to say the least. The result was a cruiser racer with impressive volume that went over big at boat shows. From a racing point of view, the extra freeboard meant that the centre of gravity of the deck and the additional topsides was not the greatest asset from the point of view of stability. The more conventional concept of a design with normal freeboard and a relatively larger cabin top means that the weight of the deck is much closer to the waterline.

There is another aspect to the question of designing low coachroofs on hulls with high freeboard, particularly on yachts of 35ft or over, and that is the question of human scale. There have been a rash of large, so called cruising boats in recent years with enormous interior volume gained through over generous freeboard. The superstructures are low and rakish and look very smart. Unfortunately when you go below the windows are all above eye level and there is no outlook. The opposite situation is nicely typified by Don Pye's design of the Oyster Heritage (it's safe enough to name names when one is being complimentary, for the others it must be a case of 'if the cap fits wear it'). The Heritage has a conventional coachroof, the windows are at average eye level and the occupants have no need of a periscope to keep track of the happenings around them.

The second factor that must not be forgotten is that the deck is also an important structural part of the yacht. The stresses, that are set up within it, must be allowed to follow logical paths without weak points. Consider the hull of a yacht as a fore and aft girder. The fore and aft rigging exerts upward forces on the ends and the mast pushes downwards in the middle. If the girder is not strong enough the hull will imitate the banana, with unfortunate results. To combat the rigging stresses the lower parts of the hull are acting in tension and the deck is in compression.

If there is a degree of continuity in the superstructure then the whole deck can absorb the stresses and the effect of the coamings is to provide an increased resistance to buckling by nature of the improved form. If there is an abrupt break in the superstructure then that point is the weak link and the side decks and gunwhale construction may have to be sufficiently strong to take all the load, ignoring the superstructure.

This may seem an over simplification, but, none the less, the designer must look at the deck very critically and visualise the stresses that will occur. Neither compressive nor tensile stresses go up or down steps at all well!

When all the conflicting requirements have been resolved and an envelope of sorts has been conceived then the most difficult stage arises. The envelope must be given a geometry, in three dimensions, that is pleasing to the eye from all angles. 'From all angles' is the factor that can cause the greatest grief. It is no use drawing an attractive profile and a workmanlike plan if the one is not in some way a reflection of the other.

The most critical line on the average deck is that created by the intersection of the coaming and the coachroof top. It is inevitably a powerful line to the eye when viewed from an oblique angle. It is of paramount importance to consider all three dimensions and to invent and impose a strict discipline upon that line, more than any other.

In the writer's opinion this discipline should start with the sheerline and the geometry of the sidedeck because, if this has not been considered in three dimensions, then even a perfectly sculpted superstructure will show up pretty oddly along the line of its roots, where it grows out of the deck.

There are no hard and fast rules for designing decks and each designer will impose a unique signature by whatever different approach he takes to the problem.

Disciplines are something that computers really understand. Whereas the writer is sufficient of a romantic to deplore the concept of hull lines being generated by a computer (he cannot afford such a machine anyway), he has been very prepared to employ computer facilities for the generation of deck geometry. The results are a table of offsets accurate to a millimetre, in advance of any drawing other than a few sketches, and the ability to impose strict values that guarantee that no horrors will arise when the deck appears in three dimensions.

These imposed disciplines start with the sheerline; the curve of which is directly related to the changing curve of the deck in plan. By employing the deck offsets to create the sheerline the curve will be in harmony no matter what the angle of heel. In fact the curve is created in such a way that there is an angle from which the sheer will appear as a perfectly level plane. In certain cases, particularly where the spring of the sheer is not too strong, it is possible to pitch the side deck at exactly the same angle so that in effect there is no curvature in the fore and aft dimension. Apart from anything else this is a most desirable feature when locating the spinnaker pole stowage. The computer is made to draw the intersection of the side deck and the coamings along a line that is once again related to the half breadths of the deck. In effect this line picks a point on each station that is a chosen percentage of the distance between the edge of the deck and an arbitrary straight base line related

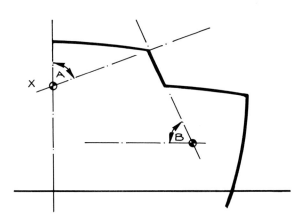

The computer generates the outline of the superstructure at the intersection with the side deck. The inputs can be varied to alter the position and angle of the base line relative to the centre line, and to vary the percentage position of the intersection. Because the half breadths of the deck edge are one basis of the calculation the two curves will be sympathetic.

Angles 'A' and 'B' are constant on all stations. Point 'X' is at a constant, or constantly incremented, height on the centre line. The controls impose a strict discipline on the fore and aft line formed by the intersection of the coaming and the cambered coachroof top.

to the centreline. By jiggling with the location of the base line and the chosen percentage, it is possible to create a side deck to suit any requirement, knowing that its curve is not so arbitrary that it will not be sympathetic with the outline of the deck.

The writer's approach to the geometry of a coaming is such that he will not entertain any thought of twist occuring. This simply tells the computer to strike a constant angle on all stations. The next part of the programme generates the co-ordinates for the top edge of the coaming where the camber of the coachroof will intersect. This is done by establishing a common denominator for that point of intersection when viewed from forward and related to an easily defined point on the centre line, the third dimension. In its simplest form this means that the intersection must fall on a line drawn from the centre at a constant angle from a given height. Such a discipline will mean that, if seen from dead ahead with the eye at deck level the intersection would appear as a straight line.

Before the advent of the computer these same strictures could be applied but that had to be constructed graphically, by very accurate drawing, and the offsets lifted on a scale ruler. This is not easy when the lines concerned are following very gentle curves with only small variations between stations. Because each angle is geometrically controlled the computer generates perfect co-ordinates in a matter of seconds. By varying the inputs the designer can manipulate the deck until it most satisfactorily encloses the required envelope.

Fashion, style, call it what you will, is an element of deck design that is ever present. Beauty may be in the eye of the beholder, but our eyes are conditioned by certain standards that we learn to consider important. We expect a cruiser racer to be sleek and streamlined. 'Handsome is as handsome does' is reversible to suggest that if the product is intended to echo the performance of some famous champion then it must at the same time reflect a similar image.

As a yacht's purpose becomes less aggressive, as racing gives way to pure cruising or even motorsailing, so one's eyes more easily accept steeper, forward facing areas of deck or wheelhouse. We accept that streamlining is no longer the ultimate priority and comfort and protection from the weather attract a higher value.

The design of the deck has a tendency to follow fairly stereotyped patterns that change subtly over periods of several years. There will always be certain exceptions, refreshingly individual approaches like the Petterson Maxis, but mistakes will still be made, particularly in the realm of converting plan and profile into a satisfactory three dimensional whole.

PART TWO

VOYAGING

Minion was designed by Laurent Giles very much in the idiom of his early JOG boats such as Sopranino.

5

Minion in Brittany

Our first cruising boat cost us £600 in 1960 and in her we had two summers of very happy cruising. These two accounts were published in 1961 and 1962 and tell the story of our first ventures to Brittany and the Bay of Biscay. They were written by my wife Pat.

Twelve Days in *Minion*

Minion is a Laurent Giles designed 2-tonner by Thames Tonnage (21ft LOA, 6ft beam and 3ft draught), rigged as a Bermudian sloop. Similar to *Sopranino*, though larger and heavier, *Minion* has a fin keel carrying 900lb of cast-iron ballast with a separate rudder on a skeg and no auxiliary power. She will sleep three, two up forward and the third in a tiny quarter berth opposite the galley. The doghouse provides sitting headroom over the galley, which comprises a two-burner swinging Calor gas stove and excellent little lockers and cubby holes.

We carry one of the Prout collapsible coracles which, on passage, lives above one of the forward bunks, where it is lashed up to the deckhead. The bottom of the cockpit floor will lift to seat level, making it self-draining through suction bailers in the ship's side. Aft of the cockpit is a large stern locker which holds all the sails and spare gear and equipment. Three 6-volt motor-cycle batteries supply nine electric points throughout the yacht, including a combined port and starboard light high up on the jumpers.

Navigation is done on the lee cockpit seat in fine weather and down below in rough weather. Twelve Admiralty charts and six of the smaller Royal Cruising Club charts, together with Reeds *Almanac* and H G Hasler's book, *Harbours and Anchorages of North Brittany*, gave us all the information we needed.

We left Lymington on Saturday, 10 September, planning to cruise to the Brittany coast in the thirteen days before us, St Peter Port our first objective. We were well aware that the strong tides in these cruising grounds would have to be treated with great respect, as we had no motor.

Leaving the Yacht Club after lunch, we set the mainsail and our invaluable Flying Dutchman Genoa to a very light south-westerly wind and let the ebb take us down past the Needles, close-hauled on the port tack. At 2000 Anvil light was sighted bearing 345° mag. and about 2 miles away, although the log only read 5.2. Half an hour later the wind backed to the S S E and we were able to lay a course of 210° mag. for the Casquets, still close-hauled. We kept three-hour watches from 2100 onwards throughout a beautifully bright and moonlit night.

11 SEPTEMBER The light south-easterly wind held all day until we were well up to the Casquets and then died away to nothing. The ebb carried us round at 1800 and by the time the flood came, and darkness with it, we had the northern end of Guernsey abeam.

Realising that we should lose badly by continuing to head down towards Les Hanois, and with the added danger of being set in towards the rocks on the young flood, we elected to work round the north of the island in the hope that we might be in a suitable position for either the Great or the Little Russell on the next ebb.

During the next six hours we ghosted across towards Platte Fougere light, and then worked our way round the rocks north of Herm with the assistance of the tide flooding north up the Little Russell. Using safe bearings on Platte Fougere and Sark lights, we arrived at the top of the Great Russell in time for the ebb. Needless to say, the hand bearing compass was almost continually in use, and there were no watches below that night. The ebb brought with it a light north-westerly breeze, which gave us a run down the Great Russell and a short beat up to St Peter Port. We entered the harbour at 0600, just before dawn, and anchored in a least depth of one fathom.

After sleeping most of the morning, it was decided to take a look at the Channel Islands in daylight. A fresh north-westerly wind gave a fast sail as we reached up the Little Russell under a reefed mainsail and giboa. This curiously named sail used to be the Genoa, but has been cut down in such an unorthodox manner that it is now neither one thing nor the other, hence the name. We had a splendid sail round Herm and Jethou once again, though unfortunately saw little as the islands were wrapped in a dismal, misty gloom.

Re-entering the harbour at 1730, we hurriedly launched the coracle to go ashore and do some shopping. A small fortune was then spent on buying batteries for torches, and a little alcohol was purchased for medicinal purposes only, of course. On returning to the coracle which we had left high and dry on the quay side, 20ft above water level, we were amazed to see a small boy about to propel it forcibly down the stone steps to its doom. However, this calamity was averted just in time.

13 SEPTEMBER Awoke, albeit rather late, to find a light northerly wind blowing – a fair wind for Lezardrieux – what luck. We left St Peter Port at 0845 and bore away for St Martin's, having set the mainsail and giboa. During the morning we changed up to the Genoa, having dried out the other, and we also set the storm jib as a mizzen staysail by running it up the backstay on the spinnaker halyard. The skipper sailed close past both Roches Douvres and Barnouic lighthouses, whilst the cook slumbered below, on a warm and sunny afternoon.

Les Heaux lighthouse, which stands between the entrances of the Pontrieux and Treguier rivers, was sighted about tea time. At 1930 darkness came upon us as we approached Les Heaux on the last of the ebb. We had by this time reached a point well west of the entrance of the Pontrieux river in anticipation of the flood. The first plan of approach was to cross into the white sector of Les Heaux, and hold this sector until we had passed eastwards into the white sector of Paon light, then sail for that, until the leading marks in the main channel could be used.

It soon became obvious that without auxiliary power we would never be able to keep in the white sector of Paon because of the strong set and the uncertainty of the breeze, which had now backed to the southwest. So out came the hand bearing compass, and with the aid of a very large-scale chart chart we worked our way round the rocks by way of the Men de Castrec Passage, passing inside Les Sirlots buoy.

Taking minute-by-minute fixes on Les Heaux, Rosedo and Paon, we crabbed our way round with the bows pointed for the rocks all the way. Confidence in the navigation grew when Vieille de Treou was found, and from there we beat slowly up the Grand Chenal, passed Gosrod beacon, passed Men Guen, and then the breeze freed. This enabled us to take a long slow tack from Men Guen up into the Pomelin roadstead, a tiny anchorage on the starboard hand, opposite La Croix lighthouse, which we entered on a stern bearing on Rosedo light.

As we went in the dinghy rowlocks suddenly found themselves on the lead line, the lead itself having decided that Lezardrieux was as good a resting place as any, and parted company with us. A fix on Men Grenn and down went the anchor, which had been ready to let go for the last six hours.

By now it was midnight and the crew having learnt the joys of hot rum and orange on a September night, we turned in, the navigator anxious for daylight to bring his first sight of this river and anchorage that we had safely entered.

14 SEPTEMBER The morning blew in with a fresh south-westerly wind. We weighed anchor at 0930 and sailed out of our beautifully safe anchorage under mainsail only, a jib being hanked on ready for use.

The tide was flooding up the river and we tacked up with it, leaving the Tranquet rock to starboard to have a look at the little village of Loguivi. Here, as the wind was freshening, we pulled down a reef. We

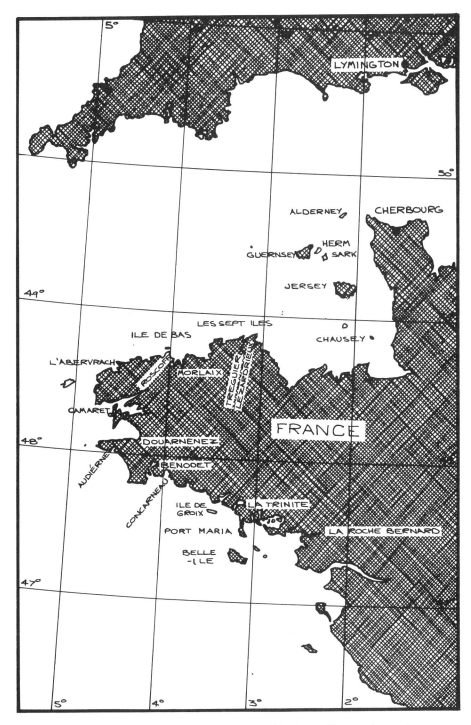

This chart of the Western English channel and Northern Biscay shows the principal ports visited during our cruises in 1960 and 1961.

met one small coaster, and a gravel barge overtook us as we short tacked our way up the river using Hasler's book, which we found excellent for showing us how far we could go on each tack.

We were off Lézardrieux by midday and sailed up to the bridge, sounding above and below it. Eventually we anchored with Les Chaises beacons in line and Min Keraoul beacon in line with a white patch at the end of a road on shore. This placed us close inshore on the south bank under the hill on which Madame Brenner has built her new hotel. Knowing the bottom was only fair, we were very glad of the 27lb Duerr anchor and three fathoms of heavy chain lent to us by friends. These, together with our own 3 fathoms of chain and 11 fathoms of 1¼in terylene, plus 15 fathoms of ¾-in terylene, sometimes used double, always held us securely. We launched the coracle in the evening and scrambled ashore over slimy rocks and boulders to enjoy our first French meal in a restaurant in the town.

15 SEPTEMBER We weighed anchor at 1115 and sailed down the river with a moderate south-easterly wind, under full mainsail and No 1 jib. To see something of Bréhat, we took the Ferlas Channel and even poked our nose into the red-cliffed entrance of Port Clos, where ferry boats taking passengers to and from the mainland were doing a good trade.

The wind veered to light south-westerly as Men Garo beacon was left close to starboard and the terylene Genoa set. We passed close outside Pen Azen and Les Sirlots buoy with the tide under us. The wind was falling light as we sailed past Les Heaux and it took a long time to reach La Jument bouy. However, by 1915 we had weathered Le Corbeau and were able to head in for the Tréguier river, whilst a fiery, fantastic sunset burnt itself out. Leaving the great white and red ringed lighthouse of La Corne to port, darkness overtook us once again. We anchored opposite the Guarivinou buoy in a least depth of 2 fathoms, still in the white sector upstream of La Corne.

16 SEPTEMBER Awoke early to find the yacht rolling uncomfortably in a fresh to strong north-westerly wind. Leaving this anchorage at 0700, we headed up the Tréguier river under the No 1 jib only, until the double-reefed mainsail was set after the first mile. On approaching the town itself we shook out one reef and handed the No 1 jib and, after doing some sounding, anchored off the quay in 3 fathoms at about 0900. It was here that our little pocket-sized transistor radio proved invaluable, for without it we should never have guessed that a depression which passed south of us originally should turn over Paris towards Dover and end up heading south-east over the Brest peninsula. No wonder we had very strong north-westerly winds, followed by equally stormy south-easterly winds.

17 SEPTEMBER The condensation was so bad during the night that

'The water was so clear we were able to place Minion's *keel exactly where we wanted it, avoiding any very large stones'.*

there were drips and dampness everywhere, which did not encourage us to leave our warm sleeping bags from which we could hear the wind tearing through the rigging and the rain sheeting down on to the deck just above. However, the forecasts promised some improvement for the following day and in the evening we sailed down the river, anchoring just upstream of Pointe Jaune.

18 SEPTEMBER Having weighed anchor at 0820, we beat down the river through the narrow entrance between La Corne and the black conical buoy called Le Taureau. A moderate to fresh easterly wind was blowing as we bore away to westward under full mainsail and genoa. Later we were to boom the genoa out to windward and had a wonderful day's sail inside the Sept Iles and the Plateau des Meloines.

After sailing close past the entrance to Primel, we bore away on to the very obvious leading marks for Morlaix. We anchored in the main channel just over a mile upstream of Barre de la Flotte buoy, with Tour de la Land bearing 252° mag. We were rather expecting a northeasterly blow, which was why we went up the main channel instead of anchoring under Penn Lann.

19 SEPTEMBER We beat out of Morlaix under mainsail and No 1 jib against a moderate to fresh north-westerly wind. Leaving the river by the Grand Chenal, we went out to the Pot de Fer buoy, where we tacked and made for the entrance of the Canal de Ile de Bas. There being insufficient water to enter Roscoff, we kedged close to the eastward of Duslen beacon and had our lunch.

At 1500 the anchor dragged as the wind increased, so we hoisted the mainsail only and sailed into Roscoff, where we made fast to a fishing boat in the Vieux Port. After some reconnaissance on our flat feet we decided to move up the wall to a shallower spot. To do this we had to tie down two reefs, for the wind had increased considerably, merely to sail ourselves 200 yards dead to windward. This we accomplished safely and made fast against the wall at the top of the harbour just beside the Douane's little hut.

The water was so clear that we were able to place *Minion*'s keel exactly where we wanted it, avoiding any very large stones. Gesticulating, though helpful, Frenchmen helped Mike to make the masthead line fast to our heavy chain which was wound round a square block of masonry. High water was at 1800 that evening and we found, as we had expected, that she was afloat for only two or three hours, which suited us very well.

20 SEPTEMBER Feeling a little weak after a pleasant evening ashore, we scrubbed the bottom with the two bucketfuls of water that we had saved before the water went away. Although this was only Tuesday and we were not expected home until the Friday, we decided to sail for England that evening if the forecast showed any signs of the very strong north-westerly winds decreasing.

At midday there were gale warnings for Portland and Plymouth, but at 1800 the forecast was north-west, 5, becoming west variable, 2 or 3, for those areas.

We thought this a very reasonable forecast for the middle of September and left immediately. We had already prepared for a rough night at sea – three reefs had been tied down in the mainsail, and the storm jib was ready. Down below the bedding was all rolled up and put away in polythene bags, except for a blanket for the lee bunk. The kettle had been filled (this is an impossible job in a rough sea) and biscuits and sweets put where they could be easily found. The cockpit was rigged to be self-draining.

Gathering speed rapidly under our very reduced rig, we sailed out of the old harbour at 1820, being careful to keep the leading marks in line astern. Once clear of the rocks bordering the entrance channel, we bore

'...we found ourselves in the middle of a NATO exercise'.

away for the Ar Chaden lighthouse.

There was certainly a big sea running outside, though height is of little account compared with the breaking crests. The log was streamed off the Astan buoy and a course of 040° set for the Needles. Once beyond Ile de Bas and out into deeper water, the seas started to come in more on the beam and the breaking crests were fewer. *Minion* behaved in an exemplary manner, lifting over each sea easily and rarely taking any great weight of water on board.

The wind was Force 7 and north-westerly and the yacht was travelling too fast for comfort. After an hour Mike went forward – we were both wearing lifelines – and lowered the storm jib, leaving it securely lashed down to the lifelines. We were both very sick and wished the yacht had two tillers, as steering seemed to be the only prevention from seasickness.

A certain amount of water could be heard swilling around in the bilges, though this makes a far more alarming noise than is usual owing to the underwater body being so flat bottomed. During this night we did two-hour watches only, sleeping, or at least relaxing, in the lee berth, the labour of removing oilskins and boots in the tiny cabin proving too much for us.

21 SEPTEMBER The wind decreased during the night and at 0400 the storm jib was reset and two hours later the third reef was shaken out. After soup and biscuits for breakfast, the Genoa was set, the wind having now gone into the west. Guernsey was in sight for most of the day.

The Casquets came abeam at 1930 and we found ourselves in the midst of a NATO exercise; two frigates and at least twenty minesweepers all steaming round in different directions at high speed. Two French minesweepers, supposed to be in line ahead, had to give way to us as we sailed solemnly through the lot.

22 SEPTEMBER During the night the wind increased to Force 4 or 5 from the south-west and we handed the Genoa soon after midnight. We must have reeled off the miles that night, as Anvil came abeam at 0600 and the Needles three hours later. We tied up alongside *Overlord* in Yarmouth to clear Customs at 1030 and waited for nearly two hours for them to put in an appearance, as they had to travel from Cowes.

September cruising poses the old question of insufficient daylight and rather cold nights. We had not intended to sail at night, except on passage, but were very well equipped, fortunately, and quite prepared to enter harbours and anchorages in the dark, given good visibility.

In harbour the cold nights forced us to shut both the cabin doors, particularly when the tide pushed the stern up into the wind. This, together with the steam from cooking, caused little drops of moisture all over the deckhead, making everything wringing wet. However, we were very lucky with the weather for the time of year, and no one could wish for a more interesting or more varied cruising ground on which to gain valuable experience.

South Brittany in *Minion*

Beating down the Needles Channel one June night, I found myself steering with one hand and fumbling for the big torch with the other. Mike found it first and flashed the light urgently as the pilot cutter coming up astern altered course to starboard and swept by at a great speed.

This was the weekend before the start of our three weeks' holiday in *Minion* a Laurent Giles-designed 2-tonner. She has no engine, and we have never bothered to fit a bracket on the stern for an outboard. Under double-reefed mainsail and No 1 jib we drove *Minion* to windward, determined to reach Torquay by the end of that weekend, for Mike's holiday did not start until the following Friday.

Coming up under Portland, Mike changed down to our smallest jib, which had recently been dyed a lurid orange colour. Short tacking inshore we found the tide was slack by the time we reached the end of the Bill. By 1400 on that Saturday the young ebb tide took us clear, and on we plunged into West Bay against a fresh to strong westerly wind.

Off watch I tried to sleep, but it was almost impossible, there can be remarkably few people who can sleep in a tiny boat bashing her way to windward. However, during the early hours the wind eased and, for a short while, died right away. When the morning breeze came we set all sail, arriving in Torquay at noon, 36 hours from Lymington.

At long last the evening of Friday, 23 June, came and by 2100 we were sailing out of the harbour. A light northerly wind took us round Berry Head, but then vanished, leaving us wallowing off Dartmouth. Here Mike managed to catch two mackerel which were duly poached for breakfast.

Off Start Point we waved gaily to a small Dutch coaster heading up-Channel but, alas, later that same evening we heard over the radio that she had been sunk in a collision in thick fog off Portland. We were very thankful to be so far west, thus avoiding the fog which was apparently widespread farther up-Channel.

On the morning of the second day the wind went round to the north, enabling us to set a new addition to our wardrobe. Now this sail has great possibilities. For one thing it is four sided and, for another, it is made out of three portions of nylon khaki parachute, the middle piece being reversed. Spinker is a real cruising sail, for once set on a downwind passage, whether on two poles or only one, no further adjustment is needed.

Forty-eight hours after leaving Torquay the unmistakable outline of Ile Vierge off L'Aber-vrach came into view through the mist. Altering course to the west, we lowered Spinker and set the genoa.

Mike had a very fast sail to the top of the Chenal de Four and when I came up at midnight I found that the weather had cleared and the lights of Ushant clearly visible under the lee bow. Knowing that the tide did not turn in our favour for another three hours, I stood off and on until 0300.

The fair wind and tide quickly whisked us through the Chenal, though we were unable to see the distant landmarks and lighthouses on the French coast. However, despite the dismal, misty gloom, Mike navigated to take us safely past the various beacon towers and buoys.

Once Pointe St Matthieu was well astern, we had another fishy breakfast and then I turned in. Meanwhile Mike found that he was going to arrive too early at the Raz de Sein. He had lowered the mainsail and furled it, jilling around under a small headsail, when I came up on deck again.

Between Tevennec and the mainland a short, steep sea was spilling over itself, but the passage through the Raz at slack water was quite uneventful. At last, Mike was able to drop wearily into the lee bunk. Somehow I managed to sail straight past Audierne, being much too far out and, for the first and only time in my life disbelieving the log. After beating back in light airs and rain we anchored close to the life-boat slip at St Evette as evening was drawing in.

After shopping in Audierne, we were under way soon after noon and had the best sail of the whole cruise – a very fast run under mainsail only. Off Penmarch we reefed down to the increasing north-westerly wind, though *Minion* with her fin keel and flat run aft does run most beautifully with a following sea.

'...we towed Minion *into Le Palais with the Dolphin rubber dinghy, thrilled to be there, five days out from Torquay'.*

During the night the wind gradually came ahead, but as we had the whole day before us we decided to explore the south and east coasts of Belle Ile. Even in this fine weather there was a swell coming in and raising quite a surf on the tiny sandy beaches, surrounded by the barren, brown rocks that make up this *sauvage* coastline.

Off Kerdonis Point we met a whole armada of brightly painted sardine boats. At least a dozen men could be seen on each boat, every one of which had two dinghies, towing close astern in the foaming white wash.

In this anti-cyclonic weather the wind deserted us in the afternoon, enabling us to plunge into the deep, blue water, which was astonishingly cold. Later we towed *Minion* into Le Palais with the Dolphin rubber dinghy, thrilled to be there, only five days out from Torquay.

For many an idle hour, cooped up in our London flat, we had studied Adlard Coles' book *Biscay Harbours and Anchorages*. Out of the many delightful places which he describes with such faithful detail, the one that had intrigued us most was deserted Ster Wenn on the north-west side of the island.

Naturally, therefore, we headed in that direction, calling first at Sauzon, a delightful little drying harbour. A hot, glassy calm persisted over much of the day and, at one time, we rather doubted whether we would get in anywhere for the night.

It was not until late in the afternoon that the tide served for going round Pointe des Poulains. Even then it would have swept us on to Les Chambres rocks if Mike had not jumped into the dinghy and done some hard rowing. Slowly we edged round the rocks. It was the merest whisper of a zephyr that kept Spinker pulling and even that died away as we headed up Ster Vras close to the high dark cliffs.

Towing once again, the steep-cut fiord of Ster Wenn opened up to starboard at last. To our surprise two fishing boats came into view first, but we were able to anchor above them at the head of the inlet. Darkness soon fell, transforming the rocky sides and clear, cold water into an impenetrable blackness, from which weird breathing noises came and went.

Next morning, after watching one of the fishing boats go alongside a rocky ledge on the far side, we left this wonderful natural hiding place in the rocks.

Fair weather for the next few days gave us some fine sailing in the Bay of Quiberon. We visited La Trinité, a big French yachting centre, and Roche Bernard, eight miles up the Vilaine river.

At Port Maria, on the tip of Quiberon, no amount of sounding from the dinghy could produce even half a fathom to lie in at low water. We therefore left at midnight, after three hours' sleep, silently sailing *Minion* round a huddle of fishing boats near the entrance and out into the darkness.

After four hours sailing close-hauled on the starboard tack Mike had to pull down two reefs. My log notes that it was 'beastly, rough, slamming sort of sailing'. I never did like going to windward.

Ile Penfret was sighted in the middle of the morning, which gave us hope, though it was another eight hours of weary beating before we were safely anchored under the shadow of the Ville Close at Concarneau.

We spent the whole day at Concarneau, buying a strange red fish, beans and luscious peaches in the market. Later we examined the brightly coloured trawlers in the Arrière port. Alas, there were no

'... passing Benodet *on the last of the flood'*

sailing tunny boats to be seen.

The next day found us entering the River Odet and passing Bénodet on the last of the flood. Sailing up this beautiful cool, green river was very peaceful, except for one moment of panic when a sudden gust of wind from astern capsized the Dolphin dinghy and very nearly resulted in an unexpected gybe.

We spent the night on one of the visitors' moorings on the west side of the river just upstream of Bénodet itself. Not far away lay *Fedalah*, whose owner, Mr. Norman Wates, kindly invited us on board for drinks.

Slipping our mooring, a delightful occupation when one normally has to deal with a muddy anchor and a mass of terylene warp and chain, we sailed out of the river, past the entrance to Loctudy and on towards Penmarch. When the wind failed we set Spinker, which so frightened the Frenchman ahead, who was also becalmed, that he immediately started up his engine.

When Mike pulled in the fishing line for the umpteenth time he found a strange eel-shaped fish with a sharp-pointed spike out ahead on the end of the line. It was nearly 2ft long, and more reminiscent of a slithering silver snake than anything. I kept well away from it. We contemplated eating it, but when we found the flesh was green, we thought again and threw it overboard. Later we learnt that it was a gar fish and said to be very good eating.

After spending the night in Audierne, I see that we were away at the appallingly early hour of 0520. My log also reminds me that it then took exactly forty minutes to do the next 100 yards, so little wind was there!

Thus, it was not until 1100 that we went through the Raz de Sein with a tearing tide under us, though the surface of the water was perfectly smooth. Spinker once again proved its worth on the fast downwind passage to Douarnenez. Here we were hailed by the local yacht club and given a mooring stern-on to the wall of the Rosmeur harbour.

After dining ashore on crabs' legs and red wine, we hardly believed our eyes when we woke in the morning to our first rain for nearly a fortnight. By now it was 9 July and we were due back in a week's time.

We spent that day beating up to Camaret, close past Cap de la Chevre and the ferocious outlying rocks of Les Tas de Pois, and on through the Toulinguet passage. At Camaret there were four other yachts, three British and one French. We anchored ahead of them just within earshot of the drunken crew of a nearby dredger.

Making an early start, we sailed across towards Pointe St Matthieu, which was hidden in a sullen grey mist. Visibility was barely a mile as we entered the southern end of the Chenal du Four. Passing Les Grands Moines, two sand barges sailed out, cutting inside the rocks as the tide turned against them.

At L'Aber-vrach we anchored east of the life-boat slip and went ashore. Alongside the quay the local fishing boats were busy unloading vast cargoes of mackerel, great fat ones, and masses of them. That evening we sailed right up the river to Paluden as it seemed likely to be more comfortable up there, should it blow up during the night.

Next morning there was a gale warning for our area, and two more yachts, *Hebe*, a 50 ton motorsailer, and *Dalua*, joined us. At this stage we had six days before we had to be back, and as the nearest West Country port was only a hundred miles away we saw no reason for worrying.

Little did we know that is was going to blow hard for the next six days with gale warnings at every single forecast for the next five. In that strong tideway we should have known that our big fisherman would not hold. At 0400 on our second day we both woke up suddenly to find that we were barely a couple of lengths from a rocky lee shore. Teeth chattering with fright and cold, we were only just in time to sail her away to safety. After that we picked up a local mooring with a very heavy chain, mooring between that and our own anchor.

The owners of *Hebe* were very good to us, asking us on board whenever they thought we needed to stand up and stretch our legs. For the rest of the time we played Battleships in the backs of our logs by the hour, and listened to the radio, which spoke of disasters at sea, one of which concerned a former shipmate being drowned in the Bay of Biscay.

On the fifth day we sailed down the river to L'Aber-vrach, but the wind was still north-westerly and very strong, making that coastline a dead lee shore. The following day we made an attempt to beat down and out of the river but gave up, realising that it was just plain foolhardiness and desperation that were making us try.

Never before has *Minion* sailed so fast as when we turned her round to go back up river. Under double-reefed mainsail she surfed at an incredible speed, with her bow wave coming up almost to deck level abaft the shrouds.

It was heart-rending to make the decision to leave our tiny boat in a French port unattended, but we had little choice. Mike was supposed to be back at work next day and I needed medical attention for a painful ear.

Three weeks later over the August Bank Holiday we returned to collect *Minion*. Sailing out in fine weather by the Malouin passage, we were off Ile Vierge on the Saturday afternoon.

We ran all night with the genoa boomed out right up through the shipping lane from Ushant to the Casquets, until a sudden squall hit us on Sunday morning. Mike quickly lowered everything. After ten minutes of torrential wind and rain the double-reefed main was set, and later the genoa boomed out again.

All Sunday we ran before a fresh south-westerly wind and revelled in it. A hundred and fifty miles showed on the log after 35 hours and then for four long hours we lay tossing without a breath.

Eventually a light southerly wind came in, enabling us to clear Customs off Yarmouth early on Monday afternoon. Twelve hours later Force 8 was reported off Portland Bill.

Then and now

Looking back on our days in *Minion* we have never forgotten what a tremendous adventure those first cruises were. It is obvious from the articles how proud we were and how we considered *Minion* to be quite well equipped.

At the time we were not concerned that we had no liferaft, no proper safety harnesses, no flares, no VHF, no engine and, therefore, no means of charging our three 6-volt motor cycle batteries. We had no standing headroom, not even stooping; there was just room for the two of us to sit up, one facing forward and one facing aft. The loo was a 'bucket and chuck it' and we had no water tanks, only carriers. We did, on the other hand, have a swinging stove. The genoa was known as the terylene genoa becuase this was its claim to superiority over the other sails which were cotton. In fact, it was a second hand sail from a Flying Dutchman, purchased for £5 including the sheets. We had a steering compass, a good hand bearing compass and an antiquated, even in those days, Walker's log. We had no RDF, no Echo sounder, but we did have a transistor radio which was the latest thing, on which we received weather forecasts as far south as Belle Isle.

Minion was like a model yacht with a parallelogram keel and a separate rudder aft. The expression, 'fin and skeg', had hardly been invented, nor had the suggestion that a yacht with that configuration was difficult to control downwind. *Minion* was superb on a run, steering easily and causing us the least effort on a downwind passage. It is because of our early experiences with *Minion* that I have always maintained that the length of the keel is not the feature by which a yacht's controlability should be judged. The answers lie in the hull lines, in the amount of beam and the balance of the bow and stern sections.

Cruising in Brittany in the early sixties was a totally different scene. The French economy had yet to recover from the war years and the explosion in sailing had not yet begun. We saw relatively few French yachts and the number of English yachts was sufficiently small that we would greet each other as fellow travellers in a distant land. There were no marinas, nor in England for that matter, we were never asked for any dues and when we came alongside it was not unusual to find a little crowd gathering with many gasps when they learnt that we were 'sans moteur'.

Cruising without an engine is a remarkable apprenticeship, particularly in the strong tides of the Channel Islands and Brittany. We had some anxious moments in failing winds when up tide of rocks and learnt to plan our approaches with the maximum safety margins. Crossing the shipping lanes was an exciting business. The tonnage of shipping was, I suppose less, and their individual speed and size less, but their lookouts were decidedly better and the rights of a vessel under sail were much more widely respected. Their preparedness to give way was more understandable, given the relatively small number of yachts that were to be found offshore in those days. How life has changed!

Navigation in *Minion* was an equally testing procedure. Passage making in fresh conditions was a matter of laying off a rhumb line on the chart before we left with a series of marks for each 20 miles to be sailed. The dead reckoning was then made largely in our heads as we judged how far one way or another we had been set by wind or tide away from that original rhumb line. The results were never a disaster, but then we never expected the accuracy that we feel should be achieved with today's sophisticated equipment.

Minion taught us a great deal. We were inordinately proud of her and loved her with a great love.

6

Blackjack Transatlantic 1981

This chapter is included here for the sake of the contrast between the simplicity of *Minion* and the sophistication of *Blackjack*. The depth of contrast is not so apparent in the sailing of the yachts but in the equipment. From the colossal power of the self tailing winches to the electronic wizardry of Sat Nav and Loran, *Blackjack*'s specification enabled two of us, the owner Rodney Barton and myself, neither of whom were any better than of average fitness for chairborne workers, to make a North Atlantic crossing in a time of 23 days which was considered fast for a 38ft yacht at that time.

Assisted Passage

It was rough – particularly that first week – but nowhere near as rough as it had been in March, when completing our qualifying mileage. Qualifying was a very unpleasant experience, but it did prepare us for heavy going, and we made none of the mistakes, nor suffered any of the problems, that had made trouble for us then.

Blackjack is rigged as a cutter with piston hanks on the main forestay and a Hood Seafurl on the staysail. Our technique in gale conditions was to abandon the main forestay and shorten down to three reefs in the mainsail and the staysail. This staysail is in heavy cloth with practically no overlap, it sheets inside the cap shrouds when behind a jib but outside when on its own. We always kept four sheets attached by leading the tail of the sheet back up to the sail. This meant that transferring from the inside to the outside sheeting position was never a problem. A fully reefed mainsail and staysail was a comfortable rig in an ordinary gale but when the wind rose into the 50s we would begin to roll up the staysail to tame the rig. Otherwise, the slamming as we flew over the back of the waves was too much. The boat might have been able to stand it but with 2000 miles still to go our nerves said no! The furling gear worked very easily when the staysail was in a slot between jib and

The original cutter rig, later to be abandoned in favour of a No 2 Genoa, except in very strong winds.

mainsail. When there was no jib and a full gale it was necessary to lead the furling line to a winch – it then wound incredibly tight, but the sail set very well.

There was trouble with other furling gears used on the main forestay of other yachts. In the sloop-rigged *Assassin*'s case her Dynafurl twisted irredeemably. This system is in effect a rotating stay, as opposed to a foil section rotating round a stay. *Assassin* was going very well until her stay failed and after that any wind forward of the beam left her seriously handicapped on her jury set up. In *Blackjack* we had spoken to her on

VHF during the first 48 hours and it was obvious to us that, at that stage, her furling gear was giving her an advantage. One of the great race winning factors in these events is an ability, or will, to get sail up again as a blow recedes. This is where the furling gear is excellent. It was so much less effort for *Assassin* to unroll sail than it was for us to change our jibs. In the event reliability was perhaps our trump card.

A word or two would be appropriate about our cutter rig and its suitability for the race. The race, believe it or not, is not about going to windward as in everyday sailing. Ordinarily on an inshore leg to windward it is speed made good to windward that is all important. Pointing and boat speed must be balanced to give the best combination in the direction of the weather mark. When crossing the Atlantic pointing ability is nowhere near so important. What really matters is boat speed all the time. If speed is sacrificed to point two or three degrees higher for 24 hours, it is possible to find that, as the weather pattern passes through, a south-westerly becomes a north-westerly. All that has been gained has served only to put the yacht further to leeward for the next 24 hours. In *Blackjack* we were amazed to find that for a very large proportion of the time we could sail more or less in the right direction. That far offshore more or less is good enough, and what matters is speed. Ticking off the lines of longitude was all important. Only in the closing stages down the Canadian coastline and across the Gulf of Maine did pointing matter, and then we were frequently able to carry the 150% genoa as a sloop. So, returning to the cutter rig, it was excellent when pointing ability did not matter. When trying to point over-sheeting the jib just stifled the rest of the rig, and boat speed fell off alarmingly.

One feature that was a success was a reef point in the luff of the No. 1 Jib (or Yankee). With the staysail rolled this enabled a reef to be pulled down shortening the luff and converting the No. 1 Jib to a No. 4 Genoa at a stroke. Set in this way it developed tremendous power on a reach with the centre of effort low down and was good for Force 6 or even 7.

Blackjack has a fairly modest sail plan and in order to offset this Hood made a light windward reacher in 2.8oz Laminar, Mylar and Dacron, which was a great success. The last few days were sometimes almost windless and this sail was a real powerhouse when needed.

While on the subject of sails we were particularly glad of our spinnaker squeezer. The working spinnaker was set whenever possible and the squeezer enabled one of us to set or hand the sail without disturbing the man below. Two points are worth mentioning. The equipment comes with a very long line attached and the natural tendency is to set this up as a double ended affair so that it can run through a block and serve as uphaul and downhall. We found, at an early stage, that this was a recipe for the most unholy tangles. Thereafter we had a separate and heavier (10mm) line which we attached as a downhaul, each time we hoisted. The great joy of the spi

Thrashing along in good Aries weather.

squeezer is that the sail is automatically packed before lowering it, and there is never an untidy heap of nylon that has to be carefully packed for rehoisting. It was a rule, instituted before starting, that all sails would be bagged on deck before they were brought below. To this end, when changing headsails, the one coming off was bagged on the foredeck before bringing it aft. We soon became used to this routine and the saving in terms of keeping the accommodation civilised was well worth while.

The mast and rigging was all supplied by Kemp Masts, and performed perfectly. The rig has two sets of crosstrees, and runners when sailing as a cutter. They were a nuisance to deal with tacking as they were led right aft with a 4:1 double whip led onto self-tailing winches. They were, however, very reassuring in heavy conditions and could be dispensed with altogether when sailing as a sloop. The only detail of the rig that we didn't like were the integral stoppers at the gooseneck. Particularly for short handed sailing they are always a bit awkward and, with four lines, identity at night is not easy. The reef pendants were operated on a centrally mounted winch on the coachroof, and four Spinlock jammers were later fitted forward of the winch, within easy reach, and these were a blessing.

We steered for about two hours after the start until the excitement had died down and after that only for one 40-minute spell when over canvassed and delaying a sail change. During the whole of the rest of the race either the Aries vane gear or the Autohelm 3000 kept us perfectly on course. *Blackjack* was designed for more than just the trans-Atlantic race and is fitted with Edson wheel steering which is delightfully smooth and light to handle. The hull design is finely balanced and free from any changing characteristics due to heel or roll. The rudder blade also has a small amount of balance area forward of the pivot, so that neither gear was ever short of power to keep her in the groove.

The great difference between the two systems is that the Aries vane gear is governed by the wind and the Autohelm by the compass. When sailing on the vane, the yacht could be settled into a groove and the man on watch could content himself with monitoring the compass to detect a serious shift. With the Autohelm the yacht steered a constant course and it was important to keep a regular eye on the sails because any change of wind would require an alteration of the sheets. This is an excellent combination, Aries coped with all the windward work and strong wind conditions and Autohelm with light airs and spin-nakering. Aries tended to allow a gentle weave downwind which did not matter with a boomed-out genoa but would upset a spinnaker. Autohelm kept the yacht on a very steady course until the wind and sea became too strong, and then Aries would react faster, and we would change over.

The operation of both systems was more complicated and difficult because of the wheel, particularly in the case of Aries. To obtain the best results it is necessary to introduce a certain amount of bias at the wheel or tiller to combat weather helm. This is a matter of declutching the wire drum that connects the tiller lines to the wheel and re-engaging it with the bias added. When tired it is sometimes quite difficult to get this right. On a tiller the bias is more obvious and much less thought is needed to couple up.

Our deck winches were all, bar one, self-tailers from Barlow. What a difference these make to one man alone on deck. A winch can be wound by either or both hands and, the moment the sheet or halyard is in, it can be left. We relied almost entirely on the self-tailers as cleats and, to our great surprise, we found that after 4000 miles of sailing there was no appreciable wear showing on the lines that could be attributed to the self-tailing mechanism. All the winches were two speed with both speeds geared and the choice of ratios always suited our needs well.

Before we had been at sea very long we developed such confidence in the self steering that we spent a great deal of our time on watch wedged into the navigator's comfortable seat by the chart table, monitoring our progress on an impressive array of electronics. The Brookes and Gatehouse Hercules System 190 was coupled to a Halcyon Compass, and the whole system was interfaced with the Walker Satnav, to give continuous updating of the read-out between satellite fixes. Two multi-function digital display units above the chart table would normally indicate boat speed and compass heading simultaneously, but, at the touch of a button, could be converted to indicate apparent wind speed, true wind speed, wind direction, dead reckoning, log or battery state. The dead reckoning computer is a useful way of monitoring the self steering to note the course achieved over a period. It would normally be reset when the noon position was noted. If, on the other hand, some interruption to the smooth running of the day occured, like a tack or a major wind shift, then the DR would be restarted. On *Blackjack* we only had one grouse, and that was that the damping of the digital speed read-out was surprisingly erratic. The boffins have programmed a very clever system of adaptive damping but to us this was not so logical as the systems we were used to on the older Harrier equipment. Sadly we suffered a loss of wind speed and direction information one dark and stormy night and the post mortem has not yet established the cause.

As already mentioned Hercules was coupled to the Walker Satnav. This is a truly remarkable piece of equipment and, particularly with the interface, is worth far more than the writer originally thought when it was first introduced. For those not used to sailing with Satnav it should be explained that there are two principle forms of display available. Display One shows the time and date and a continuously updated latitude and longitude of the yacht's position, the alternative is to display a Way Point. Up to 9 Way Points can be fed into the memories and on request the unit will display the distance to the Way Point, the bearing from the yacht, the course to steer, the ETA and the present heading of the yacht. Once again this information is continuously updated and the navigator has the option of relating the distance and bearings to a rhumb line or a great circle course.

While crossing the Atlantic we focused our attention on our 'Way Point 1' which was the further end of our great circle at 45° 30′N 50°00′W about 60 miles from the Virgin Rocks buoy off Cape Race. From the point of view of morale it was very encouraging to see the distance continuously reducing. From the point of view of navigation it was invaluable to have an instant indication of the course to steer to follow a great circle. What is more, each time the yacht is driven away from a great circle by a losing tack the instrument gives a new course, on a new great circle, from the current position. The Way Points are equally useful coasting. When short handed, it is much more use to be given a bearing and distance, from say a headland, than latitude and longitude. The only drawback that we could see was that Satnav had too high a consumption for continous operation. We really had above average battery capacity on *Blackjack* and two large 55 amp alternators on the main engine, which was used for charging. Our normal charging period of about 35 minutes a day kept pace with all other requirements but if Satnav was kept running that bank of batteries would fail to keep pace. The drain is nearly 2 amps, or the equivalent of a 25 watt navigation light bulb. When we realised that the consumption was causing a greater drain than the daily input we adopted the technique, which most other yachts used, of turning Satnav off for 24 or 48 hours at a time.

Satnav is only at its most accurate immediately after a satisfactory satellite transit and the frequency of these is very varied. There can be as much as two hours between acceptable fixes. In this respect we found that the Texas Instruments Loran C which we also carried was infinitely more accurate in the areas in which reception was possible. When we left Plymouth this instrument was a completely unknown quantity. Loran coverage does not satisfactorily include the English Channel and so we had no operating experience. In an idle moment somewhere around 35°W we put it to the test and began to obtain excellent results. Between the Grand Banks and Cape Sable results were very poor but after that they were again first class. Loran indicates from time co-ordinates that refer to a grid superimposed on the chart. The position is established from time differences of signals from co-ordinated shore stations, and is continuously corrected. From the battery consumption point of view results are available within a few minutes of switching on and very little programming is required.

In *Blackjack* we made our landfall on the Great Rip buoy on the Nantucket shoal. Our course to it lay along a Loran grid line so that once on the line, navigation was limited to keeping the numbers steady. This was done by the well known method of left hand down a bit, right hand down – and so on. The great advantage is that any tidal set is instantly recognisable by the sudden changing of the numbers. Diehards will say that it robs navigation of all its traditional skills – and they will be absolutely right. However when competing in an event where they are allowed, particularly short handed, there is no way that the traditional skills can ever compete on level terms with these sorts of electronic gadgets.

It is widely supposed that this race is a two-handed affair. Having read this far you will realise that our own efforts were reinforced by two indefatigable helmsmen, each a speccialist in his own weather condition, and at least two navigators. The one that has not yet been mentioned is the meteorologist. Coupled to the latest Brookes and Gatehouse Homer V radio receiver we had a Swiss-made Nagrafax facsimile machine with which we obtained very good weather maps four times a day. Providing the batteries were not too low the print out was of excellent quality. We soon learnt that a powerful transmission from Hamburg gave the best results for the greater part of the distance until we were within range of Halifax and could get a detailed analysis covering the last 1000 miles of the course. It is difficult looking back to identify any one moment on the race when, because of Nagrafax, we made a momentous decision that improved our time. A small yacht moves across the chart so slowly that it is generally not possible to place oneself in relation to oncoming weather with any degree of success. The weather maps that we received gave us a far greater understanding of the weather pattern around us which, we felt, helped us a lot. As a result our discussions on strategy always had a sound basis. When one has a picture of the weather and can anticipate changes one is so much better equipped to make the right decisions.

As each depression passes there are generally southerlies, followed by south westerlies, followed by north-westerlies. This is assuming that the depressions pass to the north, which they generally did. On board there are two options as the situation develops. Head up on port tack in the southerlies in anticipation of being headed by the south-westerlies. This takes the yacht away from the centre of the depression. Or, alternatively, free off in the southerlies and go as hard and fast as possible, but more towards the centre, particularly if you have a good heavy weather boat. This technique means that when the south-westerlies come, if you have been successful in moving closer to the centre, the time spent hard on port tack is appreciably reduced before the arrival of the north-westerlies to the rear of the depression. This sort of decision is far easier with a weather map in your hand and when the speed and direction of the depression is known.

We were not so hot on communications. We carried a Sailor MF, SSB, Transceiver but did not use it, preferring to save power and effort for other things. We did use VHF when we sighted a ship and enjoyed some welcome exchanges. Ships at sea appear to keep Channel 16 open on the bridge so that any call is taken directly by the officer of the watch. Two particular conversations stand out in our memories. The first was at about 51°N 29°W when we spoke to the 129,000 ton *Georgia* on passage from the Bahamas to Teeside. We estimated our distance to be two miles or less and the ship was very clear to us. There was a big swell and sea running and we only had a reduced rig set and the ship was never able to see us. They sent a message via the owners to our families reporting all well aboard which we all appreciated very much. The second memorable exchange was on the Flemish Cap, a small area of soundings east of the Grand Banks, where a Canadian Fishery Protection vessel, *Terra Nova* closed us and gave us a transatlantic welcome. It was our first contact with a Canadian accent and we had the feeling that not only were we able to get a reading on the echo sounder once more, but we had at the same time made contact with friendly natives! The *Terra Nova* confirmed that our radar reflector gave a strong blip on their screen which raised our confidence for plunging through the fog that was to come.

The Grand Banks themselves provided fairly clear visibility but the whole way down the Nova Scotia coast visibility was shocking. The fog occasionally closed right in to the length of the yacht. More frequently it would be about 100 yards to 200 yards, and accompanied by plenty of wind. It is an eerie and unsettling world that one charges through with an unpleasant sensation that the world has tipped to one side. The waves to windward show up fairly clearly whereas those going away to leeward have no definition and are swallowed up by the fog. On deck it is impossible to avoid the sensation that the sea is sloping from windward to leeward and the yacht is sliding sideways.

Competing in a transatlantic race without contact with the shore is rather like waiting for exam results at the end of term. We knew that Chay Blyth had finished in 14 days from the BBC Overseas service Sports round up. We knew we could finish in around 23 days, which was as good as we had hoped for, but where were all our closest rivals? Would they be standing on the dock saying what kept you? Or were they still at sea?

At daybreak on the last morning, as we sat motionless on a glassy sea and as the sun rose, there was *Poppy* only a mile or so astern and probably rowing hard. There was a private wager between the owners and so out came our oar, and so began the longest Monday of our lives. We always knew that *Poppy*, a High Tension 36 reduced to 35ft by snubbing the bow, would be difficult to beat in light airs. With a taller mast and less wetted surface she had to have an edge. If you have never tried rowing 7½ tons of yacht you are lucky. In absolutely dead conditions we managed to maintain 0.75 knots rowing with one 14ft sweep against a primary winch. Our 1oz spinnaker always seemed to be hanging under the bow even when an air did come – talk about navigating blind – we had absolutely no forward vision. Fortunately the breeze built up very gently from the shore ahead and at 12.38 local time we crossed the line doing nearly 3 knots and still 8 minutes ahead of *Poppy*. We did not win any prizes in our class, as one English and two French monohulls had already finished. *Poppy* got the prize for the second monohull in Class V and between us we were the second and third English monohulls to arrive overall.

7

Family sailing

The contrast in sailing over the twenty year span between *Minion* and *Blackjack* is far deeper than the writing indicates. In the early Sixties GRP was a new untried material which had yet to transform the scene. The design and construction of sails, masts and rigging had not advanced to the extent where we can now fit an almost unbustable rig.

The combination of all these features has meant that we now build yachts that continue to make to windward in really quite appalling conditions. In 1961 there were no yachts of the size of *Blackjack* that would continue to drive to windward in 55 knots of wind in the open Atlantic without suffering damage.

For my part I revel in the power of the modern yacht. I have no compunction about using all the modern aids that are on offer. I believe I appreciate them the more because I remember sailing without them and because they enable us to continue with enterprising sailing despite the fact that we are no longer in the first flush of youth.

With great sadness we sold *Minion* at the end of 1961, because we were leaving London and needed funds to buy our first house. It was not long however before we were scheming away to find the means of getting afloat once again.

By 1963 we had become a family of three and so a good deal more attention to civilised conditions was needed if we were to combine successfully our thirst for the sea with the role of loving and caring parents.

We satisfied the need for a larger yacht by purchasing a cold moulded Folkboat hull from Jeremy Rogers and completing the deck and interior ourselves. Our neighbours questioned the suitability of calling her *Whisper*. Boat building in the open was an embarassingly noisy occupation and it was to their eternal credit that they suffered so long in silence.

And the Children came too . . .

Whisper gave us a lot of pleasure and in addition to cruising in her as a family, which incidentally very soon became a complement of four, I raced in the Solent and across to Alderney. Racing was a very Corinthian and easy going sport in those days. One hoisted the sails and just sheeted them in. By comparison with today's events life was superbly relaxed. The crew were allowed to sit in the cockpit, so one sailed with fairly small crews, and one never thought of using them as movable ballast with their legs over the side. What an idea!

Before the children arrived Pat and I were always driven by ambition to sail as far as we could in the time available and we realised when *Whisper* went afloat that our increased family would present us with a much tighter rein, that would force us to curb our enthusiasm.

We were determined not to put the children off boats if we could possibly help it and, as our efforts were well rewarded, I feel a few comments on those early years of family sailing are worth including.

The most conscious decision that we made was to give sailing a purpose. I believe that young children, up to the age of eight or ten at least, find very little about the activity of sailing in large yachts to appreciate the sailing for itself alone. To this end we hardly ever took the children out for a sail that did not go somewhere. If there was the anticipation of arriving in some place that they enjoyed, preferably with a beach, then the discomforts on the way could quite easily be endured.

The smaller they were the easier we found our passage making. The carricot stage is the least difficult of the lot. The motion of a small yacht has much the same effect as a well rocked cradle. Once asleep the motion tends to keep them that way. For years we did our serious passage making at night or, at least, early in the morning. We found that, whereas they normally woke at six or half past, if we sailed at four or five, they would stay splendidly somnolent till much later in the morning.

The inevitable result of a night passage to Alderney would be two tired parents dying for their bunks and two bright and chirpy youngsters clamouring for the beach. By continuing the watch system well into the first day in harbour we managed to survive; and, oh, how they loved those beaches!

We avoided announcing any intention of taking our holiday in a specific area for many years. In answer to 'where are we going?' we would say where the wind takes us and avoid either disappointment or the horrors of fighting the elements to make a difficult destination.

When they were eight and seven we crossed the Channel in daylight for the first time. The conditions were good and with endless games of I Spy and some afternoon sleep the passage went very well. Suddenly they began to get some understanding of distance and realisation that there really was a lot of water to cross between the disappearance of

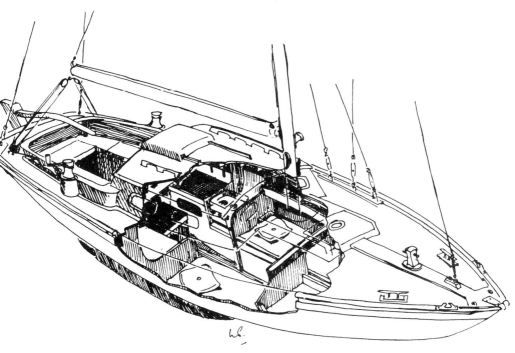

Whisper *was built on a cold moulded Folkboat hull with a straight sheer and a small coachroof aft of the mast.*

England and the first sighting of France.

It was another six years before we attempted to be ambitious as a family and allow the children to share the concept of trying to break new ground. By 1976 they were keen and useful crew members and we made a cruise to the Scillies and home along the Brittany coast that was a great success.

Sailing is like so many other sports in that the younger you start the easier you learn. I will always remember the comments that Peter Cook, editor of *Yachts and Yachting*, made when we were sailing home to Lymington after a Round the Island race in 1973. During the race the gear had been handled, as one might expect, by the adult crew members and our two children, then aged ten and nine had been supernumaries. Once the race was over and we were beating back to Lymington, they took over the primary winches and wound away at the genoa sheets with a vengeance. As Peter pointed out, one would normally be cautious of allowing children of that age, who were less familiar with the gear, to handle the potentially dangerous heavily loaded sheets of a 35 footer under full genoa. Our two, having grown up handling ropes, had an instinctive ability which meant that we never worried ourselves about the possible dangers. It also meant that they could safely help with the running of the boat from a young age.

Winches appeal to small boys and somehow it got into Richard's head that he would soon grow so strong that he would pull the clew right out of a genoa. He never succeeded but they both became enthusiastic winch winders while they tried.

The second, very important factor, that concerns sailing with the very young is the need to avoid any undue anxiety. By that I mean that the sailing that is attempted must be as free from incident; that is unplanned, unintended incident, as possible. Anxiety is terribly infectious and any doubts by the parents will be transmitted to the child and amplified on the way. Have you ever noticed that if you get lost when in a motor car, the uncertainties are invariably picked up by the young in the back seat. Just when you are trying to make head or tail of the map, junior starts up a tearful howl which comes from the unhappiness felt because, to him, the fact that the family is lost is a major disaster. In just the same way, if it is felt that Mummy and Daddy are not quite in control of the situation afloat, that sense of being lost is felt much more strongly by the young and leads to instant unhappiness.

When there were only two of us the idea of an Easter cruise that went from Lymington to Yarmouth, to the Hamble and home by way of Buckler's Hard would have seemed dreadfully tame. With two children under four it took an altogether different dimension. Not unlike the challenge faced by the crew of a cruise liner who must overcome all local hazards without alarming the first class passengers.

Looking back, these cruises were a lot of fun. A yacht's interior is like a Wendy house to a child and lends itself to amusing games. High leecloths made superb safe playpens of the saloon berths. When stuck in harbour, raising the mattresses to the top of the leecloths to form individual 'houses' was considered tremendous sport.

I believe it is important to make children feel that they are contributing as crew members, rather than passengers, from the earliest possible age. This does not on any account mean insisting on their doing things when they can not see the point. Our two learnt to steer at an early age including steering a compass course. When cruising they would take the helm to free us for some job that needed doing, but at that age they did not have the urge to steer, that has come later, and once our job was done, they expected to give us back the helm.

This 'you are needed' feeling became so well established that in later years they have been really quite surprised to find that their aged parents can in fact sail the boat reasonably successfully without them!

8

To Iceland

As with all things the cycle of life moves on and the young are no longer so young and are making their own way in the world. With less parental responsibility Pat and I find ourselves with less ties and just as much thirst for new cruising grounds as we had in our days in *Minion*.

When Rodney Barton built *Lumberjack*, also to my design, *Blackjack* became available secondhand and Pat and I jumped at the chance of buying her for ourselves. We moved to a smaller, and incidentally more convenient house, to raise the funds and count ourselves very fortunate to have become the proud owners of such a yacht.

Immediately upon becoming the owners we entered *Blackjack* for the Two handed Round Britain and Ireland race in 1985 and the Two handed Transatlantic race in 1986. When we have done these two races together I fondly imagine that we shall scrub the racing numbers off the bows and concentrate on more genuine cruising. In the meantime, 1984 was a non-racing year for two handers and we elected to take three months away in the summer to cruise in northern waters.

We chose to go north mainly because we thought we could go south when we were older and that we should tackle the more rugged prospects of Iceland and the Faroes while we were fit enough to cope. *Blackjack* is at her best when the conditions are at their worst, so we felt confident that we had the right yacht for the job. As entrants for the 1986 TransAtlantic race we needed to do a qualifying sail. For our own self confidence, we wanted to do this in the North Atlantic and short of going right across, Iceland seemed an obvious alternative.

The more we read about the country and its bird life, the more we wanted to go. Having been, we can truthfully say that we were never disappointed. Life was uncomfortable at times and some of the weather was pretty miserable, but this just made the good days seem even better and the achievement that much more rewarding.

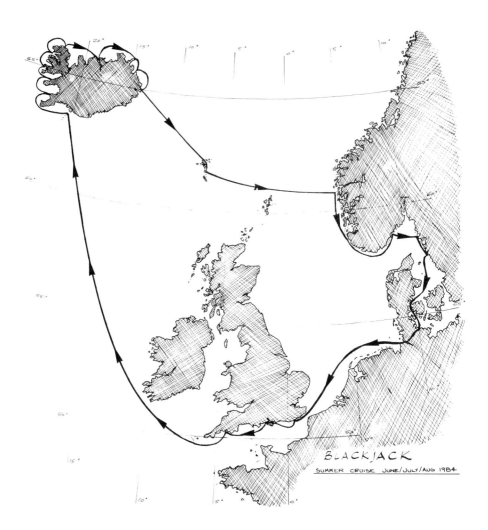

Our Northern cruise in 1984 took us right round Iceland, by way of the Faroes to Norway, into the Baltic and home through the Kiel canal.

Months of preparation, including the inevitable horrors of trying to leave one's affairs and partly completed house alterations in good order, were almost more demanding than the trip itself. In the end we got away from Lymington just in time to reach Plymouth before the OSTAR start. Dazzled by the complexity and freakishness of the mighty multis and staggered by their speed across the water we spent the weekend in Plymouth seeing to some final bits and pieces.

Our duty free stores were delivered first thing on Monday and we were off. We had an easy reach to The Lizard and then rather tedious headwinds as we made our way towards southern Ireland. It took us until Wednesday midday to make a landfall. Lot's Wife could be seen through the haze, standing guard at the entrance to Baltimore harbour. A gleam of sun shone through to light up Cape Clear Island and the Fastnet rock could just be seen as we passed to the north. This was to be our last view of the land for the next 800 miles or so and now we felt we were into the Atlantic proper.

That night we thought the Atlantic was going to live up to its name as we shortened sail to a fresh north westerly and settled down to a hard beat to windward. Next morning conditions eased again and we worked away, more westward than northward, in fairly fickle and changeable conditions. At supper time that evening we passed an Irish fishing boat and Pat spoke to them on the VHF. That was the last vessel we were to sight for the next six days.

On Friday the wind began to fail and by evening our progress had become ridiculously slow. As the evening wore on we lowered first the genoa and then the mainsail as well, to avoid the frightful slatting that would otherwise have just been useless wear on the sails. So began the Great and Absolute Calm. At 0930 next morning we rehoisted the mainsail and then the floater spinnaker and for a short while reached the dizzy speed of 3 knots. Alas, by lunch time, all was calm again and down came the sails once more.

Off the English and Irish coasts we had used the motor, albeit sparingly, in the flattest spots but out in the Atlantic we forebore. We had only limited supplies of diesel and we felt this should be reserved for emergencies. We could not motor all the way and if we had lost or damaged the rig we would have been glad we had conserved our fuel and could perhaps make the nearest harbour. And so we sat it out, rolling constantly, on an otherwise glassy surface. In these conditions we were visited by porpoises with beautifully striped side markings. With no ripples and superbly clear water, their antics could be followed easily as they chased each other around us, occasionally plummeting to, what seemed, colossal depths.

In the latter part of Saturday, occasional airs would come, sometimes incredibly locally. There was a time, for instance, when reaching under main and genoa, we achieved as much as six knots, where the cats' paws lay on the water, only to reach the end of them and run out of steam completely, as we shot into unruffled areas where the calm still persisted.

Eventually at about 0200 on Sunday a more reliable air appeared and we were underway at a modest speed once more. By 0500 this had freed and, determined to use the precious air to its utmost, we hoisted the floater once again. This magic sail hangs in the air, with little or no attendance, in conditions where the anemometer cups are having a struggle to keep turning.

By breakfast time the air had become a wind and down came the floater to be replaced by the working spinnaker. This is packed in a Spee Squeezer and so is much safer for the two of us to handle in a freshening breeze. By lunch time we had changed once again, this time to the small, heavy spinnaker. Now we were churning away to the north at a steady 6½ or 7 knots with our morale boosted and our spirits high.

To sit for so long in a complete calm is to appreciate a wind when it does come. For the wind to be a fair one was too good to be true and we meant to make the most of it.

At 2300 on Sunday night we were forced to accept that it would be prudent to change to a boomed out headsail. This we set with 117 miles logged since we broke out the floater at 0500 that morning.

On Monday morning, one week out from Plymouth, the wind was freshening so that we pulled down one reef in the mainsail. No easy task when bombing downwind at 7½ knots plus. We also have a reef in the luff of the No. 1 jib which is a high cut sail for the cutter rig. Pulling this down at the same time kept the rig balanced and checked the roll. By now the wind was a good Force 6 and *Blackjack* began to restore the average daily run to a more respectable figure.

All the time we were logging seven miles regularly every hour and Percy, our faithful autopilot, kept us happily upon a straight and steady course. Percy is a prototype of a new Autohelm and we were to send back reports on his behaviour to Nautech, the makers, from Iceland. As the weather became colder we appreciated Percy more and more. He never complained. He never wanted a spell for a warm up down below and his only form of answering back was an electric bleep to acknowledge that his buttons were being pressed.

By Tuesday, the wind was beginng to come ahead and life became wetter and therefore colder. Forewarned about the cost of food in Iceland and Scandinavia, we were carrying a vast quantity of stores and all sorts of spares and extra equipment so *Blackjack* was floating fairly deep and not rising to each wave quite so readily as at her usual displacement. This meant that, as the wind increased to Force 7, we were obliged to shorten sail, more to limit the quantity of green seawater charging aft along the deck, than for reasons purely related to sail carrying.

As the air becomes colder, and this air was coming straight from Greenland, so it becomes denser and anemometer readings become less significant. With 25 to 30 knots of true wind blowing we were reduced to a fully reefed mainsail and a partially rolled staysail. This is the rig we would normally expect to come down to in a full Force 8 or 9 in more southerly climes. Despite this the boat speed was still around 6½ knots and Iceland was becoming ever closer.

In these conditions watch followed watch as we cowered under the pramhood or monitored conditions from the repeaters at the chart table. Life was cold and rough but progress was good. So long as the gear held, the only consideration was the discomfort, the navigation and maintaining a reasonable lookout. We dread the advent of some problem on deck and we preserve our strength to deal with whatever

Blackjack *lying alongside a fishing boat in the small boat harbour at Heimaey in the Vestmann Islands.*

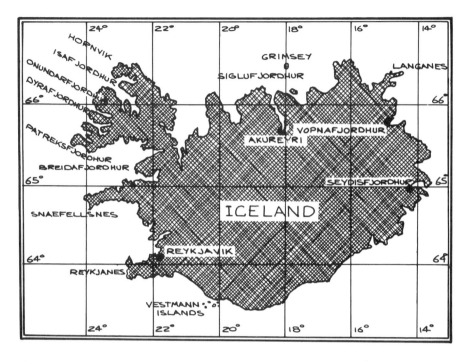

The places around the coastline of Iceland have long and sometimes unpronounceable names.

may arise. One small problem which may cause an upset of the routine can easily lead to a more major problem and from these beginnings real difficulties can and will occur. Fortunately for us our gear remained intact and we hammered on without incident.

Our intended landfall was to be in the Vestmann Islands, so named because the earliest settlers were Irishmen. These islands lie at about 7 o'clock if Iceland were a clockface and have within them the most recent volcanic activity.

Imagine our delight when at 2000 on Wednesday evening, with the overcast sky at last cleared and a pale sunshine lighting the sea, we sighted the island of Surtsey to the westward and knew that we were almost there. Surtsey is the island that rose from the sea in a violent volcanic eruption in 1963, where no island existed before.

All that evening more islands appeared and we bore away slightly for the harbour on the island of Heimaey, 20 miles to the north. It was bitterly cold but brilliant in the evening sun. The sea birds were around us in great numbers and on the mainland of Iceland we could see the great icecap of the 5000ft Eyjafjalla Jokull.

Heimaey had a major eruption only eleven years ago and the lava flow nearly closed the harbour entrance; nearly but not quite. Two hundred yards of clear water remain and we entered between towering old cliffs on the starboard hand and the jagged black lava field on the other. The land is still steaming, although quite dormant as a volcano. Such a landfall gave us the feeling that we had reached another world so weird were the effects.

In ten and a half days we had logged 1180 miles to cover just 1000 on the rhumb line. Every night was shorter than the one before, but also every night was less dark. By the time we arrived in the harbour at thirty minutes after midnight it was just getting dark, but more on account of the towering cliffs around us than the general darkness of the night.

The harbour was almost completely deserted, as we nosed our way in, and we eventually found the basin for small boats and laid alongside the most suitable looking fishing boat. This was to be our first night of cruising in non yachting waters. As a lone yacht we were welcomed into fishing harbours all round Iceland. We were always able to find a berth, either alongside a fishing boat that was not going out or otherwise alongside a vacant section of the quay. We never encountered a harbour master or were asked for any dues. Our arrival always generated interest and friendliness, with good English spoken, particularly by the younger generation.

There are yachts in Reykjavik, not in the main harbour, and also at two places on the north coast, but the numbers are really very small.

The coastline of Iceland is very inhospitable in the south eastern quarter, and this was why we had chosen to arrive at the Vestmann islands in order to start a cruise of the coastline clockwise up the west coast, along the north coast and part of the way down the east coast.

We had a deadline to make at Seydisfjordhur on the east coast. This is where the ferries arrive and we had an arrangement to meet a friend who would arrive there on July 12th. We would then sail three up to the Faeroes and on to Bergen, where a further crew change was planned.

Round Iceland

If you cruise in Icelandic waters you know for a start that you have arrived at somewhere really different. In the first place yachts are, by our standards, a rarity. There is no yachtsman's pilot book. When you reach a new harbour there is no sign to the 'visitors berths'. You must find your own way from the Icelandic and Admiralty charts and the Admiralty Arctic Pilot Volume II. Remember, that Icelandic waters were much used by the British Navy in World War II to assemble Arctic convoys, so that charts are reliable with good detail of the strategic fjords.

There is no need to be a geologist to appreciate the fantastic and sometimes grotesque features of the landscape. Iceland lies at the northern end of the great North Atlantic fault on which the Azores also feature. The division in the plates of the earth's crust passes through the Vestmann Islands and across the central areas of the country to the north coast. In Iceland the plates are actually moving apart so that the central part of the land is much younger geologically than the western and eastern ends. There are hot springs, geysers and bubbling sulphur beds to be seen and relatively recent volcanic activity means that the vegetation is, to us, sparse and immature. There are several major ice caps, snow covered twelve months of the year. We were there in June and early July and the snow on the hills was only partially melted, leaving an intriguing and beautiful pattern of purple and white, with dazzling waterfalls, fuelled by the melt water.

Rainfall in the south-west is liberal, to say the least, and any visiting yacht would be well advised to get away from Reykjavik and on up to the north without delay. The prevailing movement of the weather system gives dryer weather with more summer sunshine in the north and, quite apart from anything else, the midnight sun is an unforgettable experience. Friends have asked us whether we had difficulty in sleeping on account of the light nights. Frankly, we lived our lives so much to the full, determined to make the greatest use of our available time, that, when we did call it a day, the need for sleep was so strong that the problem never arose.

One does not go to Iceland for the beauty of the architecture, nor for the picturesque layout of the towns. Each settlement has a distinctly frontier atmosphere about the place. Urban landscaping has obviously been intended but seldom carried to completion. Roads are, with a few exceptions, unmetalled and out of town distinctly rough. The population of the whole of Iceland is only around 250,000, roughly comparable with Southampton. Reykjavik, the capital, and Akureyri in the north, are the only towns of any size, the rest are no more than villages and seldom have more than 1000 inhabitants. Communities are small and isolated and outside of Reykjavik petty crime just does not seem to exist. We soon gave up locking the yacht when we went ashore and revelled in the complete trust that seemed to prevail.

The Icelanders were very friendly. The younger generation spoke good English and we were always welcomed into their small harbours. A small crowd would often gather to view our arrival but soon disperse. Their questions were uninhibited and very direct. One of the first questions asked would be how much had the yacht cost, which is fairly natural in a country where the ownership of a motor car is generally the only major outlay that will be made, other than for their house. The children are used to having the free run of the fishing boats and visiting coasters, so that they have a tendency to come aboard and gaze in the hatchway without invitations. This took a bit of getting used to but they meant no harm and were never mischievous.

We spent three nights in Vestmannaeyar and climbed to the top of the new volcano. Even though the eruption was eleven years ago, the gound is still steaming and hot gases escape from yawning holes around one's feet. We marvelled at the thought that on the first night of the eruption, which lasted five months, all the 5000 inhabitants of the town were evacuated in their own fishing fleet. Now they are back and the fish factories are working again. By drilling into the lava beds and pumping cold water down, a hot water supply is created. The houses are all built in concrete using the volcanic ash as aggregate and the roofs are corrugated iron, painted.

The passage from Vestmannaeyar to Reykjavik was about 120 miles and leaving at mid morning, we were in for a late breakfast next day. The VHF operator provided us with an accurate English language weather forecast which was a great help. He told us that the south-easterly wind that was, at that time, quite gentle, would slowly increase and at midnight become fresh to strong south-westerly.

To reach Reykjavik we had to round Reykjanes (the 'nes' is pronounced separately like our own Ness meaning headland), so up went the spinnaker to make the fastest possible time on the first leg and avoid meeting the south-westerly before reaching the headland. In mid-afternoon we were inspected by a group of killer whales with the distinctive black and white markings. It was marvellous to see these immaculately smart creatures in their natural element.

We rounded Reykjanes with a fair tide, stronger than expected, and as we headed north the weather deteriorated, as forecast, and we reduced sail accordingly. It was cold and raining as we entered the main harbour in Reykjavik and we found a snug berth alongside the Customs launch in the north-west corner. It was Sunday and also a public holiday and the young Customs men who visited us told us we could remain alongside until the following morning. We found the Customs very easy to deal with, given coffee, they were delighted to chat and proved a great source of information. Next morning we moved across to the fishing harbour and lay alongside a boat with a broken engine. This gave us the necessary security to leave the yacht for a day and take a coach tour inland. Once again it rained, but this probably meant we were seeing that part of the country in its true colours.

Our main ambition was to reach the fjord country in the north-west so we made another long passage from Reykjavik into the Breidafjordhur. Once again there was a 'nes' to be rounded, this time Snaefellnes on which sits the 4700ft snow covered Snaefells Jokull. This time we were less well aware of the coming weather and a vicious head wind hit us in the middle of the evening chilli con carne and continued to blow throughout the night. Not only that, it blew anti-clockwise around the mountain, that we were rounding in the opposite direction. There was a steep and horrible sea caused by a fair stream and squalls of rain blotted out the visibility. Each time we hoped we might ease sheets, the wind would come ahead once again and, all in all, it was a distinctly tedious performance.

The Breidafjordhur is the one place where off lying skerries or rocky patches make the navigation less easy. In general, in the other fjords, the water away from the shore was clean and deep, but not so in the Breidafjordhur. Apart from a couple of alarmingly low echo sounder

We rounded Bjartanger, the most westerly headland in Europe in relatively peaceful conditions.

readings, where we expected deep water, we successfully found the way into the Kolgrafafjord. We were greeted by two fishermen in a fast inflatable who we asked aboard for a beer. They were keen that we should anchor close to their island, at the entrance to the fjord, and visit their house. Regrettably we pleaded lack of sleep, not liking the prospect of leaving the yacht unattended in such a position, and put our hook down well up the fjord in almost total seclusion.

The following day saw us rounding Bjargtanger, the most westerly point of Iceland, and heading up the Patreksfjordhur. One uses the expression 'a day sail' in rather elastic terms. It was broad daylight when we weighed anchor at 0400 and it was light enough to launch the dinghy and take photographs when we dropped anchor again at 2330 that night, having logged 75 miles on the way.

It was in fact the first really lovely sunny day and our morale rose considerably. The wind was never more than 8 knots true and the motor was called upon for eleven of the nineteen hours we were underway. The dreaded Snaefells Jokull, around which we had battled in such filth earlier, became bathed in sunshine, and lay to the south looking utterly innocent and benign. On such a day, visibility is fantastic and the backdrop of mountains stretched away for sixty miles at least.

It was on this day that we caught our first cod. For a yacht cod fishing has to be a light weather exercise because one must be stopped. The

Flat calm in the Isafjordhur in the extreme north west of Iceland.

Our first sighting of ice off Straumnes. As it melts the ice takes on the most grotesque and often very beautiful shapes.

technique is to lower the line, with a series of lures (in our case artificial squid) and a weight, to the bottom, preferably in over forty metres. The line is then raised one metre and jiggled until a bite is felt. Sometimes the results are immediate and at other times a total failure. The Icelanders think nothing of eating cod themselves, familiarity breeds contempt, perhaps, but freshly grilled cod steaks of ample proportions gave us great delight in *Blackjack*. Everyone agreed that the cod war was a thing of the past and we were welcome to whatever we would catch for our own pot.

In the Patreksfjordhur we anchored at the head of navigation and after such a long day at sea chose to spend the next at anchor. We climbed about 1,800ft to the snow line, took copious photos and watched the snow buntings and wheatears. At sea level the eider ducks were a magnificent sight; great flights of black and white drakes coming home low over the water, like a squadron of jets returning to base.

From Patresksfjordhur we sailed to the Dyrafjordhur; from there to the Onundarfjordhur and then to Isafjordhur. Each fjord tends to have an 'eyri' which is, in effect, a gravelly spit extending into the fjord from one shore with a deep passage off the end of it and shelter behind it. It is on these eyris that the settlements are built with their small harbours on the inland side. The eyri is echoed in the place names, such as Vatneyri, Thingeyri, Flateyri and Akureyri.

In the north-west corner we sailed up the Isafjord, spending the first night in the fishing harbour at Isafjordhur. From there we set out to explore the great spit of land that forms the northern side of the fjord. No roads penetrate this area and the only signs of habitation are isolated holiday homes for use in the summer. These are only accessible by water or by trekking on foot overland so that these are the nearest thing to uninhabited shores that one can find in western Europe.

There was plenty of sunshine to light up the awe inspiring and magnificent scenery and the wind blew either. Force 6 or 7 or Force 1 or less. We approached the Dranga Jokull from two separate directions and spent two nights away from any sign of the rest of humanity whatever at the head of the Hesteyrifjordhur. When the time came to leave for the north coast we were monitoring Channel 16 and overheard an exchange with an English ship headed past Straumnes into the Denmark Strait. The gist of the conversation was that the operator was confirming that there was eight miles of clear water between the pack ice moving in the East Greenland current and the end of Straumnes. We had rather expected there to be more like 30 miles and had not anticipated the likelihood of sighting ice.

Before we reached Straumnes, for which we had the sheets slightly eased on port tack, we suddenly saw a line of brilliant white to seaward, no very great distance from our own position. This proved too much of a draw and, abandoning hopes of reaching our chosen anchorage at a civilised hour, we hardened up and beat out to sea.

About five miles off we found a series of small bergs, none more than eight feet high and many of them in an advanced state of melt. Decay would be the wrong word for such superb pieces of natural sculpture. The shapes were grotesque but yet had a delicacy and beauty all their own. Where the thickness was more substantial they were an iridescent blue which appeared to have a brightness out of all proportion to the dullness of an otherwise overcast afternoon.

Knowing the icebergs' reputation for being far greater under water than above, we sailed with great care between them and burnt off miles of film in a frenzy of excitement. Turning back towards Straumnes once again, we now had a fair wind and with time to make up we hoisted the working spinnaker and fairly reeled off the miles. The sun came out and we tore along past a series of great capes. The guillemots, razorbills, puffins and fulmars flew around us in unbelievable profusion. Our final headland brought us to the lovely bay of Hornvik. Open to the north but, on this occasion, completely quiet, we lay with nothing between us and the North Pole. On shore the highlight of the evening was a pair of red necked phalaropes bobbing at the water's edge, the first we had ever seen. I wish I could describe the place as having perfect tranquillity, but half an hour after we had turned in, the peace was shattered by the rasping scream of a chain saw! A fishing boat from Isafjordhur had chosen the same night to come in to collect driftwood from the beach. Thank goodness they only kept the saw going for thirty

To make up for lost time we set the working spinnaker and had the most exhilarating sail through the Denmark Strait towards Hornvik.

minutes or so, and after that we were dead to the world.

It was foggy with no more than 300 yards visibility when we left in the morning with a gentle easterly that gradually died. We cleared the mighty headland of Horn and set off across the great bay that lay between us and entrance to Eyjafjordhur, 90 miles to the east. Around midday the fog lifted and gave way to brilliant sunshine and to the south of us we had a superb view of the Dranga Jokul, gleaming white. The wind came and went and we motored on and off as the day wore on. Late that evening we came upon another line of ice stretching from the north east in towards the land in a south westerly direction. This time, about 2200, the sun was shining and the colours were truly memorable. Once again we consumed film at a great pace as the only means of 'taking home the ice'.

Shortly before midnight we found a good breeze off the shore and with genoa drawing well we started the most unforgettable 'night' sail that can be imagined. Just after 0100 (we were on GMT, which is also local time), the sun sank two thirds of its disc into the horizon and for forty minutes there seemed to be no change before it slowly rose out of the water again. It was always light enough to read the chart quite clearly at the chart table and on deck it was perpetual sunshine. It was by now the night of 1st/2nd July and the longest day was ten days past; in addition, we were still some twenty-five miles or so south of the Arctic Circle.

By 0730 we were alongside some picturesque, but distinctly shakey, old wooden staging in Sigludjordhur enjoying breakfast on deck for the first time on this cruise. Nearly all the harbours have well engineered steel piling lining their harbour walls with a mass of motor tyres as fenders. Siglufjordhur was one of the few places where the old staging remained.

It is thirty miles up the Eyjafjordhur to Akureyri and we carried the spinnaker most of the way. The scenery was breathtaking, despite all we had seen before, and we arrived in Akureyri shortly after a French yacht, the third yacht we had seen under sail, the first non Icelandic, passed us beating out.

There were two small Icelandic yachts in the tiny harbour at Akureyri and later a third arrived. One was a David Thomas designed Quarter Tonner and the other two were a Swedish cruising design built under licence near Reykjavik. The owners are very keen and made us welcome. Later, when we came to leave, they sailed with us on board *Blackjack* as we beat in an increasing breeze back down the fjord. Their wives picked them up from Dalvik where we spent the night. Next

Guillemots riding a small bergy bit off the north coast of Iceland. This photograph was taken in clear sunlight at 10.00pm in the evening.

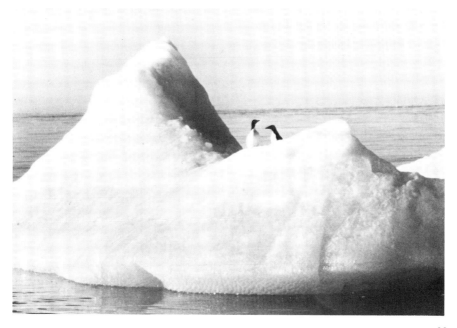

morning we beat out to the tiny island of Grimsey which lies on the Arctic Circle.

Here we were entertained by an expatriate Englishman. Having been unemployed in Middlesbrough, he had gone out into the world to seek work. He found employment in Iceland, liked it and settled down. Now he has his own fishing boat and an ample income. He has married an Icelandic girl and they have three delightful children. Their house to which we were invited for Sunday lunch was warm and very comfortable. One could not help seeing the pride and well being of this man who had made his own way in the world at a time that others reckon that the world owes them a job, come what may.

Time was beginning to run out and it was necessary to take long strides if we were to make our rendezvous at Seydisfjord with the ship from England.

With true contrariness the wind veered to the eastward and we had a long, 85 miles dead beat to Langanes, the north east tip of Iceland. Once again life was cold and tedious, and when we did round Langanes our next 70 odd miles down the east coast were in perpetual fog. Only, when, with the help of the echo sounder and RDF, we crept into the Vopnafjord did the visibility lift above half a mile. The fog lay all the way down the coast only thinning as we penetrated the fjords. Two days later we crept into Seydisfjordhur, this time with help from SatNav, just fifteen hours before the 'Norrona' berthed with our friend, David, on board. He was to sail with us to the Faroes and Bergen.

To the Faroes

It was a great pleasure to see David arrive on the Smyril Lines ferry, spot on time for a rendezvous planned months before. He had travelled by overnight coach from London to Aberdeen, then on by overnight ferry to Lerwick, in the Shetlands. In the middle of the following night he joined the Denmark-to-Iceland ferry, calling at Thorshavn in the Faroes on the way. He seemed in remarkably good form after such a long-drawn-out itinerary.

Rather than put to sea there and then, we made a short day-hop to Nestkaupstadjur, just south of Seydisfjord, to let David find his way around *Blackjack* and see a little of Iceland before we left.

There are those who would have stayed one more day to avoid sailing on Friday the 13th, but by a democratically taken decision we ignored superstition. At the very civilised hour of nine o'clock, and with visibility still short of a mile and practically no wind, we groped our way out, clearing the last headland under power by around 1030.

The course was roughly south-east and during the morning we flew the floater spinnaker. Over lunchtime we were back on the motor, and in the afternoon we got a new, if gentle, breeze from east-north-east and ambled off at 4½ to 5 knots on the genoa.

This sort of gentle, fair-wind sailing and occasional motoring lasted

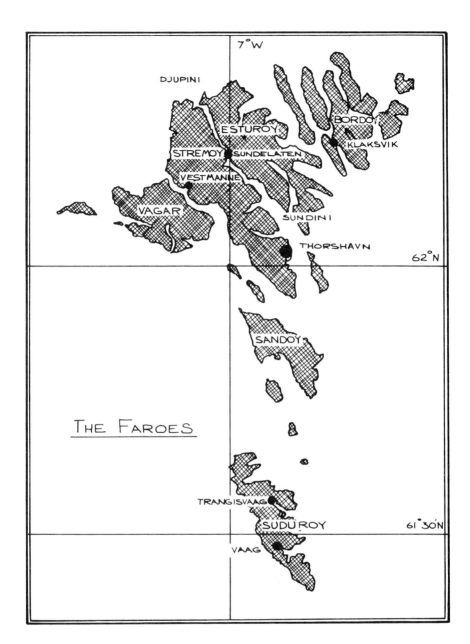

We made Klaksvik on Bordoy our port of arrival and worked our way south through the islands, departing for Norway from Vaag on Suderoy.

till breakfast time on Sunday, with no horrors or alarms and steady if not dramatic progress. RDF bearings had shown us to be fairly constantly to the south of our dead-reckoning position and when we saw our first glimpse of the Faroes, 48 hours out from Iceland, we needed to turn to the north-east to make the right approach to our intended place of arrival.

Our plan was to make Klaksvik on Bordoy our arrival port and to work our way south through the islands, making our eventual departure from Vaag on Syderoy.

In order to reach Klaksvik we wanted to enter the Djupini, meaning deep water, and to do this we had to use the motor for a short while to avoid the foul stream scheduled for the afternoon. It was a new dimension to our cruising which had not seriously concerned us since leaving the West Country. For the next few days our life would be strictly governed by the Tidal Streams Atlas. We were using a Faroese publication which is highlighted at intervals by rather alarming red arrows to indicate serious overfalls. Our digest of these was that they were not to be taken lightly. But certainly in a yacht the size of *Blackjack* they were no great worry, provided there was no contrary wind element. If a wind of any strength and the stream are opposed, one should avoid the red areas like the plague.

During the late afternoon we had a pleasant sail up the Djupini, remarking on the greenness of the hills compared with the more barren slopes of Iceland. Soon after six we had found a convenient berth alongside a fishing boat in Klaksvik and our gentle passage was over. It's funny how one can have a preconceived idea of a particular passage and how wrong one can be. Back in the winter, when planning the trip, I had always imagined making the passage east across these northern waters as likely to be a hairy downwind run with fresh winds and big seas. How wrong I was.

Strolling around Klaksvik that evening, we were immediately struck by the more affluent appearance of the town compared with any of equal size in Iceland. The roads were well surfaced and the whole place was much more spruced-up and well-to-do. Gone was the frontier town, unfinished, untidy atmosphere we had left behind.

Our first day in the Faroes was delightful, not for the scenery in particular and certainly not for the sailing, which was spasmodic and rather dull, but for the welcome given to us by the Mikkelsen family. David had talked to their daughter, Joren, on the ferry, during his outward passage. Hearing that we intended to visit the Faroe Islands she had insisted we call at the little village of Syderigote where her family lived. David's request for an address had been utterly dismissed. 'Just sail into the bay and we shall see you coming. We don't see many yachts in the Gotevig.'

True to her word, when we sailed up to the tiny quay, there was Joren and her father to greet us. We spent a delightful afternoon with them, visiting their charming house and learning a great deal about the islands. Alas, the berth was no place to spend the night and we left again at 1630, sailing gently round the southern tip of Esturoy and into the Skaale fjord. We found a convenient berth alongside a pier and took an evening stroll through the adjacent shipyard. There were three trawlers of between 300 and 800 tons under construction, two more hauled up a slip and one in dry-dock for a refit. There was a night-shift in action and the whole outfit was obviously a very going concern. Considering the difficulties in our own UK shipyards, we could not fail to be impressed with the level of activity.

Tuesday morning dawned bright and clear in the Skaale fjord, although fog was rolling over the hill from the next fjord to the east. We were to find this sort of situation very much a feature of the Faroe Islands. While one fjord may be enjoying sunshine, another may be wrapped in a blanket of fog.

As we left the fjord we turned to starboard and headed up the Sundini, which is the shallow water, the opposite to the Djupini. With a full-sail northerly breeze we beat steadily up the fjord in bright sunshine, enjoying the scene and the shoreside settlements we passed. The challenge that drew us in was the Sundelaten, a narrow passage under a bridge of questionable height which would have to be passed if we wished to go right through the Sundini instead of retracing our steps.

The lowest figure we had for clearance under this bridge was 17 metres, presumably above high water. Or was it datum? Due to some quirk of the tides, the level at the bridge apparently never varies although the stream runs through at great speed. So we could assume that datum and high water were one and the same. The height of our mast was just over 16 metres so we hoped that 17 metres was correct, but felt disinclined to take any chances. We dropped our kedge for lunch just south of the bridge where the fjord was wide and the stream negligible. We weighed again 30 minutes before slack water so we would arrive at the bridge with the stream still running against us, but with the strength weakening.

Picking our way through the shallows approaching the bridge, the least depth was 3.8 metres which was one metre more than the chart suggested. We came into the dredged channel, only about 20 yards wide, which leads under the main span of the bridge, and began to meet the strength of the stream.

'How fast can you go?' they shouted from the bank.

'How much do we need?' we asked.

'Six to eight knots,' came the answer.

Of the height they said there was no worry. But we were not so sure. With an indicated three knots from the log we inched our way ever closer, until at last we felt sure we would go through. Only when we were practically there could we be certain. Then we opened the throttle and pushed the speed up to pass underneath. It certainly did not need the full six knots but then slack water was not far away. Overhead there may have been 17 metres, but from deck-level there seemed to be only centimetres to spare and we were much relieved to emerge unscathed.

The sun stayed with us for the rest of the Sundini as we continued to tack to and fro. We consoled ourselves with the vision of a splendid run on the reciprocal course when we had rounded the north end of Streymoy. This sort of forward thinking is nearly always counter-productive and no sooner were we out of the fjord, looking up at the highest sea cliffs in the world, when the wind freshened and backed heavily. We found ourselves thrashing along under reduced sail and, to cap it all, we were enveloped in fog with visibility down to 50 yards.

Navigation in these foggy conditions is not as difficult as might be expected. In general, the waters are clear of isolated off-lying rocks and a reliable echosounder is the most useful aid.

That evening we poked our nose into the little harbour of Vestmanna and hoped to find a peaceful berth. There seemed to be an unusual amount of activity on the quayside and, as we were waved away from the most obvious berth, the reason dawned on us. Laid out on the quay in neat lines were the results of a whale hunt that was clearly only just over.

We are not active opponents of whaling and have some sympathy for both sides, but we had no stomach for such a scene. Anticipating the butchering would probably last all night, we took ourselves off to a quiet corner of the bay and dropped anchor.

The whales are herded by small boats until driven into shallow water where they are slaughtered in a fearful bloodbath. This has been a traditional source of meat for the islanders since time immemorial and has not really upset the ecological balance in the past. Traditionally the herding was done by small boats, propelled by oars, and when the spoils were divided, each family had what they could carry and preserve by traditional methods. Now the whales are spotted by faster craft. One suspects that the outboard motor is used for the herding, and the distribution and storage is made easier by the motor-car and the deep-freeze. Sadly this must tell against the whale, making survival of the species a lot more difficult.

From Vestmanna we had another foggy sail south until the sun broke through as we approached Thorshavn, capital city of the Faroes.

We liked Thorshavn, and not just for the luxury of hot showers in the seamen's mission. It is a clean, attractive city and the contemporary Lutheran cathedral a striking if not wildly beautiful feature externally, has an interior of quite dazzling simplicity and architectural genius.

In Thorshavn we met *Eilidh*, a 58ft yacht built in 1931 by Dickie of Bangor to the designs of Alfred Mylne. She had come north from her home waters on the west coast of Scotland, and her young, lively crew were delightful company. Her's was the first red ensign that we had seen for over six weeks.

We were able to exchange our empty Gaz cylinders in Thorshavn. Now we could allow ourselves toast again for breakfast and relax in the knowledge that our supplies would last us the remainder of our cruise.

From Thorshavn we sailed south to Suderoy. We first sailed into the

A typically dramatic shot of the rocky coastline of the Faroes.

Trangisvaag fjord, beating up to Tveraa and then anchoring behind an island in the Tjaldevig for lunch. In the afternoon we sailed round to Vaag where we met *Eilidh* once again. We walked to the south of the island and climbed the great cliffs, hoping to see the puffins in their nesting grounds. Alas it was too late in the summer, July 20th. The young had flown and all the birds were at sea.

The following morning, as quietly as possible, we slipped our lines from *Eilidh*, whose crew had only returned from a local dance at 5.00 am, and sailed for Norway.

Our stay in the Faroes had been all to brief. We had logged 125 miles in our meanderings and yet we had seen only a fraction of the whole island group. We might have seen more with less fog, but our experience in the way of visibility was very much to be expected. Conditions change very rapidly and frequently, both in respect of visibility and strength of wind and, while inshore, we did not set our largest genoa or a spinnaker. Settled conditions were very much the exception.

The scenery is fascinating. It is much greener than Iceland but, on the other hand, the geological formations have not the same variety. The most dramatic part is undoubtedly the great sea cliffs that face the Atlantic, while the bays and fjords have a charm of their own. For those with the physique of a mountain goat, the walking must be superb.

Scandinavia

Our passage from the Faroes to Norway was again too easy to be true. The wind only once rose to 16 knots true and was for the most part around 10 or 12 knots. What is more, it was fair the whole way and we were always able to lay the course.

For us the sight of the great North Sea oilfields was a new experience and a revelation. The great concentrations of fields, like Cormorant and Brent, are quite staggering with an eerie, almost science-fiction effect. The size of the structures is immense but passing at a distance, as indeed one must, the scale is very difficult to appreciate.

The Brent field is perhaps the most striking because of the slightly formal layout of the rigs. Four great platforms stand in an orderly line running north and south, or nearly so, spread over a distance of six miles. To the eastward of the line is an isolated flare and to the westward a spar buoy. On the chart the pattern has the appearance of a gigantic kite laid out on the sea. The pattern is so distinctive that it was easy to take a series of transits as we passed to the south of the field and create a running fix in the process. A 90,000-ton tanker was connected to the spar buoy and seemed quite dwarfed by the surrounding rigs. At one stage of our passage we counted no less than 23 structures within sight, all standing up like marauding creatures from another planet.

Our schedule meant that we must be in Bergen on July 29th to meet the good ship *Venus*, when she arrived from Newcastle. David was to return in her and Richard, our son, and Alex, a friend from university, were due to join. Our arrival in Norway on the 24th gave us a few days' grace and so we made our landfall north of Bergen, in order to see something of the great Sogne Fjord before going south.

From the charts and pilots, including Mark Brackenbury's guide, we chose to arrive at the island of Fedje just south of the entrance to the Sogne Fjord. In the event, this proved easy to approach with a secure harbour and was therefore very convenient. It was as quiet a place as can be imagined. The few locals spoke little or no English and there were no Customs. We were slightly apprehensive about this as we feared we might be required to enter formally at a clearance port. However, inquiries through the Pilots using VHF established that no one was going to lose any sleep if we enjoyed ourselves where we liked and called on the authorities when we reached Bergen later in the week.

The Sogne Fjord is vast and if one penetrates to its innermost depths, where even the Admiralty Pilot waxes lyrical about its beauties, one can be one-hundred miles from the open sea. In the time available we could not consider going that far and we contented ourselves with a brisk run

Blackjack *moored Scandinavian style in Norway's Sogne fjord.*

up to Vikum, about 16 miles from the entrance. After a night there we beat out again, marvelling at the grandeur of the scenery.

One of the joys of cruising in Norway and Sweden is to pass through the inner leads that allow one to sail for miles at a time, without venturing out into the open sea. There is a fascinating variety of broad fjords, narrow alleys and scattered islands. There are, of course, bridges and overhead cables to be considered but these are well marked on the charts and again, as one approaches, by signs on the shore. Some forward planning is necessary to ensure that wasted mileage is not made but this is really quite straightforward.

We wound our way south towards Bergen, through a wonderland of rocky channels, finding two perfect stopping places on the way. The idea of sleeping in Napsvaag seemed irresistible and indeed it was. Even more enticing, if a little trickier in the way of rock dodging, was our night in Grunna Sund, recommended by Brackenbury.

When in Rome do as the Romans and, when in Scandinavia, follow the Scandinavians' example in the way of anchoring. For each of our first three nights after Fedje, we put our bow-line ashore and laid out a stern anchor. The locals have good reasons for these techniques, not the least being the great depth of water even quite close to the shore. We suffered only one uncomfortable night later on when, having opted for a recommended spot, we became subjected to an awkward cross-wind during the night. Fortunately, we had on this occasion put our heavy anchor and chain out into the channel and taken a stern warp to the shore; nothing gave, and by morning all was peace once more.

When approaching one's chosen pitch there is some technique involved in bringing the yacht into such a situation. Our most usual arrangement was to launch the dinghy and send an advance-party ashore. They would make the head-rope fast and row back out to meet us. If we were able to judge our distance correctly, we would drop the kedge as we came in, thereby establishing an instant bow and stern mooring, which could be adjusted for distance off later. The locals are more proficient. With the advantage of familiarity, they know where they can put their bows against the rocks and send a line ashore without a dinghy.

Bergen proved an ideal place for our crew change. Yachts lie in the more northerly of the two harbours, not far from the RoRo terminal. Somehow, Richard had managed to satisfy the ferry company that his sailboard was only hand-baggage and this we stowed in its usual position against the forward stanchions.

Of the places we visited as we worked our way south, two in particular stand out. Sundal at the head of the Maurangerfjord, itself a branch of the huge Hardanger Fjord, was most beautiful, with a delightful walk to a pool at the foot of a dramatic glacier. Farther south the Lysefjord lives up to Mark Brackenbury's recommendations and, despite a lack of sun, we enjoyed sailing its full remarkable length. It

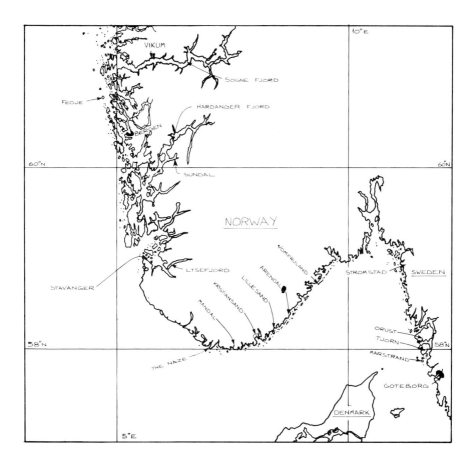

This chart shows the parts of the Norwegian and Swedish coasts visited.

was while the boys were ashore considering the climb to the Pulpit rock that Pat harvested two bucketfuls of mussels from the water's edge. From these we were able to select enough large specimens for a veritable feast of *moules* that evening, ranking as the culinary highlight of the summer's cruise.

Once south of Stavanger the coastline changes in character. There are no inshore routes and available harbours are far fewer. This seemed a good reason to make an overnight passage and get round the Naze and on to the south coast as soon as possible.

While on the west coast the weather had been changeable; some rain; some sun, but not a lot and only once warm enough for a fairly spartan swim. As daylight came off the Naze the sun rose into a clear sky and for the next six days we were to enjoy absolutely unbroken sunshine. Summer clothes at last!

The south coast of Norway has none of the drama and grandeur of the west coast, but it does have a charm and intimacy which makes it equally attractive. Mandal, Kristiansand, Lillesand and Arendal are attractive waterside towns with sheltered berths for visiting yachts. Between them the inner leads wind through delightful, narrow, well-marked channels with any number of backwaters and small islands that provide idyllic natural anchorages. The channels are so narrow that, in the main, one motors with a headwind. But given a fair wind one can sail past everchanging shores. The holiday homes of brightly-painted timber are in impeccable taste, with many private landing-stages, and the rise and fall of the tide is so small as to be unnoticeable.

We spent four happy days working our way north-eastwards along this coast. Our last evening before we made the passage across to Sweden was unforgettable. After a gorgeous day of creeping through the leads east of Arendal, we emerged off Sildeodden into relatively-open water looking for our last Norwegian anchorage.

According to the log we hoisted the floater at 1720 and lowered it $4\frac{1}{2}$ hours and 21 miles later. So perfect was the sailing that each anchorage farther on seemed more desirable than the one close to hand. Freshly-caught mackerel were consumed underway. Darkness was falling as we eventually lowered sail and tucked ourselves around the north end of Jomfruland to find a completely sheltered anchorage on the west-facing inner side.

Ten hours gentle sailing, interrupted around midday by three hours under power, brought us to Stromstad on the west coast of Sweden the following evening.

We were 11 days in Swedish waters and we enjoyed every minute of it. The Swedish archipelago from Stromstad south to Gothenburg is a veritable playground for the cruising yachtsman, and the Swedes make full use of it. Entering Swedish waters and sailing south we were immediately aware of the large numbers of yachts sailing. We entered on August 12th which was, in fact, just after the official Swedish holiday period. Yet the number of yachts under sail was still impressive. Very much like the French, the Swedes really sail whenever they can and as a nation do not readily resort to the motor. Their production designs are particularly handy and they manoeuvre under sail in situations that in UK harbours would invite the label 'show-off'.

Once again there are frequent choices of route with narrow passages through waterside settlements. Quiet anchorages or sociable harbours abound, both for overnight or lunch-time stops.

The detailed Swedish charts, bound into a turn-over book the size of a Beken calendar, are essential for full enjoyment of the coastline. Once one gains confidence in their accuracy one can sail close to the rocks and tack in and out, treating navigation more like map-reading than scientific plotting.

We enjoyed the Hamburgsund, the Sotenkanallen and villages like Gullholmen, Kyrkesund and Ronnang. We spent an entertaining night at Smogen, which is the mecca of cruising yachts on this coastline and could be said to be vibrant to a degree. Arriving in the late afternoon on a Wednesday, it was not easy to find a vacant slot. All the visiting yachts moor bows-inwards to the shoreline, which has a continuous staging along it, with anchors out astern. In the high season a second rank is formed, with bow-lines to the sterns of the front rank and stern anchors beyond theirs.

The finest evening was spent sailing in through the Malo Strommar and up the Koljo Fjord on the north-west side of Orust. Parts of this channel have been blasted through the rock and are straight as well as narrow. But the wind was kind to us and, with our sheets hard in, we were just able to lay the course. The peace and beauty of sailing gently up this fjord as the evening drew in was superb. Our chosen anchorage off Eriksberg, a tiny hamlet behind an island, proved perfect in every sense.

We spent several nights in Stenungsund, the home of Sweden Yachts. We enjoyed the spectacle and the parties that went with the Tjorn Runt, a race for 1000 yachts round the island of Tjorn, and we spent a day in Gothenburg, including a fascinating tour of the Volvo motor-car assembly lines.

No cruise on this coastline would be complete without a call at Marstrand. Mark Brackenbury, being an East Coast man, describes Marstrand as the Burnham-on-Crouch of the Swedish coast. A South Coast sailor would be more likely to compare it with Cowes. Certainly, it is a great yachting centre and has hosted many important championships. In our opinion it is a good deal more attractive as a place than either Cowes or Burnham and well worth a visit.

Home from the sea

It took us from 0730 on the 23rd till 1600 the following day to cover the 143 miles from Langedrag, outside Gothenburg, to Ebeltoft in Denmark. Admittedly, the last 20 miles took us six hours in a dying air as we crept round Hasenore and the Sandhagen bank.

We got into Ebeltoft without touching bottom but there can have been very litle room under our keel in the approach. In Denmark we became acutely aware of our draft of 2.12m (7ft). Once again we were using a Yachtman's Pilot prepared by Mark Brackenbury which, while an excellent guide, was inclined to speak of two metres as plenty of depth. Danish yacht harbours, in the Little Belt in particular, follow a fairly standard pattern with yachts moored bows to a pontoon and stern lines to a pair of piles between which one passes to enter the berth. Facilities with more than 2.5 metres were not always to be found and Brackenbury does warn one to allow some margin as changes in climatic conditions can produce half-a-metre fall over night.

It was just this lack of deep-enough harbours that gave us an interesting challenge on our second day going south. Anchored in the Maarup Vig on the west side of Samsoy we realised, in mid-afternoon, that the next decent anchorage was a full 40 miles away.

For the first time in several weeks we had a fresh breeze and, being in the north-east, it suited us well. Rapidly recovering the sailboard we got underway with mainsail and our small, heavy spinnaker. This is a strange device belonging originally to a Contessa 34 and with an extra panel to give it a more suitable height. With the cloth humming with vibration and the wind rising to a true 25 knots, we fairly rushed along.

In fact our progress was apparently so unusual that a low-flying light aircraft which appeared out of the overcast did a full 360° turn around us; the better to make out this mad English yacht charging across Danish waters. We made our chosen anchorage in the Vejle Fjord in just five hours and had our hook down in peaceful surroundings by eight o'clock. It had been a splendid sail and, after so much gentle sailing, we had all enjoyed the excitement of dashing between the islands with such speed and purpose.

We spent two more nights in the Little Belt before we reached our final Danish port of Sondeborg. This was a jolly place with its lifting bridge causing constant interest. The shops were good and the town active and alive. There was some very keen dinghy and board sailing from the sailing club to the south of the town, that evening.

Somehow as we left Denmark we felt that our holiday was over. From now on our concentration would be on passage making home. There would be no time to loiter and such stops as we would make would be for convenience only.

From Sondeborg to Kiel we had a fresh south-westerly wind and limited visibility. During the day we smelt the German coastline more than we saw it. Evidently the agriculture is very rich in this area, judging by the farmyard aromas that reached us offshore.

In Kiel we took advantage of the facilities of the British Kiel YC. This is a military establishment operated entirely for the Services posted in Germany, but they nonetheless offer a very warm welcome and excellent showers to passing civilians. Contrary to Brackenbury's advice the NAAFI shop is not open to visitors, but the club is a duty-free zone and it is not necessary to clear customs when calling. The shops are a longish walk and being Mittwoch (Wednesday) the banks were closed in the afternoon. However, in Germany post-offices will change foreign currency and so we were able to convert Danish Kroner into Deutschmarks.

From our berth at the club we were able to speak to the lock-keepers on VHF and they advised us that, if we wished, we could enter the Kiel canal at 0500. Dues of 25 marks, about £7.50, were payable as we entered and we were out of the lock by 0535. Motoring at a steady 5 knots, we reached Brunsbuttel at the western end of the canal 12 hours later. The tide suited and we locked out and went down the Elbe as far as Cuxhaven for the night. As can be imagined this was a long and wearing day, particularly in view of the fact that the passage from

Brunsbuttel to Cuxhaven turned out to be a hard 15-mile slog to windward. Comparing notes with others, it would appear that it is much more pleasant if one can enter the canal in time to make Rensburg for the night, instead of waiting in Kiel to enter in the morning, as we did.

Leaving the canal and entering the Elbe was a distinctly rude awakening. Time spent is Scandinavia and the Baltic has a markedly softening effect and emerging into the Elbe is to re-encounter realities such as, strongly-flowing streams, cold contrary winds, and fast-moving commercial shipping in an abrupt and salutary manner.

Given head winds, as we were, it would be inadvisable to expect to leave Brunsbuttel and avoid Cuxhaven altogether. The beat out to clear the Elbe must be made on a fair ebb stream and it would be touch and go to attempt the whole distance in one six-hour period. The Elbe has an evil reputation, particularly with onshore winds, and this is just what was forecast for our departure next morning. West to south-west, Force 6 possibly Force 8, was far from ideal and our chief worry was the vulnerability of the sailboard stowed against our forward stanchions.

Because one is leaving on the ebb, a head wind inevitably creates a most unpleasant sea. As we thrashed our way out we met several yachts running back in. They, probably very wisely, had decided that discretion was the better part of valour.

The commercial traffic in the Elbe is far heavier than in the approach to any UK port and there was a steady stream of fast-moving vessels coming downriver with us, making for careful judgement as we picked our tacks.

These are the conditions in which our cutter rig is really good. With a small jib, staysail and two reefs in the main, *Blackjack* had no complaints. The same could hardly be said for those of us on board. Three out of the four found that so many weeks of flat water had ruined our immunity to seasickness and the first 12 hours at sea were hardly fun, by anybody's standards.

Next morning, Saturday, the wind eased enabling us to spread more sail and by evening we were able to ease sheets slightly and lay a reasonable course.

By midday on Sunday the wind had come ahead again and we were shortening sail once more on a long port tack towards the Outer Gabbard.

Early on the Monday morning we benefited from a sizeable windshift to the westward which enabled us to tack and lay down the seaward side of the Galloper and the North Falls. In the late afternoon, after two or three tacks, we found the East Goodwin buoy in hazy sun and, soon after, the lightship itself.

With a steady 30 knots true south-westerly wind and a clear sky we just scraped round the South Goodwins and stood inshore to escape the worst of the east-going stream now running against us.

Later on that evening with the cross-Channel ferries batting in and out of Dover harbour, we resorted to an hour or so of motor sailing in order to reduce our time off the pierheads. With three reefs down and only the staysail forward we fought our way westward. It is a narrow strip of water off Dover and Folkestone inshore of the forbidden traffic zones and, with the thought of 'big brother' eyeing us on radar, we kept our tacks short all the way to Dungeness.

By midnight we had a fair stream, but, at the same time, a full gale on the nose made life particularly horrible. It was necessary to roll the staysail partially as the anemometer went into the high forties. It was with some relief we felt conditions ease in the morning, and the north-westerlies that the forecasters had been promising for days eventually materialised.

The stitching on our staysail had begun to look rather the worse for wear in the early hours and we had rolled it up and set the storm jib forward instead. As breakfast time came we were able to spread more sail and a much easier day followed. However, we were glad to put into Brighton in the afternoon to lick our wounds.

After so long away from British waters the berthing charges came as a bit of a shock. They were exactly twice the highest charge that we had paid anywhere in the previous three months and 4800 miles. Never mind, the showers were much appreciated and by the time we left for Lymington at 0500 next morning we were fully recharged and ready for a spanking eight-and-half-hour sail from berth to berth.

9

Round Britain and Ireland

When Pat and I bought *Blackjack* from Rodney Barton in 1983, we immediately entered for the 1985 Round Britain race and the 1986 Two Handed Trans Atlantic.

To me a great deal of the enjoyment is in the preparation and planning and I wanted to find ways of improving on *Blackjack*'s performance in the 1981 and 1982 events.

Having been conceived for the Transatlantic event *Blackjack* should be at her best in heavy upwind conditions. Whereas I was satisfied that the potential was there, I felt that the sail wardrobe was unsatisfactory particularly in the middle of the range of wind strength.

Sailing in the TA race in 1981 I felt that boat speed under the cutter rig was good but at the expense of pointing ability. In strong to gale force conditions this is no problem because the sea state will preclude pointing anyway.

We have always used a 150% genoa for light conditions and, depending on sea condition, this can be retained up to 20 knots of apparent wind. However the cloth weight is not really heavy enough for this sort of treatment and we would normally change to a full hoist yankee and staysail at about 18 knots and settle down to sailing as a cutter. This is a nice cruising rig but for racing particularly inshore, as in the last 1000 miles of the TA race or in the Round Britain race, it is far from perfect. The yankee is cut for a wide entry angle and in order to keep all three sails working the yankee sheet must never be really hardened in.

In fact, when cruising we believe that our progress to windward is generally just as efficient with the staysail rolled up, the yankee sheeted relatively hard and the yacht pointed up towards the wind. This is in comparison with sailing faster and freer with the sheets eased sufficiently for the staysail to be unrolled and set between the yankee and the main.

Blackjack *using a high cut number two genoa obtained for the 1985 round Britain and Ireland race. It is used over a wide range of wind speeds.*

What we needed was a No 2 genoa capable of profitable use over the widest possible range of wind speeds. Particularly Round Britain we wanted to waste as little time and energy on headsail changes as possible. The use of a roller system is a great idea with which we are from time to time quite tempted. The principal advantage is that there is never any delay in increasing sail once conditions moderate. Against this has to be considered compromises that are bound to exist. The rolled sail is maybe good enough for reaching but is really far from ideal as a windward sail. If the roller sail is to survive a wide range of strengths then the cloth weight can not be light enough to give an optimum sail when unrolled completely in light winds.

The solution which we adopted and which proved a great success round Britain was to obtain an almost full hoist No 2 genoa with a modest overlap and a high clew. The object of the high clew is that with a reef point on the luff, four feet up from the tack, the whole sail can be dropped in one movement. The area reduction is not colossal but the simultaneous lowering of the centre of effort is an added benefit. The overlap is reduced and the effect of reefing the main is much more effective.

The sail supplied by Hoods was in 8.8oz narrow panel soft cloth, triple stitched and we have been delighted with it. In 18 knots we are conscious of the lack of overlap and should change although the speed drop will not be disastrous. With the luff reefed and two slabs in the main we can power to windward in 35 knots plus. During the race this sail proved a real power house and raised *Blackjack*'s potential in the 25-35 knots apparent wind range considerably.

The other chink in our armour was in the light airs downwind department. The memories of trying to finish the TA race in 1981 using the all round working spinnaker in ghosting conditions were etched permanently in my mind. This sail is in 1oz material, rather fuller than necessary and is always used with a spee squeezer. In anything less that 10 knots apparent it is a pain in the neck and never lifts above the pulpit.

Fortunately we were able to buy from Hoods, secondhand, a Tri Star floater that had been used experimentally on the 1983 Admiral's Cup triallist *Panda*. Hoods had made a new sail for the owner and the original with 10ft taken out of the middle has proved an absolute wonder. Pat and I are happy to handle it without a sock which makes its use much more spontaneous when a free air comes along, and it flies high in the lightest of zephyrs. Not only does it respond to the least airs, it is immensely stable when set and can be cleated off without worry.

Having cruised for three months in 1984, partly with a crew of four, we realised that we needed to change our habits a bit if we were to become an efficient racing crew and in the months before the start of the Round Britain race we made a conscious effort to handle the yacht as though racing, so as to reduce the time lost in sail changing and to attune ourselves to carrying the proper amount of sail for the best performance.

We made three particular outings which were devoted to tuning ourselves and the yacht. One cold, but sunny weekend in early May, we sailed eastabout the Isle of Wight and down to Lulworth Cove for the night. We learned how out of condition we were and what a job it was changing between the two big genoas. Lulworth was delightful with only two other visiting yachts.

Later the same month, over a Bank holiday weekend, we sailed to St. Peter Port and back by way of the Ortac Channel with a few hours in Alderney on the way home. We had recently installed a Decca Navigator and I used this trip for familiarisation. The equipment was all I had expected it to be and we were extremely thankful to have it. We expected most yachts to carry the sets and those without would be at a colossal disadvantage.

Our final outing was on a Saturday, fourteen days before the start and constituted a real heavy weather trial. There was a fresh to gale force southwesterly wind blowing and an ebb tide and I cold bloodedly put a waypoint into Decca 3 miles southwest of the Needles Fairway buoy and announced that that was our objective. We put two reefs in the mainsail and set the small yankee in anticipation of unrolling the staysail to form our cutter rig. As it turned out the staysail remained firmly rolled and we had all the sail we wanted and a little more. We passed the Bridge buoy off the Needles in company with Mary Falk and Ann Fraser in *Quixote*, a UFO 34. They were not just out for a trial, as we were, but beginning the passage down to Plymouth a week early. We did not envy them the trip. Comparing notes later it appears that from both yachts it was at times possible to see the entire profile from the stem right down to the toe of the keel! The waters off the Needles with a southwestly wind against the stream are known as some of the roughest round Britain and that Saturday with 40 knots of wind, they were living up to expectations. Beyond the Fairway buoy the seas became a little longer but we were decidedly pleased to reach the waypoint and run back in. Surfing in on the face of the very steep seas off the Bridge was quite unnerving and in one great burst of speed the digitals of our speedometer indicated 14.55 knots!

As a trial it was invaluable. In the first place I learned that my oilskins were totally inadequate and needed replacing urgently. In the second place we discovered afterwards that the GRP servo blade of our Aries Vane gear had split from top to bottom. Fortunately it was repairable but it would have been embarrassing to find the weakness during the race. Thirdly we learnt that the deck repeater fitted to our Decca was an invaluable item in those conditions. Visibility was very limited and quite apart from a weak stomach I was so busy on deck that navigation at the chart table was just not convenient. With the appropriate Sail Plan programmed in, all the necessary information was continuously displayed in the cockpit.

We reached Plymouth in time for scrutineering with only minor items to attend to and so were able to enjoy the week, which turned out to be hot and sunny. It gave us an opportunity to study the opposition and to get to know some of the competitors.

It was very obvious that our class (35 – 40ft) would be dominated by the stripped out specials all of which were close to the limit of 40ft compared with our 38ft. Their displacement was generally only about 65% of ours despite their greater length and, except in rough weather, they were bound to leave us standing. This was no surprise to us, the Round Britain race is one in which the majority of competitors have only vague hopes of winning their class. Rather it is a race full of unofficial categories and everyone soon finds out who are their main rivals within a few hours of the start.

We knew that we should set our sights on racing against similar boats, the cruiser racers with proper accommodation; what one might describe as the Grand Touring Category.

As I have tried to explain in a later chapter I consider the start of a race vitally important. I do not subscribe to the idea that, with 2000 miles to go, a minute or two at the start is neither here nor there. If your performance is very closely matched with another yacht then overtaking in the same conditions is not easy. If, on the other hand you start ahead, you may find that the conditions suit the leaders and your lead may well be stretched. If that is to be the case the last thing one wants to do is to start at the back.

Pat and I sailed well out beyond the line while waiting for the start and realised that, although the wind was fairly free on the line itself, a mile or so out it would come ahead of the beam and a weather position would be an advantage. One or two enthusiasts who set shy spinnakers as they crossed the line were not so well rewarded. We started close to the weather end of the line a few seconds late but travelling at a good speed and soon found ourselves clear air. The penalties for being over the line early are so stringent that it pays to be just a little bit line shy.

The first mark is the Eddystone and as we rounded it at bout 1230 Pat's brother, Peter, closed us in a Sigma 36 with our daughter, Jenny, aboard and gave us a great send off.

Once round the Eddystone the fleet settled down into a long procession of close hauled starboard tack yachts laying a course some miles to the south of the Lizard. The fair stream was only in our favour until 1730 and as the afternoon went on we considered a tack into the bay. We noticed that *Ntombifuti*, the favourite for monohull honours in our class, had done so and we wondered whether we should follow. Starboard tack was quite definitely the winning tack for the time being. If it freed a little we would be sorry not to have gone towards the shift, on the other hand, if it freed a lot we might not need to tack at all. In the event this is what did happen. Our decision not to tack was not really based on inspiration, it so happened that *Gemervescene* and *Assassin*, whom we had identified as close rivals, showed no sign of tacking and so we soldiered on on starboard.

During the night the wind did indeed free and we had several hours with the apparent wind about 60° off the bows and we made good speed towards the Scillies. Before daybreak the wind began to drop and all the indications from forecasts and so on suggested that we were in for a fairly airless interlude. The natural reaction was to point up. This certainly increased boat speed, but it also drew one close into the islands and I was nervous of the effect of the east going tide if we failed to make it round the Bishop. Previous experience on Fastnet races and cruising in the Scillies has always indicated that in a high pressure situation the Scillies seem to attract a bubble of still air that is very local. I called Pat before her time and together we set the floater and tried to edge away towards the south. Initially we were passed by yachts that were still close reaching, *Gemervescence* amongst them, but when daylight came the dividends began to pay off. To seaward of us there were ripples, towards the islands still water. Once in those ripples the gentlest of breezes filled the sails and we began to move once more. For the next six hours we sailed ever so slowly in a great arc eventually tacking downwind in a series of gybes to pass the Bishop light.

Off the lighthouse we were in first class company, we crossed ahead of *Ntombifuti*, the first and last time we would do that. The 63ft *Quailo* and 50ft *Helmsman Inter Ocean* were not so far ahead and we reckoned that we had played the right cards at the right time. *Gemervescence* was still with us but our lead was now about a mile.

Sunburn was the worst problem to be faced that day as we flew the spinnaker very shy and allowed ourselves to go out well to the westward of the rhumb line. The wind came in from the west the following morning and our position was fortunately the right one. *Tigo V* one of the lightweight 40-footers came through in the early evening and so did *Quailo* for whom the drifting conditions had been very difficult. During the evening we heard *Ghoster* calling another yacht without success and chipped in to talk to them ourselves. *Ghoster* is a 56ft converted 10 metre sailed by a delightful Danish couple, Bent and Ulla Britt Lyman, whom we had just met in Plymouth. They were closer to Crosshaven than we were, but much further to the eastward. Bent was very cagey about who else was around, apparently on the last race he had upset one competitor by giving away his position. However when we had finished talking to Bent, Brian Wells of *Assassin* took up the exchange and told us he was 41 miles out of Crosshaven, much the same distance as ourselves, but he also was down to leeward. The westerly wind was by now quite fresh, conditions that we thought would suit *Assassin*, so we knew we had a race on our hands. As it happened we had picked up an Irish weather forecast which had suggested that the wind would go northwest, so we were hanging on to our windward position. Come eleven o'clock or so that night, the header did indeed arrive and, whereas *Ghoster* and *Assassin* were close hauled and tacking for the last ten miles, we only needed one short tack to make the finish and were in ahead of both of them, though not before receiving a substantial shock over the VHF with still about an hour to go.

Imagine our surprise when, thinking that we were perhaps doing reasonably well, we should hear the smallest monohull in the race, *Humberts*, calling up the race officers to tell them they had finished. The Trafford brothers, Richard and James, were sailing a J24, to us a distinctly inshore day racing boat, lengthened to 25ft to meet the minimum length requirement. We learned later that all the time we had been virtually becalmed they had been rowing, permitted by the rules of the race, at a steady three knots! However this leg was to be no flash in the pan as far as the Traffords were concerned and our respect for them was to grow with each succeeding leg.

In the Round Britain and Ireland race there are four stopovers of which Crosshaven is the first. Competitors take their own time as they cross the finishing line and then re-start across the same line exactly 48 hours later. So, if you finish at 0032 as we did, you start again two nights

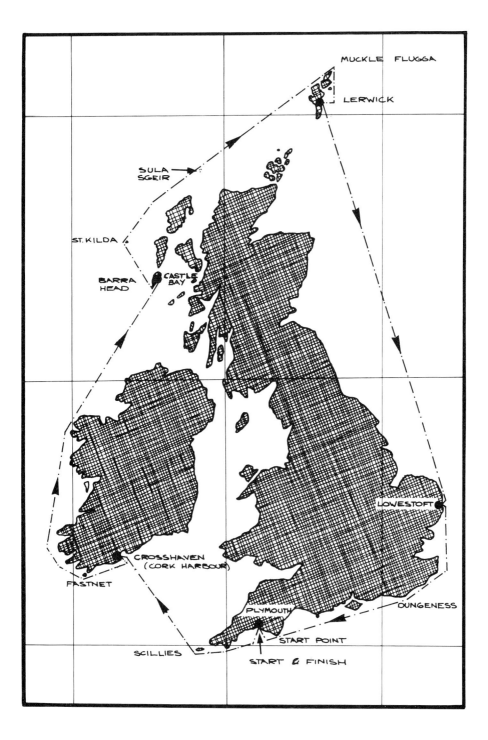

The Round Britain and Ireland race course takes in all the British Isles except Rockall and the Channel Isles.

later at 0032! We crossed the line one minute behind *Alien II*, a catamaran we knew from Lymington and as they were engineless it was the least we could do to offer them a tow into the river. Picking up the tow was no easy matter as the moment the cat lowered her mainsail she started making a fairly rapid sternboard. In the midst of our efforts we drifted back across the line almost impeding *Pacesetter* who was finishing behind us. As all this happened a voice in the darkness called *Starboard* and I imagined it was *Pacesetter* hailing us. The fact that they were on port tack did not occur to me at the time but we discovered later that the voice came from our VHF speaker and it was in fact *Assassin*, out in the darkness somewhere, crossing tacks with *Ghoster* and hailing him by radio!

The Crosshaven stopover was a lot of fun. Not many people had trouble to cope with, after light winds in the Irish sea and with the fleet not yet stretched out there was a splendid get together at the Royal Cork Yacht Club with a chance to get to know new friends.

In *Blackjack* we lay alongside *Ghoster* and began a friendship with the Lymans that grew throughout the race.

The time gained on the first leg was of far more importance than we realised at the time. When we re-started the wind was fresh south-westerly and likely to veer later. For *Blackjack* this was her chance to show her paces and within three miles of the start we changed from the No 1 genoa to our new No 2 and settled down to an uncomfortable but, as it turned out, a profitable night.

Off the Old Head of Kinsale we put in a long starboard tack seven miles out to sea and during my watch I put two slabs in the main and pulled down the luff reef on the No 2 Genoa. This was the first time I had had to do the operation in such strong conditions and I was quite taken aback at the amount of winch power needed to accomplish the reduction. A kevlar line is led through a block at the stemhead and with a hook into the reef cringle and a three part tackle back on the coachroof, lowering the sail, once the halyard has been eased is no problem. On the other hand because the whole operation is done with the sail drawing, the effort required in those wind strengths to re-tension the luff was more than I could achieve with our normally quite adequate halyard winch. I eventually got it taut by leaving the reef cringle high above the stemhead, taking in what I could on the halyard and then taking the tail of the three part tackle to a winch and applying a much greater amount of power to tension the sail downards.

Blackjack loved it and Pat and I hated it. I had stuffed myself with Stugeron and mercifully survived but, straight out from the delights of Crosshaven, Pat suffered for a while. The sufferings were found to be worthwhile next morning when talking by VHF to *Pacesetter*. They had started fifteen minutes behind us and were now seven miles astern. When we came to the Fastnet we had just managed to edge ahead of *Tigo V* who had re-started an hour before us.

Once round the Rock we were able to crack sheets and increase speed as we shot off towards Mizen Head and the Bull Rock beyond. *Tigo V*, with her length and lightness, began to regain her lead but for the boats astern of us the story was not such a happy one. As they came to the Rock the wind was already veering and instead of cracking sheets they were still hard on the wind or even beating over the same water that for us had been a reach.

The southwest corner of Ireland has some magnificent scenery which we remembered from a cruise in 1982. This time around there was no chance of refreshing our memories. Apart from one short glimpse of the Bull Rock at less than one mile, we saw absolutely nothing until the weather cleared next day off Connemara, giving magnificent views of Achill island and the north west tip of Ireland.

That day was a day of steady reaching under full main and No 2 genoa with a good deal of concentration on human welfare. We were both pretty tired from the heavy weather the day before and constant steering to make our best speed. Towards evening we got a call from *Ghoster*. They were making much better speed than us using their length to good effect and catching fast. This spurred us on to change up to the No. 1 Genoa but we could not hold them off and on they went. All this time we had been wary of the infamous Irish salmon nets that can reach for three miles across one's path. We were fortunate but others became entangled and had great difficulty freeing themselves.

From Ireland up towards the Hebrides we had generally too little wind and lost a lot on *Ghoster*. Bent had flown a shy spinnaker all night a little further to the eastward. We had debated whether we should try a spinnaker but the angle did not seem right.

Barra Head could be seen at 0415 on the Sunday morning, three days out from Crosshaven, but still 32 miles away. The short, light nights in these latitudes are a joy and reminded us of our cruise to Iceland the previous summer. The sail in past the islands at the southern end of the Hebrides was a delight in easy sunny conditions and we crossed the line at Castlebay at 1142, a very civilised hour to re-start in two days time.

We were in more than two hours behind *Ghoster,* and five hours behind *Tigo V* who was the fourth monohull in our class. We could console ourselves that only *Ghoster* and *Quailo* were ahead of us in the 'Grand Touring' category, but much less creditable was the fact that *Humberts* was still over two hours ahead and *Silk*, a Beneteau First Class Ten was five hours ahead of her.

At Castlebay all the competitors have to lie in the anchorage using their own ground tackle. The holding is poor with quantities of kelp on the bottom and when a squall comes through there is inevitably a lot of dragging. The first evening was reasonably peaceful and Clare Francis, cruising in her lovely yacht *Night Sky* had an early evening party on board which was a lot of fun.

Our only problem was the zip on Pat's oilskin jacket and with no

Yachts lie to their own ground tackle in Castlebay where the holding is very unreliable. Lumberjack *UK 45 is Rodney Barton's 45 footer, the successor to* Blackjack.

facilities available on shore, she had a long job hand stitching. There was a party at noon next day in the Castle given by the McNiel of the McNiels, in fact an American, but none the less the leader of the clan McNiel. After the party we returned to *Blackjack* and others repaired to the various hotel bars in the town. It was about this time that the wind got up from the southeast, which placed us at the lee end of the fleet with others dragging down towards us. *Assassin* was fouled by *Jemima Nicholas* and Pat and I went to the aid of the Royal Marines who, in the absence of the crews, were trying to sort out the chaos. We succeeded in extricating *Assassin* from the chaos but not before Pat had had her finger caught against a fishing boat which, as well as bruising her finger, bent her wedding ring into a square.

We decided that we were not safe with the rocks so close astern and the danger of dragging yachts descending upon us. We lifted our anchor and chose a new spot with reputedly good holding but a very long distance from the landing place. We held well but for the time being that was the end of our social contacts. In the evening the wind dropped and we rowed across to *Mobira,* in answer to an invitation and met more members of our class that we knew only as names.

Looking out about 0730 next morning I was surprised to see *Silk* sailing into the anchorage and dropping her anchor close to her original position. *Silk* had been due to re-start at around 0600 and we supposed that they must have damaged something and returned for repairs. They had some fifteen hours in hand over the second boat in their class so clearly they could aford to get things right. Through binoculars we could see no obvious trouble and no frantic activity either. The weather forecasts were quite vicious that morning with gale force winds predicted and in many ways we were glad to go to sea at our due time rather than worry about dragging anchors around Castlebay. After we had started and were heading back towards Barra Head we overheard a VHF exchange which gave us the reasons for *Silk's* return. Evidently they had obtained a direct forecast from Glasgow which had suggested that mean wind speeds of 40 knots were to be expected. Frankly, we were surprised that they should have turned back. The owner had done the race before in a slow boat and had purchased *Silk* with the express intention of winning his class. It seemed an odd choice if he had no confidence in her ability to withstand heavy weather. His caution was infectious and a number of yachts in his class stayed put in

We short tacked round Barra Head on our cutter rig expecting much stronger winds on the leg out to St. Kilda.

Running before a full gale between St Kilda and Muckle Flugga, Pat takes her turn at the wheel.

Castlebay for up to 40 hours longer than their alloted time while waiting for the conditions to improve.

In *Blackjack* we could not even contemplate such a move, she is a proven boat in heavy weather and indeed needs heavy weather to show her proper pace. Nonetheless all the chit chat made us a mite more cautious than usual and when it became a bit puffy in the lee of Barra Head we did not hesitate to change our No 2 genoa for the cutter rig in anticipation of much worse weather on the windward side. Strangely this did not materialise and after short tacking round the headland, determined not to overstand, we settled down for the leg out to St. Kilda close hauled but laying.

The gods were obviously on our side, those who had left earlier had had a head wind that prevented them laying, and this, of course, reduced their lead. *Blackjack* was going well and when our confidence returned we shook out our reefs and put back the No 2 genoa. The wind was gradually freeing as we caught glimpses of St. Kilda at 2145 and by 2300 we had the No 2 genoa boomed out to starboard as we closed the islands.

Rounding Muckle Flugga

There was the occasional glimpse of a light in Village Bay but otherwise all one could see was the ghostly outline of these remote and rugged islands. Thanks to Decca we were able to follow the shortest route and gybed just after the 0033 shipping forecast very close, less than five cables, to Soay, the tiny island on the western end of the group.

This was the beginning of the most exhilarating run I shall ever remember. The wind soon rose to a full gale and *Blackjack*, under a full main and a No 2 genoa, took off like a lightweight, surfing for long periods but always under perfect control. What the speed rose to in the bursts we shall never know because our display was tuned to a different function, sufficient to say that 103 miles came up in the first 12 hours on Decca fixes and 195 in the first 24. This is a very high average for a moderate displacement (7½ tons) yacht on a waterline of only 30ft. Conditions improved as we approached the Shetlands. The wind was still strong, but less than gale force, the sun came out and, on more of a run we were able to boom out the genoa and allow Percy, the Autohelm, to take over the steering.

Rounding Muckle Flugga lived up to all expectations. The wind was once again howling out of the south, it was raining and the swell was enormous. In fact one must also round the outer Stack which is a gaunt and desolate lump of rock standing alone to the north of the lighthouse and forming the most northerly outcrop of the British Isles.

We rounded once again as a shipping forecast was coming through. St Kilda was now 37 hours and 20 minutes and 300 miles astern. We had mercifully dropped the No 2 genoa and changed to the small yankee before hardening up and we prepared ourselves for a really hard thrash to windward for the 57 miles south to Lerwick. Bent Lyman on *Ghoster* had told us that he was already round and punching into some pretty nasty conditions. We had also overheard the lighthouse keepers passing on the rounding times for the boats close ahead of us. We knew that they would not like the conditions on offer so we raised our morale with the thought that we might catch up some time.

Sadly with some distance still to go the wind moderated and we changed first to the No 2 and then to the No 1 genoa. South of the Out Skerries we could see two sails ahead of us but without the help of strong winds, we could make little impression. Rounding Bressay and not to be outdone we flew our big floater spinnaker for the few miles left to the finish and narrowed the gap a little more.

Ntombifuti, Constance and *Panicker* were way out of reach, but *Tigo V*'s lead was now only 12 minutes and *Jeantex* a superlight, wood epoxy 40 footer, that should have been ahead all along, was in just six minutes ahead of us. *Ghoster* was nearly three hours ahead but to our great relief *Humberts* was not yet in. They had never been far from our minds in the very rough conditions of that leg and whenever we spoke to another yacht on VHF, we always agreed that we could thank our lucky stars that we were not out there in a J24! In fact they came in at breakfast time, unbowed and unscathed, and appeared to have positively enjoyed the conditions. With *Silk* now well behind we could at least feel that we were only being beaten by boats longer than ourselves. We had at this stage overtaken *Romtec,* sailed by the father and son team of David and Ben Dillistone, who were leading the 40 – 45ft class. We did not really expect to hold them off for very long.

The rounding of Muckle Flugga and the stopover in Lerwick are the highlights of the whole event. The members of the Lerwick Boating Club set out to make everyone's visit a memorable one. At 0300 we were met by a rubber boat as we approached the line. 'Did we need any assistance? Was our engine working?'

Next morning we were introduced to Alexis Gray whose family would adopt us for our time in Lerwick. We were, there and then, driven away to enjoy the luxury of their bathroom and given a stupendous lunch of pork chops. Alexis took all our dirty washing and returned it to us washed and ironed. Later that evening, after drinks aboard *Blackjack,* Alexis and her husband, John, took us on the most enjoyable drive around Mainland. It was a beautiful, sunny evening and the views of the islands were magnificent. We saw Scalloway and Voe and the grove of trees in the north that the islanders value so much on the otherwise treeless moors. The evening ended in the very

Part of the fleet rafted up in Lerwick where we enjoyed a spell of superb Shetland hospitality.

convivial atmosphere of the Lerwick Boating Club.

By this time Pat and I were becoming much more ambitious and hoping that given a fair proportion of strong headwinds on the last two legs, we might even overtake *Tigo V* and *Jeantex* and creep up the order. We were a very restricted group of yachts in Lerwick, the majority coming from Class V and with no smaller boats, other than *Humberts* coming in behind. This gap in the order was due entirely to the stay in harbour policy adopted back at Castlebay. In fact at 6 o'clock on our last evening whilst we were the hosts to a party of nineteen or so on board *Blackjack*, our good friend, Willam Ker, the veteran of the fleet, brought his Contessa 32, *Assent* in as the leading monohull in Class VI. Undaunted by weather forecasts he and his crew, Malcolm Murray, had left on time and fought their way round to Lerwick to establish a lead of 18 hours over the rest of their class. This was enough for them to maintain their position all the way to Plymouth and take the prize for the first monohull in class. We were particularly pleased because during the preceding winter William had been agonizing over the idea of cutting two feet off his yacht in order to qualify for the class below. I had advised him strongly against doing so and was delighted with his success. Had he taken a saw to his boat he would have been in the same class as *Humberts* and had to be content with second place!

The leg from Lerwick to Lowestoft is, except for the last 40 miles, totally featureless and the 470 miles seem quite interminable. After the first day we no longer saw another yacht, although we occasionally spoke to *Romtec* on VHF. There was the occasional sight of a distant oilrig. We had some fairly brisk close reaching with about 30 knots apparent and then the second evening out the wind went very light and then came up from astern. We set the floater but we should have set the working spinnaker because the wind speed soon rose and we had to peel. The run lasted for 91 miles and for a lot of that time the wind speed had risen to over 20 knots true so it was an exciting night. Just before midnight we gybed on to starboard which was no easy task. Pat steered while I set up the second pole. With the spinnaker setting from two poles we gybed the main and then took down the original pole. Until everything is properly braced on the new course the spinnaker is a lot less stable, making steering much more difficult, but we lost no time. There is a school of thought that believes in squeezing the spinnaker before a gybe and re-setting on the new gybe. This is undoubtedly much safer but, to us, the time spent at reduced speed is unthinkable.

There were periods of quite nice weather during this leg which if we had been cruising we might have enjoyed. However, our state of mind was such that, knowing there was nothing we could do to increase speed and knowing how well the lightweights would be doing, we allowed our frustration to get us down and fretted to no good result.

Pat happened to overhear a VHF exchange which amused us no end. The owner of *Jeantex*, Wolfgang Quix, had called requesting a directional bearing to be taken on his transmission as his Decca was not functioning as it should and he was uncertain of his position. This proved too difficult and the coastguard embarked on other means of helping him find his position. Wolfgang could see a red oilrig platform but could make out no markings. Nearly all the platforms are painted red so it was suggested he should motor up to it and take a better look! *Jeantex* has no engine and the rules would not have allowed its use anyway. Eventually the coastguard persuaded him to burn a white flare and requested all the oilrigs to mount a lookout and, if possible, report a sighting. Still no luck. Wolfgang was by this time highly embarrassed and quite prepared to wait for a sunsight to find his place! It turned out that his crew, Dieter, had entered all the waypoints in their Decca without using the correct key sequence for a position with easterly longitude, now that they were past the Greenwich meridian. They felt very foolish later and their wanderings cost them a place bringing them into Lowestoft an hour behind *Blackjack*. However Wolfgang found a copy of *Yachts and Yachting* in the clubhouse of the Royal Norfolk and Suffolk in which I had written enthusiastically about his boat and so he forgave us!

The approach to the Lowestoft finishing line is either down the narrow channel inside the Scroby sands or round the outside. We chose to come down the inside and thanked heaven for a fair tide as we tacked constantly on the No 1 Genoa. Because of our cutter rig, tacking is a slow process and with the big Genoa set it is necessary to go forward and hand the sail round and then rush aft to help heave it in. Never mind, we were feeling really fit at this stage and after several hours hard work we crossed the line at 1412. Three hours still behind *Tigo V* and *Romtec* but ahead of *Jeantex*; there was a fair gap before and *Tsunami* and *Mobira* were in after midnight.

The question of fitness is important but so far into the race it would be difficult to be out of condition in the normal sense of the word. However there are dangers all the way round the course. Michael Cozens of *Gemervescence* strained a tendon in his ankle very badly, doing the Dashing White Sergeant at a party in Castlebay, Barry Sanders in *Assassin* bruised or maybe cracked his ribs during an involuntary gybe in the gale off St. Kilda and Kai Granholm fell down *Tigo V*'s forehatch while carrying a sail across from his own yacht *Mobira* in Lerwick and broke his ankle. We went everywhere with the greatest caution lest we should join the ranks of the walking wounded. Shortly after leaving Lerwick I fell down our own forehatch and I will swear that as I fell I made a mental note of all the things I might break on the way. Fortunately seaboots and full oilskins provide good protection and I survived.

The Royal Norfolk and Suffolk Yacht Club was very welcoming and helpful and we enjoyed our stay in Lowestoft, contrary to other people's warning that it was a poor stopover. It is the waters just outside the harbour that are not so attractive but then we never have liked the North Sea or the East coast. The last evening before we sailed we had a very pleasant dinner in the clubhouse with the two other married couples there. Desmond and Kitty Hampton were well ahead of us in *Panicker* and Bent and Ulla Britt Lyman were still three hours ahead in *Ghoster*. The talk was beginning to turn towards future races and Kitty wanted a new boat designed to be a *Ntombi cracker*. This generated some interesting discussion and I promised to put some ideas on paper after the race.

When it came to our time to re-start, the wind was fresh southeasterly and there was a nasty sea running outside the pierheads. *Tigo V* had gone out ahead of us not entirely organised, we thought, and we caught sight of them crossing the line very fast on a heavily reefed main and, as yet no headsail. If the forecasts were to prove correct we would have a strong chance of catching them.

I reckoned that the proper place for us to start was at the extreme outer end of the line beyond the sandbanks. The local members insisted that with our 7ft draft there would not be sufficient water over the sands. For this reason we left the basin 1½ hours early and ran off to the northward to use the Corton channel between the banks and then come back down with the fair stream to the outer end of the line. We achieved this but at the cost of starting one minute late. That was of no consequence but motor sailing to get there on time in a wicked little sea we were already very wet and uncomfortable.

We had always had misgivings about the stretch that would take us across the Thames estuary and how right we were. With the strong headwinds that we had been praying for the conditions were quite appalling. One competitor described the seas as square. This is a fair description. There seems to be no regularity, no logic and no distance between them. With the wind speeds gusting above 35 knots we tried changing down from the No 2 Genoa but, without it, we could make no speed in the lulls and so we changed back again and hammered on regardless. It was a miserable night but at least we felt no-one else was going faster.

By morning conditions were a little easier as we tacked south inside the Downs, close in off Ramsgate and Deal, to avoid the foul stream. We took advantage of the respite to consume a vast breakfast before we struck out beyond the lee of the South Foreland and battled our way towards the Dover entrance. The thrash across the Thames estuary had been physically very demanding. I, for one, had some of my winching muscles complaining somewhat and in such a motion a few falls are inevitable with the resulting crop of bruises. All of this seemed worthwhile as coming past Dungeness we suddenly found *Romtec* and *Ghoster* behind us. If they were behind, we felt sure that *Tigo V* and *Jeantex* must also be astern and for a while morale was high.

The weather forecast predicted southwesterly 5 to 6 which would suit us fine but, unfortunately, there was a mention of it going southerly for a time. In short it went southerly for so long that we reached all the way from Hastings to Start Point. For us reaching is much harder work than beating. On the wind we can engage our Aries Vane gear and let it all happen. On a reach we are inevitably carrying more sail and, although the self steering systems may cope, the speed is much better when we steer by hand and pick our way through the seas. Add to all this the fact that we knew the lightweights would be having a ball and it added just one more depression to the weather system, this one centred over *Blackjack*.

Off Start the wind failed altogether and for some time we set the floater on first one gybe and then the other in torrential rain and eventually found a southwesterly and began beating once again. We had every reason to suppose that it would turn into the northwest and steered for the land without delay. The west going stream was running out so the shore was doubly attractive. Just as we approached Start we identified *Ghoster* on the opposite tack and the two of us commenced a tacking duel in pitch blackness in and out of the rocks from Start Point, round Prawle Point and into the mouth of Salcombe. Neither yacht is easy to tack in those conditions but neither was prepared to give anything away as we watched each other's lights to gauge whether or not we had room or right to cross ahead. The wind was freshening but we had to hang on to our No 1 Genoa until we could make a long tack into the mouth of Salcombe where we did a 'tack & change' to the No 2 and pulled down one reef. With this rig we just had the advantage over *Ghoster,* pointing higher and footing at about the same speed. As daylight came we sighted *Jeantex* to seaward and another sail that we feared must be *Tigo* ahead of her. *Jeantex* made the finish that little bit more exciting by using the western entrance of Plymouth Sound, when the sailing instructions allowed the use of west or east. Coming through the east passage was undoubtedly the shorter distance and *Jeantex* set a spinnaker for the leg to the line. They broached wildly as they desperately sought to hold their lead and only pipped us by a mere 5 minutes. *Tigo V* had finished less than an hour ahead and *Ghoster* was a few minutes astern of us. After 2000 miles this was an exciting way to finish and brought us in on a high note.

If Lerwick is the high point of the event the finish in Plymouth has to be the great anticlimax. A number of yachts deposit their declarations and set off home straight away, their holiday time running out fast. A number congregate in the Mayflower marina, but there is none of the atmosphere of the stopovers and there is little left to do but tidy up, go home and start thinking about the next race!

What of the results? As the reader can judge from this story we totally ignored the multihulls, treating them as in an entirely separate race. In *Blackjack* we were the 11th monohull out of 47 albeit only 6th in our class. We still reckoned that there was only one yacht, the 63ft *Quailo of Wight*, that had a proper interior and any cruising comfort amongst those ahead. We were the second married couple, having pipped *Ghoster* on the line and we were also second in a category that I had tried to promote before the race. That was the quite unofficial Century Plus class for those crews with a total age of over 100. We had been well beaten by Granville Davis and Ramon Page in *Tigo V* and we took our hats off to them for a fine effort in a new and unfamiliar boat which they freely admitted was to them a physically demanding yacht to sail.

For ourselves we do not feel the urge to do the race again. To do better we would need a more stripped out yacht, something we do not want to own. On the other hand I can well understand those who, after their first race, feel they could do better and come back to have another go. Equally there are those who, like marathon runners, are hooked on long distance events and will be there again in 1989?

10

Alas poor Archie

A fatal injury to a crew member is a serious disruption of one's holiday cruise, particularly if, as in Archie's case, he had been a valued chap to have about, who had been pulling his weight so willingly.

Of course pride comes before a fall, they say, and Archie had been showing off a bit. The accident happened just east of Kinsale on passage from Crosshaven. Archie was steering and we were just ahead of the leading yacht of a race that had started shortly after our departure. The leg was a windward one tacking towards the Sovereign Islands and the rest of the crew had been congratulating Archie on maintaining what appeared to be a fairly constant lead over a larger yacht that was obviously trying pretty hard.

As we tacked short of the Big Sovereign there was a bit of a mix-up and Archie found himself pushed on to the leeward side of the cockpit and then before he knew what was happening he had been sat on heavily by another member of the crew many times his own weight.

The rest of the crew were very nearly in tears as we sailed into Kinsale feeling rather subdued and vowing never to be so competitive again. Archie lay apparently mortally injured with a very obviously broken spinal column.

Eulogies to Archie came pouring forth. What a tireless fellow he was. He spent long hours at the helm without complaint. He never did any washing up, that's true, but he never ate anything either. What should we do without him.

We had heard of fingers being sewn on by microsurgery, but we had never heard of a spinal graft on a completely severed backbone. It was, what's more, a Bank Holiday that day in Southern Ireland and the chances of finding an expert, sober and available, who would be capable of such delicate surgery seemed entirely remote.

There was nothing for it. As he lay, Archie could only be certified as technically dead; so that, if we operated ourselves, we couldn't make him any worse.

The chart table was cleared and sterilised and Archie was dismembered and prepared for the operation. Some form of sleeve was needed to place over the ruptured vertebrae and this was obtained by cutting off the end of the fresh water delivery pipe at the gulley sink. It is an ill wind that blows nobody any good and, believe it or not, the cook is now very pleased with the shorter pipe; the kettle fitting that much more neatly underneath.

After much delicate drilling and pinning the graft was completed and the whole structure dressed with epoxy glue and bandaged with pvc tape. Archie was then placed vertically in traction for 12 hours, to prevent any complications if the epoxy flowed prior to curing and finally he was put into intensive care. Fortunately he has his own bunk in a well protected position.

On the third day it was a quiet and gentle afternoon and Archie was allowed up for some physiotherapy. He spent about half-an-hour at the helm and seemed to have lost none of his old skills. The crew could hardly believe their good fortune in having him back. Special arrangements were made that would prevent him from ever being pushed around again. He was kept on light duties for a while but gradually his confidence returned and he became once again that ever willing, uncomplaining crew member that we thought we had lost for ever – Archie, the Autohelm 2000.

PART THREE

RACING

11

The competitive urge

Racing brings out the worst in the crew and the best in the boat. There is no quicker way of learning about the performance potential of a yacht than sailing her against others on a competitive course. It is equally likely that if you, or any of your crew, have any flaws in your personality these will surely surface as the tensions grow!

Crew compatability is indeed an essential ingredient for success. Racing under the IOR is in every respect a team effort, however, like almost every other team activity there is no room for the situation in which there are too many chiefs and not enough Indians. Nor is it healthy if all the Indians are convinced that they should be the chiefs and allow this to be known.

Division of responsibility within the crew is important and each man will concentrate on his own function much better if he is not perpetually criticising the other members of the team on the assumption that he could do better.

In my own experience I have sailed with some outstanding individuals as members of my crew but, because of their intolerance of the rest of the crew, I have been more than glad to see them go.

A bit of friendly rivalry between two watches is a very healthy idea, provided the rivalry remains friendly. Once good humour is lost then the rivalry acquires a bitter taste and a good skipper will see that that does not happen

To be a good skipper is a very difficult challenge but, make no mistake, it is vital for success. It is a management, leadership problem that is worth a lot of serious consideration.

The problem is at its most acute for the owner who is financially wealthy yet poor on experience. To win he must pick a team who will pull together and contribute advice on a sensible basis. He can of course abdicate the position of skipper and concentrate on keeping his cheque book dry. This is to my mind a rather feeble attitude, except at international levels of competition, which can only give limited satisfaction. The position is very similar to that of the chairman of a company who relies on the managing director to look after the day to day running of the business.

If there is a lack of success there are two options, re-tool, in other words, buy a new yacht; or have a management shake out. With regard to the first option it cuts two ways. Poor management, that is a poor crew, will never buy success by new investment; sometimes they may even go slower. Equally it is completely counter productive if half the crew have no confidence or loyalty to the yacht. If they think their boat is a 'dog', then they would do much better to step ashore and let someone else have a go

It is an unfortunate fact that other boats, seen across the water, can give a greater impression of speed than is being felt board one's own boat. Nothing is more upsetting, to the helmsman in particular, than the voice from the weather deck that innocently marvels at the performance of a competitor. If indeed the other boat is going faster, the first thing to discuss is whether some adjustment would help your own boat to match his speed.

There are two ways of organising the crew. In the first boat there is a proper division of responsibility and a continuing dialogue involving the whole team that concentrates on developing good boat speed and sound tactics. In the other boat there is an establishment afterguard who make all the decisions and the rest have come along for the beer. At the aft end the conversation may centre on the problems of the race, but out along the weather deck the chatter will be general until they are called upon to do their bit. These are the crews who only notice that the spinnaker sheet is under the pole end when the skipper is already calling for a gybe. While they compare notes on their other interests they are unlikely to anticipate a gybe, whereas a more involved crew would be rehearsing the next manoeuvre long before it occurred.

On inshore races it is likely that one man, very probably the owner, will steer throughout the race. This is the owner's prerogative and a very reasonable one providing he concentrates. Concentration on the need for boat speed should be the sole preoccupation of the man at the helm and, whereas quite a number of people can maintain a good standard for a limited period, there are only a few who can keep it up all day.

I am against the concept of everybody 'having a go' because there is a distinct differential in boat speed between one person's handling and another and this is not limited to the windward leg. In a seaway the helmsman who concentrates on maintaining a straight course will be half a knot slower, at least, than the person who has a feeling for taking the boat through the waves with the least loss of effort and in the general direction required.

It is difficult to make the right tactical decision at the best of times, except for those to whom it appears to be intuitive. In close quarters situations, on a starting line or while rounding a mark, I believe the helmsman must also be the decision maker. Reactions have to be so instant that communication between tactician and helmsman is too slow. On all other parts of the course it is far better for the helmsman to concentrate on boat speed and for someone else to monitor wind shifts, keep an eye on the opposition and suggest the tactical moves.

Relatively junior members of a crew can contribute much more than they think during the apparently inactive parts of the course. A great deal can be learnt from the mistakes of others and, unless you are on the leading boat, it is well worth watching the leaders to see if their choice of course was necessarily a wise one. At the same time a good crew member should, as has already been said, be rehearsing the next move and looking at the gear to make sure that some horror will not occur which could be avoided with a little forethought.

The following chapters were inspired by talking to a less experienced owner whose attitude has prompted me to put pen to paper. The owner concerned had admitted to me that he kept out of the way at the start feeling that he had a fast boat and could make up the deficit later. I persuaded him that, with the handicap he had to carry, he could not afford to do this and so he began to be more enterprising with his starting techniques with a corresponding improvement in his results. It raised the morale of his crew and generally resulted in a much happier boat.

12

The start

How often does some innocent crew member comment on the speed of another yacht which is already a hundred yards ahead within minutes of the start? Does he stop to consider where that yacht was when the gun went? Does he realise what totally different conditions the other yacht is sailing in? Clear winds and undisturbed water do wonders for boat speed and the skipper can then go for the best tidal stream and settle down to sail a boat in which morale is high. The crew of such a boat know that until the higher-rated boats overtake they have not even started to build up the lead that will be needed to win on corrected time. The shorter the race the more crucial the start, particularly for the larger boats. Many people will apply this theory in reverse to long races and tell themselves that they are going to be racing for one or two or even three days – so, what does the odd second on the start line matter? The truth is that it matters a lot. There is bound to be a crowd of boats around at the start and the one which can get clear of the crowd will gain hand over fist. The fast boat with a bad start will have to wait for that crowd to disperse before it can begin the long haul of catching and overtaking the leaders. Even though the course may be long there is often a mark or obstruction to pass early on and if the speed is greater once past this obstacle then any advantage is immediately multiplied and one length becomes three as the procession pulls away on the next leg.

There are of course occasions when the reverse happens and those in front run up against foul tides and head winds. The fleet turns itself inside out to the dismay of the early leaders and to the satisfaction of the cautious whose lack of aggression on the starting line has been rewarded for once.

The measure of a good start is not so much the boat's position when the gun fires, as how she stands 30 seconds later as the fleet settles down. The ability to tack early may be critical, in which case an apparently first class start may come to nought on account of another competitor a length behind, but far enough to weather to dictate tactics. If the port tack is really critical then it may pay to start a few seconds late but in a position to tack immediately.

This is probably the hardest part of starting; this need to analyse the situation and know just where to put the boat as the gun goes. Even with committee boat starts there is almost always a bias towards one end or the other and if there is a tidal stream involved then the committee may have introduced an intentional bias to counter the tidal advantage of one end. There are a number of recognised techniques for identifying bias but they are nearly all of them much easier for a dinghy sailor than the skipper of a heavy cruising yacht ploughing up and down on a crowded line. If it is not possible to decide by looking at the flags of the committee boat or club flagstaff, then sail closehauled over each end of the line in turn and try to decide whether it would be possible to cross ahead of a yacht on the opposite tack at the other end. If in tidal waters study the streams well in advance and if there is a difference between one end of the line and the other decide which end offers the greatest advantage, or least disadvantage, and, if all other things are equal, go for it. Think about the other competitors and try to forecast where the scrum will be. With a fast boat there is no need to be afraid of the scrum, providing you know your rights, and providing you will be granted them. If sailing a tiddler and racing among a lot of bigger fish then too much infighting will result in being sat on rather heavily. If you know which are the good boats then keep one eye on them and do not be too proud to crib a bit. Reading a starting line correctly is largely a matter of experience so pick out the better boats and see where they are manoeuvring.

Keeping an eye on things is a full-time occupation and it is as well to remember that the skipper's eyes are not the only pair on board. In the writer's experience the best starts are often made by involving the whole crew. Give the more reliable members some definite responsibility so that the operation becomes a team effort; one man to call the time, one man to watch the line, one to watch for wind shifts, one to leeward to give warning of right-of-way yachts, and so on. On no account allow five or six self-appointed skippers to undermine confidence by trying to tell the real skipper when to tack and when to gybe. If he knows what he is trying to do then he should tell them, and will then get much more co-operation, even if he abandons the plan at the last minute. Above all get the crew wound up in good time, keep them occupied, keep sailing up and down the line as much as possible. Make sure they realise the importance of the situation and that they do not suddenly disappear down below for an extra jersey or to go to the heads just as the five minute gun goes.

It is of course vitally important to know and understand the boat, both for her manoeuvrability and her acceleration, or lack of it. The

Shortly after the gun, during the 1984 Half Ton World Championships. 584 appears to have a clear wind and be going well, but it looks as though the majority of the fleet have opted for the port end of the line. They could perhaps be right.

latest breed of IOR designs are mostly pretty light and nimble. They turn fast and they pick up speed fast. They can stay closer to the line easing sheets to check their speed knowing that they can pounce on an opportunity and be away in a flash. The older heavier boats take longer to wind up. They can cross the line within one second of the gun, but if they have not got full way on they will be trampled on by those who have taken a run at it. So if sailing an S&S 34 or a Contessa 32 do not fall in behind a J24 and try to follow suit, it just will not work.

For a heavy boat nothing pays better than a timed run from a known point, practised beforehand and repeated to perfection in the closing seconds before the gun. However there are pitfalls. If the practice runs have been sailed with, so to speak, a flying start, then timing the start of the final run is almost as difficult as timing the start itself. Much better to time the runs from a point at which the yacht can be held stationary, taking the time from the moment of sheeting in. In this way the final run can be started exactly when the clock dictates knowing that time has been allowed for the necessary gathering of way. Of course it must be realised that rights of way have a considerable influence on the ability to follow a chosen line when the time comes. A long run in on port could easily be upset and once a detour has been made then a late start is almost a certainty.

Timed runs are fine in rivers and estuaries where mooring buoys, alternative transits and other features give a positive starting point.

When the start is from a committee boat entirely surrounded by open water there is little opportunity for making a timed run. If it is possible to be sure that the boat's speed will be the same both ways then sail away from the line for half the remaining time, turn and sail back and, in theory, cross with the gun. In practice speed is seldom equal both ways particularly if there is a tidal stream running and it is even more likely that, just when the turn is needed a right of way yacht will prevent it.

In the majority of cases the only answer is judgement which comes from experience and knowledge of the boat. In this respect there is a strong case for staying close to the line in the closing minutes so that the distance concerned is relatively short.

Staying close to the line necessarily demands a clear knowledge of the rules relating to starting. In simple terms they are the same as in the rest of racing; port gives way to starboard, and windward yacht keeps clear of leeward yacht. The port and starboard situation leaves little doubt in most people's minds but the interpretation of the windward yacht keeping clear is far less well understood. Rule 40, luffing before starting, should be read carefully but, broadly speaking, the intention is that a yacht can hail any windward yacht for room to luff and sail a higher course except that she can not luff beyond closehauled unless the windward yacht's helmsman (sighting abeam from his normal station) is abaft the main mast of the leeward yacht. According to the rules the windward yacht must be given ample room and opportunity to keep clear. In practice, it is extremely difficult to convince a jury that room and opportunity have not been given. So the lesson is to treat the yacht to leeward with the respect that her position deserves. It is not legitimate to bear away across another yacht, and the hail 'water for the line' which has been heard is utter nonsense.

The second rule that should be written in 6ft high letters for all to see is 42.4 which says: *At a starting mark surrounded by navigable water.* When approaching the starting line to start and after starting, a leeward yacht shall be under no obligation to give any windward yacht room to pass to leeward of a starting mark surrounded by navigable water, but, after the starting signal, a leeward yacht shall not deprive a windward yacht, of room at such a mark by sailing above the compass bearing course to the first mark or above closehauled.

This rule is addressed at the 'fan starters' of this world, the little knot of boats that gather up to windward and then come boring in at high speed expecting to be given room to slip round the mark. The yacht to leeward can shout 'No water' and sail close past the mark forcing the fan starters to pile up on the committee boat or tack away. The moral is that if trying to gain that pole position at the starboard end of the line, just make sure that it is clear to leeward and that nobody can squeeze you into an impossible position.

The other rule which although not specifically relating to the start is nonetheless very relevant is Rule 41 Changing Tacks – Tacking or

Gybing. It is an essential part of pre-start manoeuvring to be able to tack or gybe close to other competitors, and to do so legally requires forethought. The critical point involved is that if by tacking or gybing you become the right of way yacht and it is better not to tack unless you are, then until the tack or gybe is completed the other yacht is under no obligation to take avoiding action. In other words the rules do not expect a yacht to anticipate another yacht's manoeuvre. So when is a tack or gybe complete? According to the Definitions in Part 1 of the Rules 'A yacht is tacking from the moment she is beyond head to wind until she is borne away, when beating to windward, to a closehauled course; when not beating to windward, to the course on which her mainsail has filled'. In the definition of gybing, the gybe is completed when the mainsail has filled on the new tack. In a modern yacht, turning fast, the action of tacking or gybing is almost instantaneous. Experience has shown that it is very difficult to protest successfully against another yacht for tacking or gybing too close unless she is positively caught in the act.

With a little practice it is possible to play the close tacking manoeuvre to considerable advantage. The general flow of yachts in the build-up to a windward start is frequently anti-clockwise to leeward of the starboard end buoy as each yacht prepares to approach closehauled on starboard. If the yacht is on the outside of this circle she is going to be

As the yachts settle on the first leg, 23 is safely on top of 30 and will probably pull out clear of 28.

to windward at the start and in a dangerous tactical situation. If she is on the inside of the circle and the timing is good then she is going to be in the leeward position and entitled to luff – and free from interference on her own leeward side. However to get into this position will very likely mean tacking under another yacht's lee bow. This has to be done close enough to the windward yacht so that the attack is not sailed over and yet clear enough to remain within her rights.

On the subject of turning, remember that it is far easier, except in very strong conditions, to gybe than to tack. Gybing takes much less way off the boat, it should be easier on the crew and by gybing it is often possible to avoid working up to windward when this is tactically wrong. So if there is room to leeward consider the choice carefully and do not instinctively turn to windward.

One of the hardest parts of starting is being able to judge how close to the line the boat is in the closing seconds. When starting on a shore transit this is only a problem if there is a bunch of boats between the yacht and the transit. Much the greatest difficulty exists at a committee boat start when the definition will probably be 'an imaginary line between the mainmast of the committe boat and the outer distance mark'. The first thing to try is to sail past each end of the line and look for a natural transit that coincides. The further away from the shore the harder this becomes, and the closer to the middle of the line the more difficult it is to judge position.

It is easy to be misled by an inner distance mark. In tidal conditions it is quite often impossible to lay the buoy close to the starting line. When it is beyond, on the course side of the line, it invariably acts like a magnet and draws the fleet out towards it.

One thing should be remembered and that is that the race officer, who is standing on one end of the line probably has a perfect view and unless it is a matter of mistaken identity, arguing about an early start will gain absolutely nothing.

If starting in tidal waters then two things are certain. If the stream is fair for the first mark then the fleet as a whole is likely to be early. The last seconds will seem like a hundred and if the yacht is too close to the line there will be all sorts of trouble. If the stream is foul the last few seconds will go like lightning and you will probably wish you had cut it a whole lot finer.

There is no single answer to the negotiation of starting lines. There is, in fact, no substitute for experience, from which comes judgement and nerve. Nerve relies on confidence in boat and crew, on practice and on familiarity. In the writer's experience some starting lines will be found much worse than others, and not necessarily for any tangible reason. The one thing that will be rewarded is perserverance. If you have the will to improve starts, then get in there and try. Sooner or later it will pay dividends, and then will come the realisation of the enormous advantage which is there for the taking.

13

Around the course

Particularly inshore, races are won by the crews who know their boats and know their rigs. The winners are the ones who come round the leeward mark and set off up the beat with the right headsail, sheeted in the right position, with the right amount of halyard tension and the

IR 5453 and K 5391 are well sorted out and going well. IR 421 is in a most unhappy state and still sorting out the chaos of the last mark rounding. She is driving to leeward fast, through lack of weight to windward, and will lose badly.

Part of the fleet rounding St Catherine's during a Round the Island race. Correct reading of the conditions at this point will gain or lose any number of places.

mainsail traveller already in the right position and so on. The losers are the opposite, they may have a fast boat but it takes them much longer to get into top gear and by the time they have done so the others are preparing for the next mark rounding some way ahead.

Racing offshore is rather different in this respect there is a case for constant tinkering in search of better boat speed, although even this is often over done. One crew member who sailed with me in many races was a great enthusiast and did not feel he was justifying himself if too great a time went by without adjusting something. The great thing is to know when there is room for improvement and when to leave well alone.

Having successfully, or otherwise, negotiated the horrors of the starting line and set out upon the course there are many aspects of racing that have nothing to do with trimming the sails and extracting the best boatspeed. This is not to say that boatspeed is a secondary consideration but it surely goes without saying that it must be applied in the right direction. On passage races and for offshore events there should be a navigator, responsible for advising the helmsman which way to point the yacht. Round the buoys, however, the solution is often less obvious, and many a fast boat has been made to look foolish by the more canny and devious strategies of foxier competitors.

The essential factors that must be considered in formulating a plan of action on each leg of the course are: the conditions of wind, tide and tidal stream and the changes that may be anticipated; the tactical situation with regard to other yachts, particularly on arrival at the next turning mark; is the thumb line really the quickest way to the next mark or could boat-speed be increased sufficiently by sailing a dog leg to justify the extra distance?

Much is spoken about local knowledge in relation to tidal streams but quite often this can just as well be purchased in the form of tidal stream atlases. If sailing on strange waters it is of tremendous importance to study all the available information in advance; agreed, the local skipper has an advantage as his knowledge is more intuitive and his tactics more automatic, giving him more scope elsewhere but just occasionally the locals come unstuck by making an automatic reaction to a foul stream when a visitor by calculation can decide to ignore the flow and sail direct. This is particularly apparent in The Solent when visiting teams have caused some eye openers in recent years. The rule to remember is that the value of tide cheating depends directly on the rate of the foul stream in relation to the speed of the yacht. On a fast downwind leg the detour involved in search of slacker water may not be justified, particularly if two extra gybes are added by so doing.

In slower conditions it may even be that once in slack water the speed over the ground is doubled and then the boat out in the stream can be

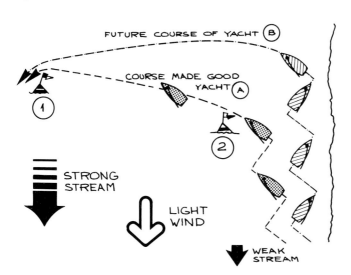

Because the wind is light, Yacht B may choose to sail extra distance in the slacker stream, ignoring Mark 1, in order to cross the stronger stream at a greater speed than Yacht A.

bade farewell. Cross tides are the most difficult of all and judging the right angle to steer is always a worry. If the strength of the wind and stream could be guaranteed to be constant throughout the leg then trial and error in the first few hundred yards would suggest an optimum course. So often the course is crossing or setting out into a deep water channel, where the stream may be considerably stronger half way across. The skill comes in allowing for this in the early stages. It is always a good insurance to keep uptide of the objective if at all possible and drop down as the yacht closes the buoy. You are far less likely to come unstuck at the last minute, clawing up frantically while the others come swooshing in from above.

One must in many cases think about the tidal streams beyond the next mark. On page 149 Yacht A has rounded Mark 1 in light airs and set off for Mark 2. She is forced to point up and sail slowly to avoid being set down by the stream. Yacht B has ignored Mark 1 and has continued to work the slack water until much further to windward with the object of reaching across the stronger stream at a higher boat speed. The success of this ploy will depend entirely on the difference in strength of the stream between the deep and shallow water and how fast Yacht A can sail in the critical stage approaching Mark 2.

If the wind is constant in speed and direction over the whole race area then we have an uncomplicated situation that in practice seldom occurs. The weather forecast may have given an indication of an anticipated shift and if so watch the clouds for a change of pattern and maybe the shift will come with it. If beating to windward, stay on the side of the course from which the shift will come. If, on the other hand, the wind is just plain flukey and there seems no telling where it will shift to next, stick close to the rhumb line and work the shifts.

Much so-called weather lore is no more than common sense. If it is a hot, sunny day with no breeze, look for the thermals on the shore and if there are high trees or hills around keep out of their wind shadow. Remember that the crew love watching all the other boats, however far away. Train them to notice the signs of a change so that you are ready for it.

Whole books have been written on yacht racing tactics but to many the subject never really seem to apply to them. In Cowes Week, for instance, crews are forever judging a situation by whether it seems fair from their view point, without considering the wider implications of the rules involved. The commonest example of this is the frantic situations that arise when short tacking along a shore on the port side of the course. The yachts approaching the shore are on starboard tack and have right-of-way. A yacht sailing away from the shore on port cannot hail 'water' at a starboard tack yacht. Every year it happens.

'Starboard' you call.

'Water,' they reply, 'we have only six feet, what else can we do'.

The hard fact is that Rule 43 (1) refers to two yachts *on the same tack*;

if a port tack yacht leaving the shore meets a starboard tack yacht and is unable to bear away and pass astern then, however shallow the water, she must tack and then hail the starboard tack yacht for water. With this in mind you must when approaching the shore anticipate such a position before it occurs and be prepared to tack away from the shore early enough to cope with the situation of being forced back again by a right-of-way yacht. These short tacking situations can be very fraught and there are times when three or four boats find themselves in step, with each tack becoming more frantic than the last. The canny skipper is the man who somehow manages to get out of step, to be in when the others are out, and find the necessary hole each time to wriggle through on port when the others are going in.

Picking one's way up the windward leg is never straightforward unless already way out in front with a clear wind. Even then the shifts must be watched and an eye kept on the compass. Too much tacking is the worst thing for a yacht with a large genoa and a weak crew, conversely a fractionally rigged boat with a nimble crew may lose so little by constant tacking that the gains may be significant. Before tacking, think whose dirty wind the yacht may be in and how it can be avoided. If another yacht has crossed ahead sail on until well across her wake before tacking.

This chapter would not be complete without some thoughts on covering tactics to windward. Perhaps the most difficult aspect is to maintain a sense of proportion. In a match racing situation, the skipper who fails to cover is considered foolish. On the other hand, in a crowded fleet, it is far more sensible to concentrate on finding a clear wind for oneself, than to become obsessed with directing one's own dirty wind at the competitors. If all other things are equal, it might be as well to time the tacks to give someone dirty wind, if only to increase the present advantage. The commonest pitfall is to tack unnecessarily, purely to cover another yacht. Unless there is some particular reason for singling out another yacht for attack, then nine times out of ten it is better not to get involved. If ahead, it is essential to insure against wind shifts favouring those behind. Having selected those boats that represent the greatest threat, then the golden rule is to time the tacks so that you stay as much as possible between them and the next mark.

Approaching the weather mark, think hard about the likely situation on the buoy. Whenever he can, a competent race officer will try to set the course so that the weather mark is left to port. Marks to port are nearly always easier to negotiate than marks to starboard. When beating up to a mark that is to be left to port an approach on starboard tack is generally quite safe and in a crowd a port tack is verging on the suicidal. That long column of starboard tack yachts has absolute right-of-way and if you tack to leeward the wind will be so cut up that you may fail to weather the buoy. The only alternative is to put the helm up and go looking for a gap in the line. If the mark is to be left to starboard the

COURSE TO NEXT MARK

WIND

STREAM

The leading yacht can be trapped on the 'wrong' tack as she is prevented from tacking by the next yacht astern. She will be carried away from the mark by the stream as she awaits her turn to tack.

situation is very different and being the leading boat is not necessarily the happiest position, particularly if the stream has been fair and will be foul as the fleet rounds on to the next leg. Rule 42.2 (c) says: *A yacht clear ahead which tacks to round a mark is subject to Rule 41 (Changing Tacks, Tacking and Gybing). 42.2 (b) says a yacht clear astern shall not luff above close-hauled so as to prevent the yacht clear ahead from tacking.*

Too many competitors assume that, because they have arrived first, they must be allowed room to tack disregarding the fact that having done so they may be on port tack and vulnerable to a hail from the yacht astern. On Page 152 a typical Cowes Week situation is illustrated. Taken to extremes these circumstances can completely reverse a fleet so that the last become first and the first last in true biblical fashion. Race committees should avoid setting courses that result in this situation early in a race if they possibly can. There is no proper way of avoiding trouble and the resulting schamozzle very often results in heavy penalties on yachts that are largely the victims of circumstances beyond their control.

Running towards the leeward or gybe mark is equally difficult and requires much forethought. It makes little or no difference whether the rounding is to port or to starboard. It does, however, make a world of difference if there is a strong stream with or against the fleet as it makes its approach. Rule 42.1 requires the outside of two overlapping yachts to give room for the inside yacht to round the mark. That is a simplification of a rule that is too long to quote here and should be read many times by all skippers to understand it fully. In practice the difficulties that arise afloat stem from establishing the existence of the overlap at the proper time and the physical problems of the chain reaction that is necessary when ten or more yachts arrive together and the outside boat does not know until the last minute whether he must allow room for three boats or thirteen inside.

Rule 42.3 is quite clear that the overlap must be established before the leading yacht is within two overall lengths of the yacht from the buoy. This is difficult to judge from the yacht astern and the onus of proof that the overlap exists is his to establish. In practice the yacht astern asking for water will call 'water', or the leading yacht will call 'no water'. If as the leading yacht you shout 'no water' and the yacht astern removes your stern lamp as he alters course to pass outside the evidence is likely to go against you. If the reverse is the case and, as the leading yacht, you claim that an overlap that has existed is broken then this must be proven and at the same time those two lengths are the guiding factor. It is when competing yachts are surfing on a seaway that the greatest difficulties arise. Overlaps are established and broken very rapidly as each yacht accelerates and decelerates. In the general excitement it is very difficult to judge the precise two-lengths moment as the yacht rushes up to the buoy. It is as well to remember whose responsibilty it will be to justify the claim before you push your luck too far.

When racing on a tideway and particularly in a crowded fleet policies must change with the state of the tidal stream. On Page 153 the fleet is approaching the leeward mark against the stream. If that stream is strong then the all-important thing is to get round as soon as possible

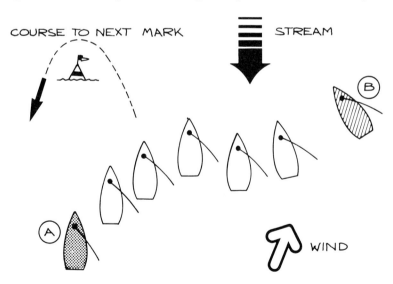

Approaching a downwind mark with a foul stream, Yacht A will be lucky to receive the water to which she is entitled. Yacht B may well be able to reach round clear of the inevitable pile up on the buoy.

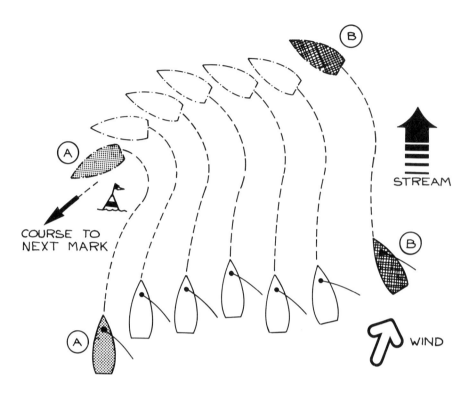

STREAM

COURSE TO
NEXT MARK

WIND

With a fair stream the gaps between the yachts will widen more quickly. 'A' should receive the water to which she is entitled. 'B' will be swept downstream and would have been better advised to slow up and drop astern of 'A'.

even at the risk of starting the windward leg in a shambles. In other words keep the spinnaker up until the last possible moment because otherwise the last few lengths up to the buoy will be very slow. Yacht A has the right to claim water but with all the yachts slowing up as they bunch together the chances of her getting it are by no means certain. As they all round the buoy the stream is forcing the outside boats inwards. Any amount of protesting and waving the rule book will never make up for lost time. Yacht B on the other hand is free to sail her own race and in many cases can actually round the mark faster by reaching in beyond the crowd with spinnaker still drawing and if it takes a few minutes to tidy up on the wind at least the boat is still in one piece and on a fair stream, so what does it matter if perfect trim is not instant

Look now at the above. The situation is much the same except that the stream has been reversed. This time the stream will sweep the outside boats way past the buoy and Yacht B will be a hundred yards or so downtide before she can begin to go to windward. Yacht A on the other hand will be much more likely to get her water and will be perfectly placed as the windward leg starts. This is the occasion to have the spinnaker down in good time. It is much better to be the inside boat of the second bunch then the outside boat of the first. This time the windward leg is against the stream and the crew must have the decks clear and the rig set up for windward sailing as the yacht rounds the mark.

On the free legs of the course races can become horribly processional and try one's patience sorely. It always seems to be hard to overtake and easier to be overtaken. Getting involved in a luffing match seldom does either party much good. At the same time it is as well to avoid giving the impression of being a soft touch who will not defend his weather side. On a broad reach any fool can reach up to weather of another yacht, take half the other's wind, and then steam close down the weather side. The luffing rule (Rule 38) is there to protect the overtaken yacht from the inevitable if the overtaking yacht comes too close. If you are faced with a yacht that imagines he can get away with coming so close to windward that he is going to stop you dead, then the only answer is to luff and luff hard and let him know you mean business. Half-hearted luffing never did anyone any good. Equally, picking quarrels is a silly waste of time. If another yacht is sailing faster and standing off a reasonable distance let him go. If, on the other hand, they can see you edging over in good time to defend yourself then your bluff may well be called and they will choose to go off to leeward. Very often if your speed is only marginally better than the yacht ahead you may find there is just no way round and patience is your only weapon. Long detours to avoid a wind shadow or a defensive luff can often result in an increase in distance and a loss of boat speed as you come back on to the course to the mark. As you approach the mark your opponent is still there and if he is a better thinker he is going to be on the inside asking for water, and will start the next leg a length-and-a-half up.

At school we were always taught that the shortest distance between two points was a straight line joining them. We all know that we cannot sail up the windward leg in a straight line, but what about the offwind legs? A small alteration of course, say 5° or 10°, can very often create a significant increase in boat speed. When that increase can be seen to outweigh the added distance then the diversion must be worthwhile. On a long leg in light weather it is frequently worth more to sail fast in the general direction of the next mark than to stick rigidly to the rhumb line at an unhappy angle to the wind. This is frequently the case when running in a large fleet. The dead run in light airs can be very dead and overtaking difficult if there is the risk of being luffed. In these circumstances tacking down wind can be proved to be a great advantage; 10° or even 15° away from the dead run and a well trimmed spinnaker will develop so much more power. Providing the crew's gybing techniques are efficient, significant gains can be made and, if the timing works out, one ends up on the most advantageous wing of the fleet coming into the leeward mark. However be warned, if the majority are on port gybe you will be horribly unpopular as you cut across on starboard and your requests for right-of-way may take a little while to sink in.

There are times when a reaching leg is best sailed as a dog leg. With the apparent wind too far ahead to fly a shy spinnaker climbing out to windward until the course is significantly free to break out the kite is frequently profitable. On the other hand hanging on to a shy spinnaker until you are well to leeward of the rhumb line, on the assumption you can climb back later, is often a disaster.

Fortunately the finish of a race is generally the simplest of problems. It is, however, remarkable how many yachts make a hash of it. Nearly all finishing lines have a bias to them and one end will be closer to the last mark than the other. In the case of a windward finish it is necessary to identify the leeward end and go for that. Remember that all that is necessary is for some part of the yacht (in its normal position) to cut the line. It is not even necessary to cross the line (Rule 51.5). In this respect there are many times when a gigantic luff or tack will take the yacht over seconds sooner than sailing without tacking.

Finally it would seem worth pointing out that whatever one's feeling towards the race officers the rest of the time, the finish is the one time when some co-operation may pay dividends. Look up at the sail numbers and make sure they can be read by those who are judging the line. If there is any doubt alter course or re-sheet the sail as soon as you have finished to make their life easier. There is nothing worse than slaving all day to get round the course only to find that you have not been identified and nobody has taken your finishing time.

14

Pointing high

Sailing to windward is a very wide subject and one on which a great deal has been written. What follows was written mindful of the broad range of factors that bear upon the efficiency or lack of it when sailing to windward. The writer offers no excuses for approaching the subject of sailing to windward principally in terms of pointing. So many claims are made on behalf of various designs to promote their superior pointing ability that it seems quite justifiable to devote some thought to this particular aspect of windward sailing.

To arrive at Vmg (Velocity made good) to windward we know that the wind angle is only one factor and that boat speed through the water is also vital to overall progress towards a windward mark. There are, however, special circumstances where an ability to point high is a particular advantage. For example, when sailing in a crowded fleet the yacht that points high can very often climb into clearer air more easily than one that foots faster but not so high. Often, when sailing along a shoreline in an effort to avoid the tidal stream, a high pointing yacht will be better able to hold her course along the bank than a lower pointing yacht which will be forced to put in more tacks – and so spend longer in a stronger adverse stream.

So, if we accept that there are times when despite the Vmg calculations we may wish to sacrifice some speed in order to point as high as possible, what are the limiting factors? Why will one yacht apparently sail 2° or 3° higher than another?

If a curve of speed against the wind angle is plotted it can be seen that as the wind angle becomes smaller the rate at which boat speed tails off accelerates until it reaches what might well be described as a precipice. The point of sailing we are concerned with is very close to the edge of this precipice. Speed has been lost in return for high pointing ability, but not so disastrously as would happen if we took another step closer to the edge.

What makes going to windward so different to all other points of sailing? This can probably best be answered by describing the situation in terms of a profit and loss account. The credit side of the account is never very far ahead of the losses when going to windward and so the speed range of the yacht is always very limited. When running the influence of the wind is 100% profit, there are no drag factors arising out of the rig. The moment that the apparent wind comes forward of the

Peter Johnson's Highwayman *powering upwind in the smooth waters of the Solent.*

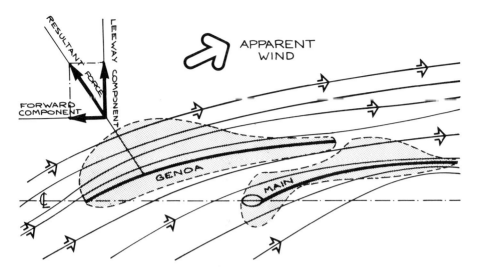

This diagram, based on a flow diagram by Hood Sails, shows the cambered surfaces of the mainsail and genoa presented at an angle to the wind. The airflow can be seen together with the pressure distribution curves (dotted lines enclosing the shaded areas). The resultant driving force is sub-divided into a forward component and a leeway component by the parallelogram of forces shown top left.

beam the loss account is opened. When hard on the wind the losses are at their greatest and every increase in speed is countered by a further increase in drag. When the yacht is trimmed for pointing high, and the helmsman starts to pinch, boat speed drops off but the losses do not. The profit becomes marginal and progress is suddenly very small indeed.

Turning now to the mechanics of windward sailing we can express this in simple terms by drawing a diagram of the rig (above). The sails are cambered surfaces presented to the wind so that the airflow is divided by the leading edge, creating a depression to leeward and pressure to windward. This results in a force that can be divided into a forward component and a leeway component. Underwater the keel surface generates a sideforce to combat the leeway and the yacht moves forward at an angle to the wind. The limiting factor for reducing that angle is the angle at which the leading edge of the headsail can be profitably presented to the wind relative to the centre line of the yacht. Any adjustment to the sail in search of a flatter entry that results in a reduction in camber, is bound to result in a drop in speed. For any particular condition in which the yacht is sailing there will be a certain minimum amount of camber, below which there is no longer sufficient power being generated to overcome the losses and keep the yacht moving profitably to windward.

As any student of economics will tell us, it is important to examine each side of the account in order to arrive at an overall improvement in the net profit figures. So before we look at the sails and how they are set let us look at the losses in isolation. Some of these may be controllable, others may have to be accepted.

Drag in all its forms is directly related to the amount of power required to keep the boat moving at a satisfactory speed. Any reduction in drag will ease the lot of the man who is trimming the sails. As the power requirement is reduced so he can concentrate more on sheeting the sails for a fine entry angle and thus provide the helmsman with a chance to point higher.

So what are the drag losses that should be considered? Drag from hull form is a complete subject on its own. Once one is the owner of a yacht there is not much that can be done except to understand the limitation of the particular type. It goes without saying that a long, lean, shallow hull is more easily driven than a short, fat, deep one, but what about fore and aft trim? When giving another yacht a tow, notice how the bow wave increases when one or more of the crew comes forward. In just the same way the stern wave will become exaggerated if there is too big a concentration of weight aft.

Returning to the factors that can be controlled, how about the state of the bottom? Losses due to fouling are very serious and the initial deterioration due to a less than perfect finish is remarkable. In the same way consider the propeller. A fixed propeller is never more of a handicap than when trying to go to windward. Two otherwise identical yachts sailing to windward, one with a fixed and the other with a folding propeller, will have a very noticeable difference in performance. The latter will either sail faster on the same course or, if the sails can be trimmed to produce a narrower entry angle, she will point higher at the same speed as the one with the fixed propeller.

Let us now turn our attention to the keel – without which our yacht would not go to windward at all. It is, nonetheless, a drag and its efficiency is expressed in terms of a lift to drag ratio. In this instance lift really means sideforce generated to resist leeway although some leeway must exist before the sideforce can be generated. To be correctly suited to a yacht a keel must be large enough to generate sufficient sideforce to reduce leeway to an acceptable minimum and for optimum performance it must generate that sideforce for a minimum of drag. Modern racing keels look rather like aircraft wings and it should be recognized that they are there to do a very similar job. The keel of a yacht is there to resist leeway created by the sideways element of the force of the wind on the sails, in the same way as the wing of an aircraft is resisting the downwards force exerted by the earth's gravitational pull. Sufficient to say, in this article, that the search for high lift in relation to drag has led to deeper, higher aspect ratio keels. What the writer would like to emphasize is that the design of the keel, as such, has far less bearing on the ability to point than is generally realised. A number of times one will hear people compare similar yachts of differing keel configurations, maintaining that yacht A pointed just as well as yacht B. What is so often overlooked is that A may be making far more leeway than B while pointing, in terms of bow angle to the wind, just as well. Some years ago the writer assisted in some very interesting trials carried out by Westerly. Two sloop rigged Conways were available. One had the standard 6ft 0in draft with an iron keel, and the other had a lead keel of appreciably less draft but equivalent righting moment. Sailing together each would be holding the same compass course as the other. The course made good by the deeper keeled yacht was, however, always dramatically better than the shallow version. In fact, the tacking angles measured on the steering compasses were to all intents and purposes, equal for both yachts. Had the shallow draft version been sailed alone, without the comparison presented so forcibly by her deeper sister, then purely from the simple instruments aboard, it would have been much harder to appreciate how poorly she was making to windward. As a result of these trials the lead keel was not put into production.

Nothing speeds development so strongly as competition. The IOR establishes a base draft for any size of yacht and imposes a correction positive or negative for a measured draft that is greater or smaller. When a yacht is being designed specifically for racing, where windward ability at close quarters is at a premium, then it is very frequently worth accepting a penalty for what the rule considers an excessive draft.

There are a few keels in existence with characteristics that give very poor lift at low boat speeds. It is this failing that means that such boats must keep their speed high when sailing to windward. When this is the case, pointing must be forgotten and the yacht must be kept footing fast all the time.

Let us move on to the rudder and its relevance to efficiency to windward. Fundamentally this is directly related to balance. It is important to realise why a yacht needs to carry a trace of weather helm to be at her most efficient to windward. When the rudder is mounted on the trailing edge of a long keel it is like an aileron on an aircraft's wing which, by being raised or depressed, either decreases or increases the lift of the wing. The application of the rudder creates an asymmetrical foil section which, when suitably proportioned, increases the lift in relation to drag very satisfactorily. This occurs when the tiller is held slightly to weather and the opposite occurs when it is held to leeward.

The modern yacht has a separately hung rudder either on a skeg or as a swivelling foil or spade, well aft of the keel. Properly designed it provides an additional lifting surface that makes a significant contribution to windward efficiency. It has been stated earlier that the keel produces no sideforce unless leeway exists. The reason for this is that, for the sideforce to be generated, an angle of incidence is necessary

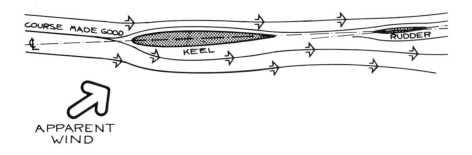

COURSE MADE GOOD

KEEL

RUDDER

APPARENT WIND

The angle between the centreline and the course made good is the angle of incidence of the keel. Because of the slipstream off the keel, a small angle of weather helm is needed to create an efficient angle of incidence on the leading edge of the rudder.

on the leading edge of the keel. This angle of incidence is directly related to the amount of leeway that is effective (above). The independently hung rudder is acting in the slipstream of the fin keel. This means that the flow angle is bent round so that if the rudder were fixed amidships the angle of incidence in relation to its fore and aft axis would be smaller than that of the keel, and quite likely too small for worthwhile lift to be generated. A small angle of weather helm restores the proper angle of incidence and is therefore a benefit, in allowing the rudder to make a contribution to the overall sideforce generated. So, trimming the mainsail or raking the mast to provide a trace of weather helm will improve overall lift in relation to drag and open the door to a better pointing angle, if this is required. At the same time it makes the helmsman's life easier because the necessary feel is transmitted which will enable him to hold a high pointing angle.

Now we should take a look at the drag factors above the water. When going to windward air drag is a major loss – for the power created by the wind on the sails which is devoted to driving the yacht forward there is a lesser amount of drag created by all the surfaces exposed to the wind other than the sails.

Designers have for years set their minds to reducing the windage aloft as much as possible. A big, fat mast and oversize rigging may give relative peace of mind but when the sails are close reefed the losses are fearful. With three reefs in the mainsail, up to 40% of the mast is a dead loss, serving only to drive the yacht backwards. It is not difficult to see what an advantage the smaller mast section can give, always providing that it stays up there. Because of the speed gradient between the deck and the masthead windage is more serious the higher one goes. The present fashion for a masthead that looks like a Christmas tree is excellent for information and communications, but it does not do the windward performance of the yacht any good at all. Things like mast steps, steaming lights and radar reflectors are all creating windage as well as turbulence on the sails. They all mean that the sails must generate that much more power to overcome the losses and this will inhibit the use of a narrow entry angle.

Having considered all the losses we should now turn our attention to the sails, because their contribution to the windward ability of the yacht is more fundamental than anything else. We have already seen that each sail is a cambered surface set at an angle to the wind. For the purposes of this chapter it is not really necessary to differentiate between true wind angle and apparent wind angle. Twice the true wind angle is that angle through which the head of the yacht will pass when we tack, which is, in isolation, a measurement of how well the yacht can point. Suffice to say that there is an angle between the luff of the headsail and the centreline of the yacht. If this angle can be made smaller while still generating sufficient drive then the wind angle can be reduced and the yacht will be pointing higher.

For the man on deck trimming the sails the problem is to select a sheeting angle (below) that enables the sail to be sheeted in so that the entry angle is satisfactorily small but the camber is retained. At first this appears to be an argument in favour of the narrowest possible sheeting angles. Indeed it is; but it has to be recognised that even with very short crosstrees there is a limit to bringing the genoa lead inboard. The leech of the genoa must be in sympathy with the lee side of the mainsail for the slot to remain effective. This means that limitations are imposed by the ability to flatten the mainsail, and for the yacht to accept the loss of drive that will arise from the flattening process. The complementary effect of reducing the sheeting angle is that, particularly with

The chord of a sail is the distance from luff to leech at any height. The camber is the maximum depth from a straight line chord to the surface of the sail. The sheeting angle is measured on deck between the yacht's centreline and a straight line joining the forestay attachment point and the fairlead.

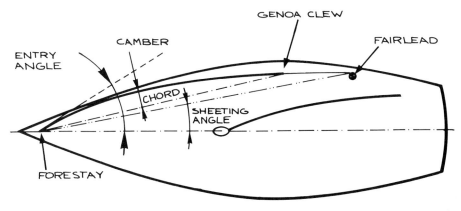

overlapping genoas, the effect of closing the slot is to increase the heeling moment. If the boat is stiff enough to stand it, then she can be made to point higher than a more tender design on which the angle must be opened up sooner to free the slot. It is also worth remembering that halyard tension controls the fore and aft position of the point of maximum camber. The effect of too much tension is to draw the camber so far forward that the entry angle is increased and the pointing ability reduced.

Nothing has been said so far about the sail itself and the sailmaker's contribution towards pointing ability. One cannot make a silk purse from a sow's ear anymore than one can convert a standard low price cruising sail into a grand prix racing sail. The price of a headsail can vary (probably at a ratio of about 4:1) between the most expensive, carefully designed sail in the very best materials, and the common or garden, very ordinary, standard sail in the least expensive Terylene sail cloth. The point to be made is that too often a yacht is condemned as pointing less well than another purely because there is no way that her headsail can be adjusted to provide drive at a sufficiently narrow entry angle to compete.

In a well designed and properly trimmed sail the entry angle will be controlled for its full height to match the wind gradient. It can, therefore, be seen that one sail may be fully efficient for a much greater proportion of its height than another, where this proper twist is not achieved. Any sail is only as good as the rig on which it is set. It may be accepted that headsails can be cut for slack forestays but if pointing is the number one priority then there is no doubt that the sailmakers' task is much easier where the sag is least.

When one reads a boat test of a yacht tacking through, say, 75° it means absolutely nothing unless the conditions in which the observations were made are objectively and accurately described. What can be achieved in moderate conditions in smooth water cannot be compared with a rough water situation and strong winds. As we have already seen the generation of a sail's power from depth of camber and the maintenance of a narrow entry angle are two fundamentally opposed requirements. So it has to be appreciated that as the drag losses increase from wave motion in a head sea, so the ability to point is destroyed by the need to maintain a higher power output from the sails. To this end the top flight racing yachts will tend to carry two No. 3 genoas. One will be a high aspect ratio, non overlapping sail designed to be sheeted to a very narrow angle, perhaps only 8°, and to present a very flat entry. In smooth water this sail develops sufficient power and enables the yacht to point exceptionally high and tack through a very small angle. Offshore, however, with a short steep sea this same sail does not respond to the easing of the sheet to generate more power. For these conditions a lower aspect ratio sail with a larger chord is designed to give greater power without the option of pointing as high.

Having analysed all these factors that contribute to, or detract from, a yacht's ability to maintain speed at a high pointing angle this chapter will be of more value if we look at some authoritative figures on windward performance.

The curve of Vmg against true wind speed (below) has been supplied by Rex Turner (Managing Director of Brookes & Gatehouse). It was prepared from a mass of data accumulated from performance figures from a number of yachts of proven high performance. It is this curve that was used for the percentage performance indication of the Hercules System 190 Computer. The instrument compares the Vmg achieved with a scaled equivalent from the graph and expresses it as a percentage above or below 100% depending on the performance of the yacht relative to the predictions. The interesting fact is that the scale employed is based directly on the square root of the rating. This graph is that of a One Tonner rating 27.5ft. To convert to, say, a Half Tonner rating 22.0ft read the Vmg from the graph relative to the wind speed, divide by $\sqrt{27.5}$ multiply by $\sqrt{22.0}$. This curve suggests that the One Tonner reaches a peak Vmg of 4.75 in 15 knots of true wind speed. Equivalent speeds for

The continuous curve is the optimum Vmg for a given windspeed used as a base for the Brookes & Gatehouse Hercules Computer. The scale of the graph is drawn for a 27.5 ft rating yacht (a One tonner when Hercules was introduced). To interpolate for lower ratings, transfer the vertical scale to the appropriate column. The dotted curve is for a typical Twelve metre at the same scale.

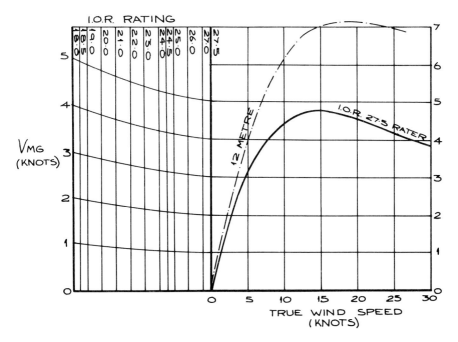

smaller boats would be Three-Quarter Ton 4.48, Half Ton 4.25 and Quarter Ton 3.90 knots. These figures have been obtained in ideal, almost smooth water conditions, and so represent the best that can be expected. One should not expect a reading of 100% when slogging to windward in a short steep sea. Equally the calculations for Vmg do not take account of leeway, they are a direct conversion of boat speed and true wind angle.

A conversation with John Oakeley brought some very interesting figures and comments to light. Sailing the Twelve Metre 'Lionheart' in absolutely ideal conditions it was possible to tack through as little as 56°. Normal conditions such as the racing in Long Island Sound would involve angles of 64° to 65°, whereas sailing in very light and sloppy conditions could mean an angle as high as 100°. In *'Kriter Lady'*, the three-masted *Freedom 65* that John sailed in the trans-Atlantic race, the best angle was 85°

The IOR fleet hardly ever reaches the tacking angles achieved by the Twelves. 65° between tacks would be exceptional. 70° to 75° is probably fairly average for top class boats in smooth water. Brookes & Gatehouse figures for optimum Vmg curves not infrequently corresponded with an angle close to 80°.

The table below can be used as a ready reckoner to relate Vmg, boat speed and tacking angle. Reading from left to right it will be seen, for instance, that a Vmg of 4.0 knots can be achieved by sailing at 4.62 knots at the unlikely angle to the wind of 30° or 6.22 knots at 50°. So, the next time you hear a member in the bar claiming that his Half Tonner will do 6¼ knots while tacking through 75°, a Vmg of 5 knots, you will know that he has either won all the club trophies – or he is more likely talking through his hat.

| | | \multicolumn{9}{c}{Angle between tacks} |
		60°	65°	70°	75°	80°	85°	90°	95°	100°
	5.0	5.77	5.93	6.10	6.30	6.53	6.78	7.07	7.40	7.78
	4.5	5.20	5.34	5.49	5.67	5.87	6.10	6.36	6.66	7.00
	4.0	4.62	4.74	4.88	5.04	5.22	5.43	5.66	5.92	6.22
	3.5	4.04	4.15	4.27	4.41	4.57	4.75	4.95	5.18	5.45
Vmg	3.0	3.46	3.56	3.66	3.78	3.92	4.07	4.24	4.44	4.67
knots	2.5	2.89	2.96	3.05	3.15	3.26	3.39	3.54	3.70	3.89
	2.0	2.31	2.37	2.44	2.52	2.61	2.71	2.83	2.96	3.11
	1.5	1.73	1.78	1.83	1.89	1.96	2.03	2.12	2.22	2.33
	1.0	1.16	1.19	1.22	1.26	1.31	1.36	1.41	1.48	1.56
	0.5	0.58	0.60	0.61	0.63	0.65	0.68	0.71	0.74	0.78
		30°	32.5°	35°	37.5°	40°	42.5°	45°	47.5°	50°

True wind angle
Boat speed for Vmg against tacking or true wind angle

15

The lee bow tide myth

In the original draft of the previous chapter I mentioned that some benefit was to be gained by pointing high in a tideway and gaining from the 'lee bow tide effect'.

This did not pass unnoticed by the editor of *Yachts and Yachting*, Peter Cook, and he and I entered into an entertaining discussion on whether or not the lee bow tide was a magic formula or not. Peter said it was a myth and I felt sure that it could be scientifically proven that it was a very real phenomenon. The article was heavily edited, the editor holding all the cards in such a situation.

I wrote all sorts of programmes for my Hewlett Packard and churned out volumes of figures and, in the end, I was reluctantly obliged to agree with Peter. Mind you, there are still times, when I feel that 'eating up to weather' sensation when we get the bow above the tide, that prompts me to wonder? Peter wrote:

'With the national coaches of Britain, France and Germany, as well as countless experts in Europe and in America, propounding the theory it is hardly surprising that "every competent racing man knows" of the benefits of lee-bowing the tidal stream. Sail on The Solent or at Burnham, or indeed anywhere which offers confined waters and strong streams, and barely a weekend will pass without someone doing well by being able to lee-bow when others cannot, he being swept bodily to windward while his less fortunate rivals flounder and wallow with the stream on the weather bow, only to be swept down tide to leeward and oblivion. Next weekend, the lesson is well remembered and, as we round the leeward mark and the great debate about which tack to take begins, someone on board is sure to point out that starboard (or port, as the case may be) will be better. It is the lee-bow tack. Thus are myths born, believed and reinforced'.

All the best myths have an element of truth, and so it is with the Great Lee-bow Tide Myth. There are indeed times when it pays to put the stream under the lee-bow, and the classic passage upwind from Cherbourg to the Needles, with its inevitable about-faces of tidal stream directly across the desired tack is the most oft-quoted example. There are, too, times when it pays to pinch up a bit when sailing into the tidal stream: sneaking along the wall at Burnham or the Green at Cowes; almost fetching the elusive, uptide, upwind mark, whose own roaring wake and bow-wave in the sluicing stream offer dramatic testimony to the forces waiting to sweep us off downwind should our concentration flag. Every time a helmsman exploits such a technique and gains a place or two there will be someone – sometimes himself – to remark how the stream carried him to windward. And since successful helmsmen are usually best at most things, including tactical pinching, more often than not the helmsman who lee-bows to the best effect is the one who wins most often.

Thus, the facile and attractive myth of a mysterious tidal god lifting the closewinded to weather and pushing the sagging and the careless away to leeward finds ready acceptance. Some heretics, however, do not accept the myth of the lee-bow tide. They argue that boats that will point higher for no speed loss go to windward better than boats which do not, and that the same holds true for helmsmen. They argue that squeezing up to slip round a mark instead of throwing good ground away by having to tack twice is a useful ploy irrespective of tidal stream. Stuart Walker, American Olympic sailor and the first American to win the Prince of Wales Cup for International Fourteens, writing in Advance Racing Tactics, put it thus:

'In its effect, uniform current may be likened to the movement of a rug on which a fleet of toy boats has been placed. When the rug is moved, all the boats move together regardless of the size or shape of their keels, regardless of the direction in which they are headed, regardless of whether they are lee-bowing or windward bowing the direction of movement of the rug. Although their apparent winds are affected differently, there are no attitudes to the movement of the rug that will result in dramatic differences in performance. There is nothing magical about the lee-bow effect.'

Bob Bavier, the great American keelboat sailor, is more cautious. In *Sailing To Win* he explains how he used to believe in the great lee-bow tide myths, and even expounded it in the early editions of his book. Gradually, however, careful analysis caused him to qualify his view until he says 'it pays to sail your boat just as you would if no current existed. The effect of lee-bowing the tide at the cost of pinching . . . . . . will not offset the loss in speed caused by pinching'.

Fact or fiction

The first aspect of practical application of a lee-bow advantage is a familiar one for cross-channel sailors. Let us start in Cherbourg with the wind from the north, which is within 10° of the course for the

Needles. If we assume that our yacht makes good a course at 45° to the true wind, we have the choice of sailing 315° on starboard tack or 045° on port. For the purpose of this analysis we will simplify the tidal stream to the point where it flows west for six hours and east for six hours at an average of 2 knots.

As we clear the breakwater we have to decide which tack to take. We will agree that the forecast has said that it will continue to blow from the north for the forseeable future. Neither tack will be very encouraging. Starboard will take us to Lyme Bay, port will take us to Brighton. The tidal stream has another three hours to run towards the west – which way is the least evil?

Let us suppose we have two yachts A and B. A believes in the benefits of lee-bowing, B does not. A sets off on port tack with the west-going stream; under the lee bow and in three hours time he tacks onto starboard to get the east-going stream under his lee bow once again. B, in the interests of proving that he is right, does the opposite. He goes off towards the north-west for three hours and then tacks back again towards the north-east.

Assuming there is no difference in performance and each yacht is doing 4 knots through the water, where will they be in relation to each other after six hours?

A will have sailed 045° for 12 miles and 315° for 12 miles and been set by the stream 6 miles to the west and 6 miles to the east which, mathematically, means that he should be 16.97 miles due north from the starting point. B has sailed 12 miles on 315° and 12 miles on 045° and has also been set 6 miles in each direction so he is also in theory 16.97 miles due north of Cherbourg, grinning from ear to ear, and saying, 'I told you it would make no difference'.

Yet plenty of cruising and offshore racing readers will know that, time and again, there is a difference – why does the theory not prove it?

If A and B were motor boats then it would have been possible for them to zig zag at 45° to the rhumb line at equal speeds and cross each other's path after six hours. But we are discussing sailing boats, tacking to windward: motorboats do not normally zig zag all over the Channel.

Remember that an earlier paragraph began, 'Assuming there is no difference in performance'. This supposed that there was no difference in potential performance on the basis that we were comparing like with like. Shall we say two sister yachts with equal ability in each crew. We also assumed that both boats would be equally capable of pointing at 45° to the true wind, regardless of the tidal stream. This was the fallacy in the argument.

The wind was due north to the man standing on Cherbourg breakwater, we will say blowing at 12 knots. If A and B had stopped their boats in the water to measure the wind direction, with the stream going west at two knots, the effective wind would not have been the same as the true wind. From the vector diagram below it will be seen that 2 knots airspeed due to tidal drift to the west combined with 12 knots true wind from the north gives a combined vector of 12.17 knots on a bearing of 350.5°

Our original assumption was that A and B would sail at 45° to the true wind. This was wrong. They will sail at 45° to the effective wind related to the surface of the water they are drifting on. With the stream going west they are effectively sailing with a wind from 350.5° and when the tide turns east the wind will effectively alter to 009.5°.

Let us now re-plot the tracks of A and B (bottom). Remember that the stream was flowing west as they left, so with an effective wind of 350.5°,

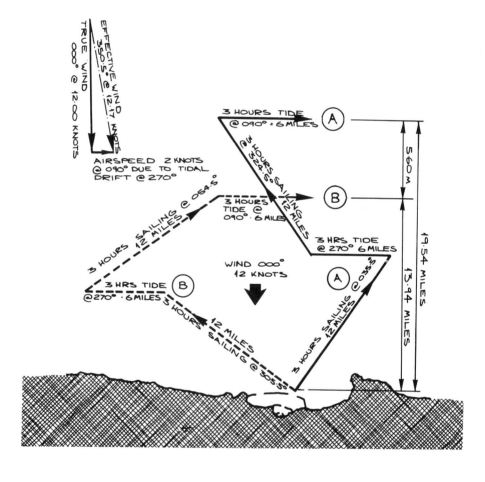

The vector diagram at top left demonstrates how the tidal stream effects the true wind and shows the effective wind felt by a free floating vessel. The track chart demonstrates how the yacht with the tide always under the lee bow gains by virtue of the improved effective wind.

A will make good a course of 035.5°. When he tacks onto starboard the stream has changed, the effective wind is now 009.5°, and A will now make good 324.5°. After six hours the drift on the tidal stream will have cancelled out, as before, but the DR position for A will be 19.54 miles due north of Cherbourg. B, on the other hand, will have made good only 305.5° and 054.5° on each tack and will have a DR position only 13.94 miles north or 5.6 miles behind A on the way to the Needles. Lee-bowing the tidal stream does, indeed, give an advantage in these circumstances.

The fundamental at issue is that there is an effective wind shift at each change of tidal stream and in a cross tide situation, such as our example above, the shift is working in favour of the boat that keeps the stream under the lee bow as frequently as possible. In our example two boats which were assumed to tack through 90° in still water were effectively tacking through 71° and 109° depending on whether they were lee-bowing or not.

There are many variations on the combination of true wind and tidal drift that will produce an effective wind that is more or less at variance with the true wind. Because, in our example, we assumed a tidal rate that was fairly high in relation to the wind speed the effect was quite dramatic. It follows that only half-a-knot of stream in a 40-knot gale is going to make little or no difference, whereas $2\frac{1}{2}$ knots of stream in a gentle 5 knot air would be so influential that the effective wind shift would be 53°.

When we consider combinations of wind and stream that are not at 90° to each other then the effective wind speed will continue to vary and the change in direction will grow less. When the tide is flowing in the same axis as the apparent wind, either directly against or directly with, then direction is unchanged and effective wind speed will vary by twice the maximum speed of the tidal stream.

Let us digress from theory to seat-of-the-pants feel. Why does the lee-bow tack feel so much better than the other? When the stream is under the lee bow we think we can feel the boat pointing up and eating her way to windward. When the stream is on the weather bow the helm feels soggy and the skipper gets irritable and all is moaning and groaning. Is this all imagination or is it something happening that is actually giving the boat a better performance in one condition and not the other?

When afloat and sailing the writer is as susceptible as any other to the belief that there is a dramatic change between a lee-bow condition and its opposite, yet however hard one tries to prove this feeling to be scientifically justified, the theories all seem to debunk the idea altogether.

The first analysis to understand is to divide the possible situations into two categories.

Category 1 is a situation where the wind and tidal stream are constant in relation to each other and the course of the yacht is varying in relation to the stream. For example, a helmsman, sailing directly into the stream, can luff up closer to the wind and bring the stream under the lee bow or bear away and create the opposite effect.

Category 2 is a situation where the wind and the course are constant in relation to each other but the course is varying in relation to the direction of the tidal stream. For example, a helmsman, sailing at a constant angle to the wind that has an oscillating shift characteristic, may find that he is forced to sail alternately with a lee-bow or weather-bow tide.

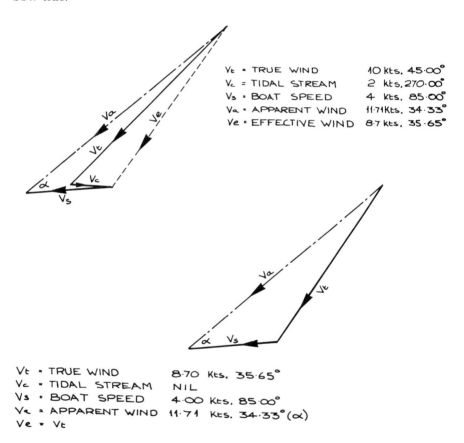

V_t • TRUE WIND	10 kts.	45·00°
V_c = TIDAL STREAM	2 kts.	270·00°
V_s • BOAT SPEED	4 kts.	85·00°
V_a • APPARENT WIND	11·71 kts.	34·33°
V_e • EFFECTIVE WIND	8·7 kts.	35·65°

V_t • TRUE WIND	8·70 Kts.	35·65°
V_c • TIDAL STREAM	NIL	
V_s • BOAT SPEED	4·00 Kts.	85·00°
V_a • APPARENT WIND	11·71 Kts.	34·33° (α)
V_e • V_t		

The upper diagram shows the combined effects of a true wind of 10 knots at 045°, boat speed of 4 knots at 085° and tidal stream of 2 knots at 270°. Apparent wind is 11.71 knots, 34.33° off the bow.

The lower diagram shows the same yacht sailing at 4 knots at 085°, in a true wind 8.7 knots at 035.65°, the apparent wind is 11.71 knots, 34.33° off the bow. Note that the arrows on each vector represent the direction of the airspeed due to each element. It must be appreciated that for the boat V_s and the tidal stream V_c this will be the reciprocal of the course and tidal direction.

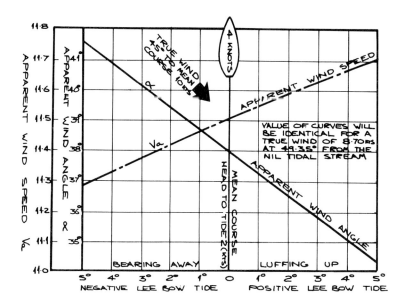

Variation in wind speed and direction for 10° of course direction — true, for a yacht sailing 5° above or 5° below the line of a stream of 2 knots directly against the mean course of the yacht. The true wind is at 45° to the stream. This diagram is equally true for a yacht sailing in nil stream and a true wind of 8.848 knots at 49.35° to the mean course.

Category 1 can be dismissed as providing wind conditions and therefore one supposes performance reaction entirely consistent with an adjusted wind and still water. This is demonstrated by Figures (a) and (b) (opposite), where (a) is a vector diagram for the combined effects of a true wind of 10 knots at 045°, boat speed of 4 knots at 085° and a tidal stream of 2 knots at 270°. The sum of the vectors gives an apparent wind, across the deck of 11.71 knots at 34.33° from the bow. Figure (b) is a vector diagram for the same yacht sailing at 4 knots on 085° with a true wind of 8.70 knots at 035.65°, which results in an apparent wind across the deck of exactly 11.71 knots at 34.33° from the bow. The simple solution to the situation is that if you look again at Figure (a) the dotted line marked Ve is what we have chosen to call the effective wind and its value is the 8.70 knots at 035.65°. This, one feels, proves conclusively that for any fixed combination of wind and tidal stream there is an equivalent still water situation. Apparent wind speed and direction will vary with similar characteristics in each case. There is therefore no justification in the belief that there is an abrupt change in condition because the lee-bow angle changes from positive to negative as the boat luffs. As an illustration the variation in apparent wind speed and direction for 10° of course alteration shown on page 173 is true for a yacht sailing 5° above to 5° below the line of a stream in ten knots of true wind at 45° to the stream running at 2 knots against the yacht. It is also

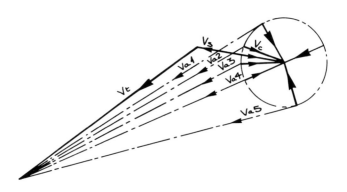

The tidal stream V_c, rotating in relation to a constant course V_s and the wind V_t. V_a1 and V_a1 and V_a5 are the greatest variations in apparent wind angle from V_a4 which is the apparent wind angle for nil tidal stream and for maximum and minimum apparent wind speed, when the stream angle corresponds to the apparent wind angle or its reciprocal. V_a2 and V_a3 represent the apparent wind for $10°$ of leebow stream or $10°$ of negative lee bow respectively.

true for a yacht sailing in still water in a true wind of 8.848 knots at 49.35° to the mean course.

Our Category 2 is much more interesting. In order to draw convenient vector diagrams it is necessary to show the true wind and the boat's course as constant and rotate the tidal stream around the yacht. The Figure above illustrates the whole range of vectors for the 360° that the tidal stream direction can vary in relation to the course.

Graphically it will be seen that the greatest apparent wind speed is when the tidal stream angle is directly opposite to the apparent wind angle and least when its angle corresponds to that same apparent wind angle. This angle is incidentally exactly the same as the apparent wind angle with zero tide. The range of apparent wind angles is that between the two vectors that are tangents to the circle with the tidal vector as radius.

The mathematics professors amongst the readers will know immediately that if, as in the Figure opposite, we plot the variations in apparent wind speed and angle against the full 360° rotation of the tidal stream direction we get two delightful sine curves. At 28.9°, the apparent wind angle is equal to the negative lee bow angle and the apparent wind speed is at its minimum. It should also be noted that this is also the point of maximum gradient on the apparent wind angle curve. At the reciprocal of 151.1° positive lee bow angle the reverse situation exists with the apparent wind speed at its zenith. The speed of the yacht has been assumed constant throughout.

For the purposes of this argument we are particularly interested in a narrow band close either side of the zero tidal angle. It is at least significant that the rate of change of both apparent wind speed and angle are both relatively high. As one would expect they are increasing as they cross from negative to positive lee-bow angle.

Before drawing any conclusions let us look at one more diagram, page 176. This is a magnification of the first ten degrees of positive and negative lee bow condition. This time a variation in boat speed has been included in anticipation of the changing conditions. The apparent wind speed has only a very slight curve but a range of $1\frac{1}{4}$ knots over the ten degrees. The apparent wind angle is varying over only $\frac{1}{8}°$. The nature of the curve has been so affected by the changing boat speed to appear unrelated to the original sine curve with a plateau at about 4° of lee-bow and a descent of increasing gradient as it passes through the zero tide angle towards a negative lee bow condition. We should not read too much into this feature as the variation of angle is exaggerated by the choice of scale. It must also be remembered that the speed increase would not be maintained at greater angles.

The only conclusions that the writer feels prepared to draw are these. First, there is no abrupt change in conditions as the tide angle passes from one bow to the other, however much it may feel that way. Second, depending on the strength of the tidal stream in relation to the wind any change in their relative angles can be responsible for very pronounced effects on the apparent wind felt on board. These effects are, however, progressive over a range of angles and not particularly related to the change from one bow to the other.

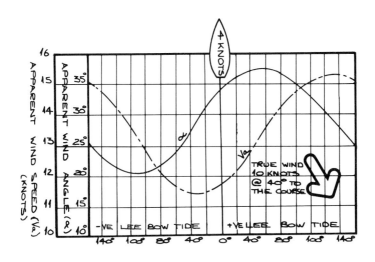

Values of apparent wind speed V_a and angle α for 360° rotation of the tidal vector in relation to a yacht sailing close hauled at a constant angle to the true wind.

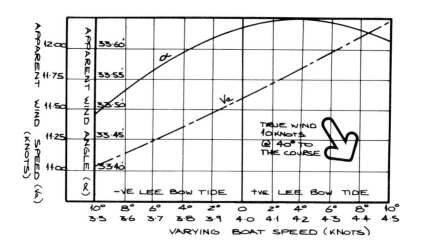

A magnification of the tidal stream angles either side of dead ahead. A realistic variation in boatspeed has been included in the computation of V_a and α.

16

In trim

I have always been intrigued by that wizard of seamanship, Captain Horatio Hornblower, who, on taking over a new command, had the sternchaser re-sited, or the roundshot re-stowed, thus improving the trim of the ship. In his case the results were invariably dramatic improvements in speed or manoeuvrability and his ship would, at a stroke, become the star of the squadron. I wonder how he would have fared in Class 1 nowadays?

Correct trim is a subject close to a designer's heart.

On The Level

The yacht whose performance first prompted these thoughts on trim was some way behind others of similar rating and from across the water it was easy to see what was obviously less easily felt by those on board. The wheel was placed right aft and behind it stood the more than ample figure of the owner. He was obviously a popular owner, perhaps with a fund of good stories, and the crew were all gathered around the cockpit, the more to enjoy the social banter in the sunshine. The stripes along the waterline told the rest of the story. Well clear of the water forward, they were firmly immersed aft, not a good recipe for boatspeed in light weather.

Designers draw their boats to go fastest when the waterline is horizontal, and a racing crew ought to try to maintain that condition as often as possible. There is, of course, an exception to this rule of which more later.

The crew weight aboard the average contemporary IOR racing yacht is an appreciable percentage of the whole, in extreme cases as much as 20% but more often around 12½%. It is, therefore, vitally important to distribute the crew sensibly fore-and-aft. Some skipper have an intuitive feel for trim and will shunt chaps to and fro continuously.

Others need to make a conscious effort to consider the problem and experiment to find the right arrangement.

Not everyone appreciates why in different conditions it is right to move forward or aft and a few words of explanation might help. In the first place there is, as mentioned before, the one exception to the rule about keeping the waterline horizontal fore and aft. In the lightest ghosting air, when there is not even a chuckle under the bow, it often pays to put weight well forward in order to raise the stern. Combined with weight to leeward to induce a few degrees of heel, this reduces the wetted surface and the energy required to gain at least some boatspeed. The mistake that is so often made is that as soon as a possible improvement has been made the weight forward should be gently, very gently, eased aft. A good rule would be to say that as soon as the bow wave is audible one should start to bring the trim back towards the flat and level.

As soon as the wind picks up and the boatspeed with it, so the need arises to pull weight towards the stern. This is not in order to lift the bows like a speed boat, it is in order to prevent the bows dropping as is most likely to happen if some preventive measures are not taken in good time.

The contemporary IOR yacht is very fine forward and relatively full aft. As speed increases towards maximum hull speed, a trough appears between the bow wave and the stern wave, taking away support in the middle of the boat. This, in turn, places more dependence on the bow and stern sections to provide reserve buoyancy. The stern, with its fuller sections, has a greater reserve than the finer sections of the bow and so, all other things being equal, the bow will drop. It is up to the crew on deck to ensure that all other things are not equal by crowding aft to restore a horizontal trim. In more technical language, as speed increases the centre of buoyancy moves aft so in order to maintain a level trim the centre of gravity must be moved aft an equal amount. As the crew are the only ballast that can be legally shifted while racing, moving them aft is the only way of adjusting the centre of gravity.

The majority of recent designs have a tendency to go bows down as they heel. Each yacht has its own tolerance to heel angle. It is those whose trim alters most radically that have the least tolerance and must at all costs be kept upright. There are however many occasions when one must reluctantly accept more heel angle than is really desirable and this is when the crew along the rails should shunt down towards the stern to counter the dropping bow, in the same way as at high speed in a more upright condition.

It should be remembered that weight distribution has a significant effect on pitching motion in a seaway. It is no use the designer and builder going to a lot of trouble to keep weight concentrated centrally in the boat if the weight of the crew is not going to be equally concentrated. Just as in dinghies, the crew on the rail should in most

Itzanother Purla, *well trimmed, going to windward in a full sail breeze. The stern wave is leaving the yacht without immersing the transom.*

circumstances sit tight together so as to make the pitching action easy and less energy absorbing. By all means call one man aft to compensate for the foredeck man when hooking up the spinnaker but, except in flat water, do not make a practice of spreading weight out unnecessarily.

Having said all that one must end with a plea for moderation. By all means throw everyone out of the cockpit in light airs, but make sure they don't all take to the foredeck. A word at the same time, to the chaps who do go right forward; for goodness sake lie down if you are trying to go windward. Windage and turbulence along the foot of the genoa are distinctly non-productive. Equally you must be sure that the conditions and the speed really do warrant the rush to the transom that some crews are apt to make at the least hint of a high speed run. If the stern wave is halfway up the transom then the damage may well be as bad as an over-immersed bow.

If in doubt fit some form of fore-and-aft level gauge and trim the boat at rest so that you can mark the point at which the waterline is parallel with the surface.

17

Spinnaker broaching

I can remember comparing notes with another skipper after the 1967 Fastnet and finding that on the other yacht they had eventually given up spinnakering because they were broaching at fifteen-minute intervals. They believed, probably quite rightly, that they were losing more than they were gaining during their brief periods of control. I had been sailing a Giles designed yacht of impeccable manners, if rather less than top class potential, and these descriptions rather horrified me.

Since those days the racing scene has advanced through a period of fast but highly unmanageable designs to even faster boats which are now showing signs of improved controllability.

Maintaining Control

When a yacht is moving through the water, in an upright condition, making no leeway and travelling at modest speed, the water flow around the hull is splendidly symmetrical. Steering and control are no problem whatever. Yet as soon as she begins to develop real power from her rig three things are likely to be happening that will afftect that water flow.

First, she will heel (except on a dead run) so that there is no longer a symmetrical shape for the water to negotiate. Second, as speed increases a surface wave pattern will be generated which takes water, and therefore support, away in the troughs and replaces it by crests at the bow and stern. Third (again, except on a dead run) the force of the rig will generate leeway, and the water flow will meet the hull at an angle of incidence. This angle will depend on the efficiency of the keel and its ability to generate a sideforce. Each of these three effects create complicated reactions on the hull which do nothing to ease the problems of control.

In order to be absolutely correct it has been necessary to qualify the first and third items by the expression 'except on a dead run'. From the point of view of the practical application of this subject to the yachtsman at sea, it is important to realise that it would be foolish to believe that this in any way means that dead running is easy.

The sector in which a running yacht is unaffected by heel or leeway is very small, and inevitably, in a seaway the yacht is bound to yaw beyond these limits – and this is where control problems are most acute. As heel and leeway are freshly generated, the responses needed at the helm are changed quite rapidly, and this is where control is only maintained by intelligent anticipation.

It is because the effect of yaw produces quite varied, and often opposite, reactions on the helm that a course 15° or more from the dead run is altogether easier to manage

The designer's problems in creating a hull shape which is capable of maintaining a constant helm reaction throughout the build up of speed and heel angle are based largely on attitude – by which we mean the attitude of the yacht, not the personality of the designer. In simple terms, if the effects of heeling or wave action result in a notable re-positioning of the centre of buoyancy (due to the re-distribution of the water around the hull) then the yacht will no longer trim parallel with the designed waterline. In the majority of cases the centre of buoyancy moves aft and, assuming that the centre of gravity cannot be moved accordingly, then the bows will drop.

Let us consider first the effect of heeling. When the designer is analysing his work, his calculations will tell him where the centre of buoyancy lies in the fore-and-aft dimension. By judicious, juggling of the weights within the yacht, particularly the ballast, he creates a situation where the centre of gravity of the whole yacht coincides with the centre of buoyancy. If this is satisfactorily achieved then equilibrium is obtain and the yacht floats on a level waterline. There are smiles all round and the designer gets a vote of thanks.

Once fixed, that centre of gravity can only be adjusted by marching an army of crew members to and fro along the deck. The centre of buoyancy, on the other hand, will move immediately the yacht heels. Unless the designer has repeated his buoyancy calculations for, say, 20° of heel, he may be in for a nasty shock. The writer has always rejected any design in which the centre of buoyancy at 20° heel moves more than 2% of the waterline length, generally arriving at a figure closer to 1.5%. The tendency is always for the centre to move aft and if it is not controlled the bow will drop as the yacht heels with a consequent upset in water flow around the hull.

The centre of buoyancy also moves sideways when a yacht heels, and this is the whole essence of stability. The very fact that the centre of gravity and the centre of buoyancy move apart laterally creates a lever arm and a righting moment is generated.

From the designer's point of view the problem here is to make the centre of buoyancy move to leeward evenly over the length of the yacht.

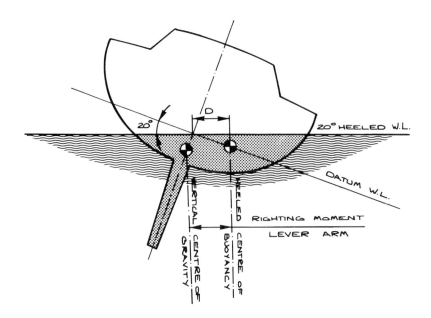

The midships section has been drawn intersecting the Datum Water line on the centre line. Calculations for most yachts will show that the immersed volume below such a waterline will be 115% to 120% of the volume below the Datum water line when upright. Provided these figures are not exceeded the extra buoyancy is acceptable.

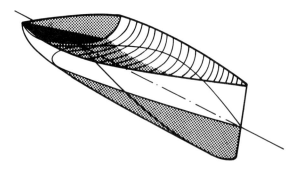

A stylised drawing of a racing dinghy illustrates the double wedge shape – broad and shallow aft and deep and narrow forward. This shape is fine when upright but is severely unbalanced when heeled.

If we measure the moments of the centre of buoyancy on each station (D opposite above) and plot them as a curve relative to the centre line, we are in effect carrying out a metacentric analysis. Clearly if the curve that is plotted has more than a certain degree of asymmetry then the effect of heeling is going to create a pronounced tendency to yaw. An underwater body that is in effect wedge shaped in both the horizontal and vertical planes will perform successfully as a racing dinghy (opposite below) which is always sailed upright.

Directly heel occurs, however, the broad flat sections at the stern produce a massive sideways movement of their centres of buoyancy, while the sharp narrow sections forward have little or none. The result is that the stern yaws out to leeward and a massive amount of weather helm is required to bring the main axis back into the required direction.

The second effect which we have identified is the effect of wave action on the hull. For these purposes it is sensible to consider the yacht sailing at or near to her theoretical maximum. Let us remember for a moment why such a maximum exists. A wave moves across the surface of the sea at a fixed speed related to its wavelength, the larger the wavelength the faster the speed. When a yacht is moving fast it is creating two waves, a bow wave and a stern wave, and these remain, so to speak, constantly attached to the yacht

It follows, therefore, that the wavelength of those waves is related to the length of the yacht. At the same time the yacht's speed is limited by the speed of those waves because, unless she planes, she cannot become detached from them. The mathematics of the situation state that this wave condition is achieved when the speed of the yacht in knots has reached 1.4 times the square root of the waterline in feet. Taking a 25ft lwl yacht, the square root is 5, multiply by 1.4 and the speed is 7 knots. The steepness of these waves is very simply expressed as being related to the disturbance caused by the parting of the water at the bow, and by the abruptness with which the stern is terminated – allowing the sea to rush back in and fill the hole created by the passage of the yacht.

This wave effect is much more pronounced on some hulls than others, and the simplified explanation in the last paragraph only touches on what is a very complex problem. From the designer's point of view, if he can draw a yacht that slips through the water with the least amount of disturbance he will have achieved his goal in two respects. First, the wavemaking drag will be low, so the yacht will sail fast easily. Second, by keeping the waves as slight as possible he will reduce the amount by which they can affect the control of the yacht.

When a yacht is described as 'ploughing along' she is obviously a fairly heavy displacement type with substantial waves leading off from the bow and stern. Between the high wave crests will be a deep trough. Viewed from alongside a yacht with a steep wave formation will expose a large area of antifouling amidships, and at the bow and stern the waterline will be well buried (page 184). Consider the implications of

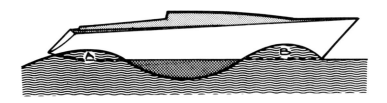

The buoyancy gained by immersing areas A and B must equal the losses where the underwater body is exposed – as indicated by the shaded area. If, because the bow sections are less flared than the stern, B provides less buoyancy than A, then the bow will drop. In this instance the Datum Water line will not remain horizontal unless the centre of gravity is moved aft to compensate.

this for a moment. For part of the underwater body to be exposed it must mean that in that area the hull is not enjoying the amount of support from the water that it would in a static condition. This is compensated by the build up of the wavecrests against the topsides of the bow and stern creating fresh buoyancy.

Now, if we have a yacht that is very fat in the middle and fine at the ends, the result is going to be that the fresh buoyancy at the bow and stern created by the waves is not going to replace the losses on the midship section caused by the trough. However, equilibrium must be achieved so the yacht will sink lower into the water until losses have been made up. Sinking lower into the water only serves to increase the resistance of the bow and the turbulence at the stern, and so the waves become steeper and the trough grows deeper, and the situation gets even worse. If, on the other hand, the hull has a more evenly distributed buoyancy, with relatively full ends, and not such a concentration amidships, then the situation is much easier. The reserve buoyancy in the ends is able to take care of the losses amidships. The yacht does not sink appreciably and the waves do not build up to the same degree.

In designers' parlance we have highlighted the problem of the prismatic coefficient. That is the means whereby we measure the relative distribution of the volume of the underwater shape. If one takes the area of the largest section and multiplies it by the length of the waterline, then the resulting volume would only be correct if the section is constant from bow to stern. Except in the case of a floating shoebox, the volume is always less than the amount by a factor which we call the prismatic coefficient. The shoe box would have a prismatic coefficient of 1.0, but the average yacht is closer to 0.56 or so.

To make the designer's life a good deal harder, it is a fact that a yacht with a high prismatic, that is with relatively full ends, may be a good performer at high hull speeds, but below maximum speed resistance is less for those with finer ends and, therefore, a lower prismatic. This is only half the problem, for with yachts of average proportions it is difficult to push volume into the ends while at the same time preserving a fine entry and slack run.

From the point of view of control the most important aspect of a yacht moving at or near her maximum speed is that the reserve buoyancy at the bow is nearly always less than it is at the stern. If the bow and stern waves build up evenly then those extra reserves of buoyancy in the stern take more than their fair share of the displacement and the stern rises as the bow drops. This is why pictures of racing yachts running hard so often show the crew concentrated as close to the transom as possible. If the bow drops the bow wave is increasing its resistance and this gives the yacht a wicked tendency to try and sail round the bow – as would any object with all its resistance at the forward end.

The third factor which we listed at the beginning was the effect of the leeway created by the sideways component of the rig and the sideforce generated by the keel to resist it. If we ignore dead running then there is no such thing as zero leeway. Nor, for that matter, is there any keel so efficient that it positively forces the yacht to windward. For the keel to generate lift or sideforce there has to be an angle of incidence between the centreline and the water, however small. The efficiency of the keel, and we should also remember the rudder, is measured as a lift/drag ratio. That is how much sideforce is created for a given amount of drag.

The question in the background is of course – how much leeway do we need to eliminate? As the yacht becomes more efficient, so it is necessary to design a keel that will generate lift at a very small angle of incidence without at the same time increasing the drag.

To concentrate more on the question of control, it is very important to consider the part that the rudder plays in the generation of sideforce during straight-line sailing. The arguments for or against a long keel with an attached rudder will probably never go away. From the point of view of a sideforce generator, when the rudder is attached to the keel its value is like that of a trim tab. It creates an asymmetrical section, by virtue of its position as a trailing edge flap. This is particularly beneficial at low boat speeds.

Those who believe in the long keel configuration quite rightly focus their attention on the fact that a yacht will turn much more sharply round a short fin than a long one. This is borne out by the almost impossible task of trying to steer a fin keel boat that has lost its rudder blade altogether. Assuming, on the other hand, that no such disaster has occurred the yacht with the rudder right aft has two advantages. For a given amount of wetted surface the distribution of the lateral area is over a greater length and, therefore, so long as the rudder is not free-swinging should have good resistance to turning. Secondly when the rudder is required to turn the yacht off course, or return it to the course following a yaw, it is at its most efficient because of its longer lever arm from the centre of rotation.

This leads to the idea that directional stability is not primarily a question of the length of the keel. It is much more a question of spreading lateral area over as great a length as possible. This can be achieved by a modest keel, coupled with plenty of area in the skeg and its root, more effectively than by putting all the area into one long appendage. Remember that the more directionally stable the designer makes the yacht, the more is asked of the rudder when it is necessary to alter direction. In a modern world of crowded harbours and marina berthing there seems the strongest case for having the rudder close to the end of the water-line where its power, when needed, will be greatest.

Having looked at these various factors, this article can only be constructive if we consider for a moment what options the designer has open to him, if directional stability and steady tracking are fundamental requirements, as they undoubtedly should be in any cruising yacht.

The answer to many of the factors considered would, one might suppose, lie in designing a yacht that was as symmetrical as possible in the fore-and-aft sense. O'Brien Kennedy's delightful little canoe sterned Slipway 5 tonners went a long way toward that ideal. However experience has shown that in plan form, the ideal shape for the waterplane, fine forward and full aft, is the exact opposite to those waterlines that are more deeply immersed; these ending in keel sections that are blunt forward and fine aft. If an easy transition from one shape to the other is to be achieved then symmetry is not so obviously to be displayed as on a yacht like the Slipway 5 tonner. Cunningly handled however, it is possible to maintain symmetrical diagonals despite the changing shape of the waterlines and sections and this may indeed be more significant, particularly in a heeled condition. The ease with which the diagonals can be controlled depends to a great extent on the beam to length ratio. It is far easier on a narrow boat than a broad one.

The advent and influence of the IOR has led to a state of mind where one has been inclined to look at the bows and sterns and mid-sections independently, rather like items in a catalogue, as the importance of measurement points has tended to favour certain sections for their rating values. This is never more apparent than in the adoption of flared aft topsides, which are designed to maximise the beam aft measured across the deck. The rating benefits of a large value for this measurement outweigh any disadvantage that may occur from immersing that flare as the yacht heels.

To achieve a hull form that is going to be well mannered at all angles of heel and while sailing fast means that the designer must relate the bow to the stern. This is where strict attention to the behaviour of the diagonals will be rewarded by a harmony that will run throughout the length of the hull. Because diagonals run up into the topsides they inhibit the choice of badly matched bow and stern sections.

Losing Control

The yacht appears to be on her beam ends, the helmsman has the tiller round the back of his neck, the crew have their arms locked round some previously vertical – and now nearly horizontal – deck fitting, the sails are flogging themselves to death and the yacht is probably going nowhere fast. As the rest of the fleet go sailing by, there is often little time to consider how it all happened. However, it is pretty obvous what

The embarrasing result of a leeward, broach and total wipe out. Notice how high the yacht floats at this angle of heel lifting the rudder, prop shaft and the root of the keel clear of the surface. The halyard appears to have been released. This is wise as well because until the yacht comes upright and re-immerses the rudder the helmsman is entirely impotent.

has happened. In some way the helmsman has been unable to resist the yacht's determination to round up. Having succeeded in rounding up she has been flattened by the fact that the sails set are far too big to be carried at the new angle to the wind.

In those leather armchairs in the clubhouse, the older members are nodding their wise old heads and remarking that if the yacht had a decent length of keel the problem would never have occurred. Are they right?

Let us consider for a moment the racing yachts of the previous generation and see how they differed. They did indeed have long keels with the rudder, hung as a flap on the aft end.

There were also a number of other important ways in which they differed, all of which are equally important in their claim to more lady-like behaviour. In the first place, in the good old days they had a safety valve in the form of the rig. Masts and particularly sails were not engineered so scientifically as today and any tendency to drive downwind as we do now would have resulted in gear failure before the yacht broached. Entirely related to this is the fact that present-day crews are so much stronger than their forbears, not physically superior but rather armed with winches and hydraulics which give infinitely greater power to their arms, enabling them to set far larger sails in relation to the wind strength. Last, but by no means least, the greatest difference is in the increase of beam and decrease of displacement.

In the writer's opinion the combination of these last two factors is far more relevant than the area of the keel. In the last chapter we dwelt on the need to maintain a reasonable control over the displacement characteristics as the yacht heels. While this can be fairly easily managed on an IOR yacht at up to 15° or 20° of heel it becomes increasingly difficult as heel angle goes beyond these limits. The influence of the rule has produced yachts with flared midship sections and flared aft sections, and bow sections relatively devoid of flare. As the yacht rolls the flared areas become immersed and the centre of buoyancy moves aft. At the same time the centre of buoyancy is moving away to leeward amidships and aft, out of proportion to the movement of the bows. The resulting tendency to yaw towards the wind is therefore increased.

As soon as the heel angle goes beyond 20° the potential buoyancy of the typical IOR design increases alarmingly. If one calculates the buoyancy of a typical IOR yacht when heeled to 35° one finds that, if measured to the same waterline as in the upright condition, the volume has increased to around 165% of the upright value. Inevitable the yacht must climb out of the water until the situation is corrected (opposite). Taken to extremes the same calculation for 45° of heel produces a figure of 185%. Whereas for a non-IOR, relatively moderate displacement, moderate beam design, the volume even at 45° may well be no more than 130%.

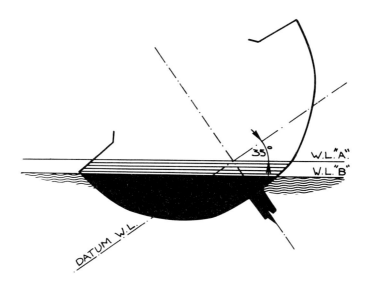

As soon as the heel angle goes beyond 20° the potential buoyancy of the typical IOR design increases alarmingly - at 35° it can have increased to around 165% of the upright value. By the time the heel angle has reached 45° the potential buoyancy may be as high as 185%, compared to, say, 130% for a moderately proportioned non IOR design.

The IOR boat cannot, of course, float to its datum waterline if the immersed volume has increased by these amounts. As she rises out of the water, riding up on her bilge, the control surfaces, that is the keel and the rudder, are no longer sufficiently immersed to maintain an adequate grip on the water. From then on the elements take over and there is little that the helmsman can do until the crew get the wind out of the sails and the yacht comes upright again.

The rudder of a modern racing yacht is a very powerful affair. Designers recognise the value of the blade as a lifting surface when sailing to windward and skippers and designers agree that it is preferable in normal steering to turn a large blade through a small angle rather than a small one through a large angle. The end result is that the helmsman has a great deal of power available to wind on the moment when he senses that the rig is going to take charge. With the best will in the world, however, the intensity of the competition is such that however big the rudder, hard driving is going to result in even the best crews coming unstuck if the conditions are hard enough.

How does it all begin? The trouble inevitably starts in the rig which probably consists of the mainsail and spinnaker. Overpowering of either of these will inevitably create weather helm, and so the means of 'dumping' the load must be examined. As far as the mainsail is concerned, there is as much need to throw off, the kicking strap and

The author and family sailing Starlight Return *on the edge of control on a hard spinnaker run in Cowes week 1978. Close cooperation between the helmsman and the spinnaker sheet trimmer was vital and all six crew are sitting up on the weather rail.*

allow the leech to slack and the sail to twist off, as there is to release the mainsheet and spill the whole sail. Spinnakering successfully in heavy weather requires two considerations to be borne in mind. The spinnaker must be stable. The moment it starts to oscillate the oscillations will generate a roll, and the helmsman will be in all sorts of trouble. This means that all controls must be kept taut, particularly the pole hoist and foreguy. If either of these is slack the pole can rise and fall and induce instability into the sail as a whole. The sheet should generally be over-tightened to avoid any flutter. Leading the sheet well forward on the rail exerts a downward force which will keep the sail stable over the whole height. Finally the pole angle is vitally important, and here the helmsman should overrule the enthusiasm of the crew if he senses that their attitude is not in sympathy with his problems; keeping the yacht tracking in the narrow path between control and total disaster. Pulling the pole aft, as one would for the same apparent wind of less strength, is going to generate forces to windward which will induce roll and spasms of lee helm which are difficult to anticipate. Conversely, carrying the pole too far forward and the sheet too far aft is going to generate vicious weather helm. This is why a heavy-weather spinnaker should be flat and narrow so that trimming to fill it is not critical and an angle can be found that is acceptable to the poor chap at the helm.

One of the commonest causes of broaching is the over-enthusiastic sheet trimmer who watches the luff of the sail with total disregard for other things. Ideally he needs eyes in the back of his head. When the sail begins to lift it certainly means that the apparent wind has come ahead. If, however, the helmsman is heaving on the tiller with all his might it is obvious that he is trying to refill the sail by bearing away. If the man on the sheet winds in, he is taking sides against the helmsman by increasing weather helm and making his chances of bearing away a lot slimmer. At the risk of collapsing the sail altogether a judicious veer at the right moment is a much better way of making friends with the helmsman.

In the previous article we recognised the need to pull weight aft to compensate for the tendency for the bow to drop as speed increases. No boat ever broached because the weight was too far aft, but too many crew on the foredeck is a popular recipe for disaster. Keen, but in-experienced, crew find it very hard not to rush forward to help when they see one man struggling against fearful odds on the foredeck. Going to his assistance may make his life easier, but it certainly does not help the helmsman or the speed of the yacht.

Broaching in flat water is nearly always a case of becoming over-powered, either through faulty timing, or lack of anticipation. It is, of course, far more likely while completing, or failing to complete, a gybe. Until the spinnaker has been settled down on the new gybe everything is against maintaining control. The crew are, by necessity, out of position and the spinnaker is for a while some way from the end of the pole which is far from stable as the guy is not taut. Oscillations reign supreme.

When the yacht is being driven hard offshore there is the added complication of sailing in waves. When the yacht is perched on the crest of the wave, bow slightly dipped and surfing merrily, life may indeed be a bowl of cherries. Unfortunately it is not easy to maintain so much speed that one sits on one wave enjoying the ride for very long, and it is the times in between that are not so easy. As the yacht surfs she is temporarily freed from the influences of the stern wave and the helm is probably fairly neutral. Directly the speed drops, back come all the influences of displacement sailing. Because the speed has dropped the apparent wind speed increases and the turning influences of the rig are correspondingly increased.

The variations in buoyancy characteristics, which were predictable in flat water, are far less predictable in a confused sea, and the tendency to yaw is worsened. Undoubtedly the most difficult moment, when running or reaching hard, is the period when the crest, which is travelling faster than the yacht, overtakes. It lifts the stern and if the yacht fails to accelerate it passes under the hull, subsequently lifting the bow before going clear ahead. As the stern lifts there is generally a sudden and severe increase in weather helm. Once overcome, this neutralises almost as rapidly. The experienced helmsman anticipates the actions in advance so that he is not winding on lots of rudder, and therefore brakes, just as the yacht is keen to accelerate and begin surfing.

Up to a point the modern, beamy yacht is in her element when driving hard downwind in a seaway. The broad shallow sections amidships and astern give ample form stability in an upright condition. Because that stability is so largely generated by form and is not reliant on massive amounts of ballast the power-to-weight ratio is conducive to sustained speed and regular surfing. Directly that upright condition is lost then the newly-immersed areas present a very different shape for the overtaking wave to pass under, and a small amount of heel can soon be multiplied as the yacht rounds up against the will of the helmsman.

One often hears quoted the dictum that one should keep the yacht under the rig when steering downwind. Taken literally by a novice helmsman the effect can be hilarious or disastrous, depending on conditions. The theory, though, is absolutely right. As the rig begins to hang out over the water the helmsman's problems can become very acute unless he or the sheet trimmers can bring the situation under control.

Undoubtedly the most frightening of all is the reverse broach, because it can all happen so fast. If, on a downwind run, the yacht begins to heel to windward through the oscillations of the spinnaker and too many crew members on the weather side, then there will be a strong onset of lee helm. The helmsman sitting on the weather side is falling away from the tiller which he is trying to push hard away from him. If there is any risk of this happening then it is essential to have an

Samuel Pepys is seen here maintaining control during a very satisfying burst of speed. Note how the spinnaker sheet is lead well forward and the crew are well spread in anticipation of the drop. The boat has been held nicely upright and despite the man (just visible) in the stemhead the bow has not dropped!

alert and willing hand on the opposite side of the cockpit who can grab the helm and haul the yacht back on course before the inevitable occurs.

It is not always possible to choose one's course so freely but the probability of broaching increases rapidly as the dead run condition is approached. If it is remotely possible, it will pay every time to luff up sufficiently to be positively reaching on one gybe. The influences on the yacht are then at least constantly in one direction, if variable in strength, and the helmsman and crew can concentrate on keeping the speed up with a greater hope of survival.

PART 4

OFFSHORE
DANGER

18

Fastnet '79

There have been many milestones in the history of yacht racing and the Fastnet race of 1979 will remain one of the most significant for years to come.

On shore we could hardly believe the reports of the disaster and rescues that occurred that night. Our son, then only sixteen, was in the race aboard an OOD 34. He was part of a very strong and experienced crew and we comforted ourselves with the feeling that they would be the last to make a hash of things.

The full shock only came home to us when we learned of their safe arrival in Crosshaven and of their experiences in the height of the storm. That they had survived was indeed a credit to their own resources, but that they had suffered such a severe hammering, including a 360 degrees roll was the result of a combination of circumstances which were, at the time, almost beyond comprehension.

The immediate reactions of the media, some of which should have known better, was, I suppose, inevitable. Before any of the facts were known there were those who were blaming the trouble on weakly constructed boats, built to satisfy the demand for speed at all costs. It turned out that this was wholly unjustified. Structural failure was in no way limited to extreme designs.

The BBC immediately latched on to the high incidence of trouble in the OOD 34s and pilloried the builders unmercifully. It was true that numerically the OOD 34s featured very strongly in the list of casualties but, in their defence, they were concentrated in one of the worst areas and they were one of the most prominently represented designs in the race. The fact that the same builders, J C Rogers of Lymington, had built the Contessa 32 of which the only finisher in Class V was an example, went unreported.

The only previous life lost in the Fastnet race was in bad weather in 1931. In 1979 there were 303 yachts which started in the race of which only 85 finished. Twenty four yachts were abandoned, of which 19 were subsequently recovered. Fifteen lives were lost and this would have been far greater if it were not for the superb efforts of the search and rescue services.

The report of the inquiry set up by the RYA and the RORC was published before the end of the year and I was asked to write the article which follows as a review of the report. My article was published in February, 1980, six months after the race, by which time we were all recovering from the shock and looking at the tragedy to see what it would teach us for the future.

Storm Seas Survival

Crossing the Solent on a Sealink ferry is probably one of the least hazardous ways of going afloat. Ocean racing is certainly one of the most dangerous. Just as Grand Prix motor racing would lose its charisma if it became totally safe so would ocean racing lose some of its magic if the element of danger were removed.

It would be wrong to portray the ocean racing fraternity as a group of devil-may-care desperadoes needlessly risking their lives every weekend. However, unless one has been a part of it, driving downwind on a thick black night, for instance, one can have little idea of the narrow margins of safety that have existed for many years. So long as the will to win exists skippers and crews will accept the dangers and press on as long as they dare. These are the sort of dangers that occur in ordinary races and, as a competitor, it is perhaps amazing that the instance of tragedy has been so small. Fastnet '79 however was an entirely different sort of danger. There is no suggestion arising from the report that it was the press-on spirit that caused the trouble. There may have been a reluctance to retire but it would appear that the great majority of competitors devoted their thoughts primarily to survival and, for those still sailing the course, the race was a secondary consideration. Returning again to the acceptance of danger as a necessary part of ocean racing we must all recognise that the same circumstances may happen again and there is no way that we can expect to be totally safe if they do.

It would be irresponsible to give the impression that Fastnet '79 with its tragic death toll, was to be accepted as an inevitable ingredient of the sport. Due to a sense of false security, born of a long period of more temperate conditions, the great majority of the fleet were unprepared for the severity of the storm. The whole purpose of the official inquiry was to examine the evidence and extract from it the lessons that must be learned. These lessons will not prevent competitors sailing close to the margins of safety in their drive to be winners. The lessons must however be used to ensure that, if there is another severe storm when the RORC fleet is at sea, we are all fully prepared to meet it and prevent a repeat of 1979's tragedy.

The official report of the inquiry set up by the RYA and the RORC was published early in December and has been a talking point ever since. It is easy enough to pick holes in it but quite useless to do so. Much of the written text is very pertinent but the great majority of the data analysis seems of much less value. The conclusions and recommendations are very limited. This unfortunately seems right because despite the fullest possible co-operation from the competitors and the rescue organisations the evidence is still conflicting and inconclusive. There is something very impersonal about computer analysis of questionaires. Having talked to a large number of those involved the writer believes that survival was a very personal affair. Survival depended on the collective seamanship of each skipper and crew both in the preparation of their boats and their strategy at sea. This was an element that could not be set out in tabulated form and expressed in percentages, and yet was in many cases an overriding factor at the time. Seamanship is not a quality that is easily described on paper and readers should not translate these remarks into a suggestion that all those who came to grief did so purely on account of a failure to exercise good seamanship. A sequence of events can inevitably overtake the precautions of even the most experienced seaman. This was never more true than in the case of yachts which stood by others and then suffered set-backs which would never have occurred if they had only had their own salvation to consider.

I was not on the race but I have been fortunate to talk to a fair number of those who were. I count among these many of my friends and my own son and in general I respect their views and opinions very highly. Together with the contents of the report I am drawn towards certain conclusions and it is these that will be my guide in forming my decisions in the future.

It is of little surprise to any of us to read that the severe or B2 knockdown is the fundamental horror that is the greatest danger in the circumstances such as Fastnet '79. The term B2 should, perhaps, be explained. In the questionaire, Question B1, asked *'Did you experience a knockdown to horizontal or almost horizontal during the storm?'* Question B2 asked, *'Did you experience a knockdown to beyond horizontal (including a 360° roll)?'* Readers can, from this, see straight away the origin and definition of B1 and B2 knockdowns. 77 out of the 235 yachts analysed suffered B2 knockdowns or 33%. Included in these 77 were 22 of the 24 yachts that were abandoned. There is a suggestion in the report that because the incidence of knockdowns was higher in the smaller classes, the relationship between size of yacht and wave height was a factor. It is difficult to accept that the state of the race did not have an equally significant bearing on the figures. Analysis shows that the incidence in Classes 1 and 2 was indeed much lower. It was however remarkably consistent in Classes 3,4, and 5. In general the largest boats were mostly round the Rock at the height of the storm but

Class 3 and below were not so fortunate. Many of the knockdowns recorded in the smaller classes appear to have been sustained while still fighting their way north-west towards the Rock.

It might help to try to reconstruct the probable sequence of events that result in a B2 knockdown. Being laid flat by the effect of the wind is a situation which, though unpleasant at the time, is not generally catastrophic in relatively small seas. However if the yacht is flattened as it rises to the crest of a vertical or near vertical wall of water 35ft high, the likelihood of being thrown off that wall by the effect of the crest is very great. Such a tumble must inevitably contribute to the heel angle, which, as experience has shown, will exceed 90° and may be the first stage of a 360° roll. This probably sounds like an over simplification by an armchair observer who was not even there. All the evidence however points to the existence of exceptionally steep wave fronts several times higher than the beam of the yacht. Whatever the reasons, yachts were obviously frequently unable to stay on these nearly vertical slopes and began to slip towards the trough. In this situation the lateral resistance of the keel, as opposed to its righting moment, is a positive disadvantage. Because the keel and rudder cannot slip sideways at the same speed as the hull they serve to increase the angle of heel progressively. If, at the same time, the crest is breaking there is nothing to prevent the yacht being driven into the trough with several tons of water behind her. As soon as the lee deck is immersed the final angle of heel will rapidly be increased and in a number of cases in the Fastnet resulted in the completion of the full 360° of roll.

For any of us who were not there, the size and steepness of the seas encountered by the Fastnet fleet is difficult to appreciate. The crew of *Windswept*, which had rolled in the early hours of Tuesday morning, had *Mickey Mouse*, a sister yacht, standing by for a short while. They said that to see a replica of themselves in the same waves made the yacht look so small and the waves so large that the effect was infinitely more staggering.

The report carries an annex from the Institute of Oceanographic Sciences on severe wave conditions during the Fastnet Race. Their conclusions are that the significant wave height may well have been 33ft, it could have been as high as 46ft. The significant wave height is defined as the average height of the 33 largest waves in every 99: quite difficult, to evaluate from the deck of a yacht with a thousand other things to worry about at the same time. What is really frightening is the statement which says that the *highest individual wave every three hours would be close to about twice the significant wave height.* They also say that the waves could have had *steep or near vertical sided profiles* and crests would have travelled at 30-40 knots. The size of the seas meant that when a yacht fell, she fell far enough for the impact loading on decks, rigs, heavy items stowed below and on crew members brought up short at the end of their harnesses, to be a crucial factor. Add to this the confused nature of the sea due to the very rapid change in wind direction and it is easy to realise that if the yacht was flattened when climbing a sea from ahead or as it passed under from astern her direction of fall was also uncertain. There are several accounts of knockdowns that have resulted in the yacht having reversed her course by 180° before recovery.

As far as the future is concerned owners must face two problems. If caught in similar circumstances how do they handle the yacht so as to limit the risk of a B2 knockdown? And, assuming that the knockdown is going to occur, what steps does one take to limit the damage to the yacht and injury or loss of life among the crew? Some yachts lay a-hull and were knocked down and rolled, suffering damage in the process while others lay a-hull battened down and survived the storm relatively unscathed. Others ran before the wind, some towing warps, some not and again, in each case, experienced knockdowns. Some felt that they were running too fast and others wished they had had more speed. Clearly the RORC fleet represents a very wide variety of hull types and what was sauce for the goose may not, in this case, have been sauce for the gander. There is a feeling that experienced skippers who really know their boats perhaps have an instinctive feel for doing what is best. The more competitors from Fastnet '79 one talks to the more this same point comes home. To survive successfully one had to adopt the tactics that were suited to one's own type of boat. It would be very dangerous to generalise but two opposite extremes seem to illustrate this point.

The first account came from a man sailing a Rogers 39. These boats are light for their length, with a shallow profile and a relatively clean, flat run into a fairly full stern. His answer was to keep sailing hard and fast under a fully-reefed main-sail and storm jib. Before the Rock, while still close reaching, this was evidently a very rough passage and it is tremendous credit to the construction of the yacht that she withstood the hammering that it entailed. Once round the Rock, they maintained the same sails and drove down wind with the seas on the quarter at fantastic speeds, surfing on the crests for long periods. They were a strong and very competent crew with very good helmsmen. He was however prepared to agree that this strategy depended on the hull form of the yacht providing an exceptional degree of controllability at high speed. His view is that had they been more cautious and carried less sail they might have survived less well. The opposite illustrations came from several of the owners of heavier displacement yachts with deeper hull profiles and finer ends which lay a-hull without trouble. They felt that their particular types would not have run easily and could certainly not have been driven hard down wind.

The Report is inconclusive on the subject of survival tactics. On the other hand it does say: *'There is, however, an inference that active rather than passive tactics were successful and those who were able to maintain some speed and directional control fared better'*. Obviously those who lay a-hull successfully will have faith in their own yacht doing the same thing again. But, for those who have doubt, the question of maintaining some speed and control is worth a lot of thought. It would not be flippant to compare the situation of meeting a near vertical wall of water with the 'wall of death' at the fairground. The speed of the motor cycle glues it to the wall of the cylinder by centrifugal force. If a B2 knockdown involves falling off the face of a wave, then perhaps there is some merit in suggesting that, climbing that wave with some forward momentum will help to provide a force against the face of the wall for long enough to enable the yacht to climb out over the top. These comments do not, of course, have any relevance to the yacht that is running before the sea, for which the critical period is the moment the stern begins to lift to a new wave. On seas of the size of Fastnet '79 the stern has to rise a sickeningly long way and the bow will appear to drop and drop and drop. This is the time when the speed is critical; too little and there is not enought bite on the rudder for the helmsman to keep the line he wants, too much and the surfing when the crest is reached is too wild and a broach is inevitable. If you broach in these sort of conditons the period of the waves is so small that the next wall of water is upon the yacht before she can recover, leaving her entirely at its mercy. To run before successfully it is important to use the best helmsmen, for everybody's lives are in their hands. By instinct and experience they must very rapidly discover the best angle to the wind and sea and the optimum speed for maximum control. If warps are going to be streamed astern the general consensus is that they must be very long to maintain a constant drag and have something heavy on the end to give maximum immersion. This means that as the stern is rising the end of the warps should be back in the trough behind the approaching wave. By all accounts, anything less than 10 fathoms would have been ineffective, and 15 fathoms would have been much better. Others believe that shorter warps, sufficient to dampen the swing of the stern, are more effective.

It is perhaps worthwhile considering objectively the actual state of affairs that exist in wave conditions. A wave travels across the surface of the sea at speed. We have already seen that the experts suggest that in Fastnet '79 the crests may have been travelling at 30-40 knots. What must be realised is that the water itself is not moving, except vertically. An object such as a yacht drifting in waves will be carried up the face of the wave because the surrounding water is rising with the passing of the crest. As the wave goes roaring by the yacht settles in the next trough and, apart from her drift due to windage, she is substantially in the same place and in the same water as before.

How often do people speak of sailing down the face of the waves when running off? Stop to think for a moment, and it will be realised that in normal circumstances the yacht is actually going backwards up the face of the wave and her speed through the water is delaying that

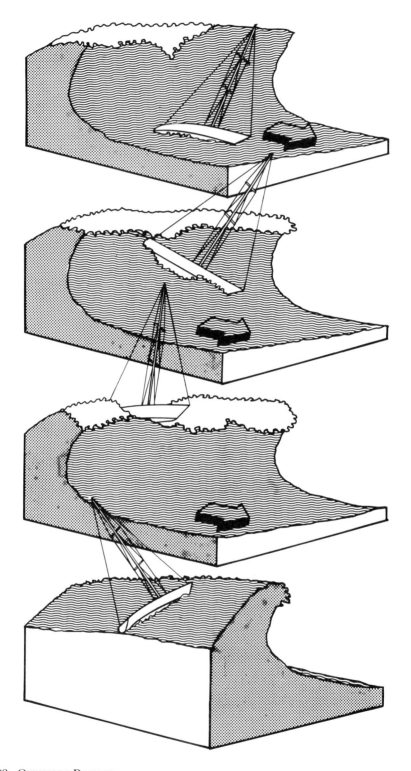

action. While the stern is up and the bow is down the impression of sailing downwards is very real. The ability to overtake the waves is very rare indeed. Of course, surfing on the crest is another condition altogether and involves achieving a balance between a combination of sail power and the forces of gravity, which are propelling the yacht forwards and downwards, and the effect of the rising water on the face of the wave, which is forcing the yacht upwards. That long exhilarating sleigh ride nearly always ends with the bows going up as the speed drops and the wave goes chasing on ahead. If it ends with the surfing forces producing a speed in excess of the wave crest then disaster is not far away and a B2 knockdown is imminent. The experienced helmsman, traverses the face of the wave and if he feels the risk of overdoing things he luffs away to increase the amount of traverse, eventually dropping back and then lining up for the next wave. Bearing off again as the yacht begins to rise will increase boat speed and as the crest is reached surfing is resumed once more. It is this traversing technique which accounts for so many skippers' comments that bringing the wind and waves more on to the quarter created a happier and more controllable situation.

Some yachts even in the smallest classes succeeded in continuing to windward or close reaching under very limited sail and, in this respect, the new ORC requirements for Categories 1 and 2 are a welcome provision. The assumption that is now drawn is that without a trysail it is not possible to achieve a satisfactory minimum sail plan that is also balanced. In 1980 under Category 1 and 2, and this includes most RORC races, the storm jib became mandatory with an area of $0.5 \times IG^2$ also a Trysail, 35% of the area of the mainsail (.175 x P x E), and a heavy weather jib of $0.135 \times IG^2$. What must be emphasised is that these are maximum sizes and careful thought in consultation with sailmaker and designer should be given to determining the correct choice.

On a masthead rig yacht of typical IOR proportions the maximum size trysail will be only about 73% of the maximum size storm jib. This combination would surely be a mistake and that if the two are to be used together, the storm jib should be reduced to the same area or less than the trysail. To those of us who can not speak so familiarly of winds continuously at 60 knots plus this is going to seem like a pretty small

As a wave - perhaps travelling at 30-40 knots - overtakes the yacht she can be thought of as climbing its face backwards. Her speed through the water is significantly less than the speed of the waves and merely increases the time it takes them to overtake her.

As the breaking crest overtakes a yacht she may surf wildly for some moments in water which is actually moving forwards. Then the wave roars past and she falls back on to its rearward slope.

storm jib for use on other less frantic occasions. Serious decisions will need to be made to choose the right size for the heavy weather jib for use in ordinary gales. On the fractional rigged boat the balance of maximum size is much better and with the very much larger mainsail the need for a trysail is much more inherent in the type anyhow. The evidence of the report shows that 22% were carrying trysails but only 8% used them. It is not known how these boats were distributed throughout the fleet but there is evidence that some skippers were not prepared to expose their crew members to the risks involved in setting trysails. This emphasises very strongly the need for much greater attention to the drills involved in the use of heavy weather gear.

If the trysail comes on deck still wrapped in polythene and neatly folded by the sailmaker, storm conditions are not the time for the trials that should have taken place at the beginning of the season. The trysail should have a tack strop spliced on and sheets permanently attached so that only one bag need be found which will contain all the gear that is needed. Sheeting arrangements should be permanent and marked, and the main halyard should have a shackle that is easily handled with cold, wet fingers so that it can be transferred to the trysail quickly and safely.

It was surprising to learn immediately after the race that a very large number of yachts appeared to prefer to take off their mainsails altogether and continue under storm jib. Looked at from the deck the storm jib looks far smaller than the mainsail fully reefed; but, in practice it is very often much the more powerful of the two. In the writer's experience to take off the storm jib and leave a well flattened fully reefed mainsail transforms a yacht. From being a leaping flying thing intent on becoming airborne on the back of every wave she becomes almost hove-to and the speed is reduced to far less than if the storm jib had been retained and the mainsail stowed. Think again of the yacht climbing the wall of water in danger of being thrown back into the trough. Sail area right forward is threatening to push the bow off as it rises to the crest, the most critical moment of all, just when lee helm is the last thing the helmsman wants to feel.

It is interesting to note one of the reasons that the OOD 34s as a class suffered so much trouble. Because the Class Association decided that the OOD 34 would not carry the full number of headsails permitted by ORC regulations they were not bound by the maximum size limit relating to the storm jib. The size chosen by the Association was 27% bigger than the IOR maximum of $.05 \times IG^2$. Only one of them had a small enough storm jib to cope with the conditions. That one owner was fortunate in having on board a storm jib left over from a previous yacht and was very glad to use it. One other OOD 34 survived very well under fully-reefed mainsail only. They plugged on until they could no longer gain ground and then ran off under the same rig and went into Cork. The class Association has now added a spitfire jib that is 3.2% of IG^2 to the outfit of sails.

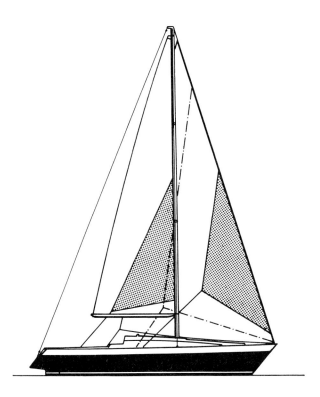

A masthead rig sail plan showing the maximum sizes for the trysail
(1.75 × P × E), storm jib (.05 × IG²) and with the heavy weather jib (0.135 × IG²)
shown dotted. It must be emphasised that these are maximum sizes.

In Fastnet '79 the build up to disaster was very strongly influenced by circumstances. Those short of the Rock very naturally continued to try to follow the course as long as they could. Those round the Rock were heading south-east in any case and were much more likely to keep sailing if only under bare poles. Those with the least to lose probably retired soonest, they may also have been the least prepared to risk the damage that is inevitable in racing though gale conditions. Many, however, will have pressed on having been conditioned to the idea that the modern yacht was capable of surviving more than we now realise it is sensible to assume.

In no case does it appear that lack of sea room was a primary cause for concern. Next time this situation may be very different.

When the next occasion arises the weather forecasting may give no greater warning than last summer. None of us, however, can disregard the dangers involved and forget the tragedy of 1979. Faced with a wind force in double figures and a sea of rapidly growing ferocity each skipper and crew will have to decide upon a strategy for survival and hope that their preparations for it have been adequate.

There is apparently a degree of steepness of wave profile that makes lying a-hull or bows towards the weather unacceptably risky. Faced with similar circumstances we must either attempt to judge the moment when the steepness of the sea is our greatest danger and then change tactics and run off, or remain lying a-hull and believe in the strength and integrity of the hull to withstand a severe knockdown should it occur. It should be possible to prepare the yacht to withstand most of the worst effects of a knockdown though it is perhaps not practical to suggest that this can necessarily extend to the rig. To lose the mast is unfortunate but not in itself the ultimate disaster. We are all aware of the damage that the loose spar can do the hull, though there is little evidence of it occurring. The important point is that the crew should be able to survive inside a dismasted yacht. When conditions improve it may still be possible to motor, set a jury rig or accept a tow.

19

The aftermath

There has been fine tuning to the ORC regulations since 1980 but no major changes. Heavy weather sails are more clearly defined but the fact remains in 1986 that Classes V – Vll are only required to satisfy Category 3 of the ORC regulations for the Morgan Cup and the Cowes – Dinard – St Malo races. Category 3 does not make the provision of a storm jib mandatory and the logic of this is entirely beyond understanding

As far as ocean racing is concerned the designer is, in general, concerned primarily with the conception of race winning designs and, although one would suppose that none are so rash as to consciously jeopardise the lives of the crew, there is a margin of safety which must not be crossed. It is right and proper that this margin should be controlled by the authorities in order that the fleet is meeting a common and therefore fair, requirement.

To regulate design the ORC is bound to resort to the provisions of the IOR and by the use of penalties and rating factors discourage unhealthy trends. There has been since 1980 a gradual re-tuning of the rule that now directs designers towards lower centres of gravity and a reduction in beam.

The work of the Wolfson Unit in Southampton has contributed strongly towards a better understanding of severe wave conditions. The article that follows was written following the publication of their report in April 1984.

The Breaking Wave

One of the immediate results of the severe weather, damage and loss of life which accompanied the 1979 Fastnet race was a loss of confidence in the direction taken by the development of the modern offshore racer. This spawned a number of reports over the intervening years, all of which have focused attention on improving the breed – and on encouraging techniques for surviving severe weather.

The latest, and by far the most thorough, report has recently been published by the Department of Ship Science at the University of Southampton, which subjected an extensive series of models to breaking waves in a test tank to see whether it was possible to correlate the easily calculated hydrostatic and geometric features of a hull with its actual behaviour and propensity to capsize.

By using a total of nine models, in two basic families – one fin keel and the other a traditional long keel type – and then having wide and narrow beam versions, plus a high freeboard version of the fin keeler (complete with its own wide and narrow sisters), the authors of the report were able to determine how each variant coped with large breaking waves.

The results give designers a clue to ways in which ultimate safety can be improved and at the same time lend weight to some of the survival techniques which are now practised. The findings are also, in many ways, critical of contemporary IOR race-winning designs.

The International Technical Committee, which recommends rule changes to the Offshore Racing Council, has already been paying attention to the results of a similar study and report made in the United States, and this latest report will surely reinforce the trend. The much-criticised crew limitation rule is in fact the first step in a move to encourage less reliance on maximum beam and it will probably be followed by further amendments which will encourage a lower centre of gravity by adjustment of the CGF Formula.

Much of the RORC fleet is crewed by large, strong crews and for them the option of an 'active' technique for survival is a possibility, and the report does give some merit to these techniques which involve the crew sailing the boat at all times. However, the smaller crew of a cruising or short-handed racing yacht will be forced to adopt a more passive defence against disaster, and it is with this category in mind that the findings of the report need the widest possible publicity and understanding.

The hydrostatic analysis of the designs used for the tank testing is something which will bear some explanation if the full understanding of the report is to be appreciated. Page 209 shows a stability curve. The horizontal axis indicates the angle of roll from 0° (mast upright towards the sky) to 180° (mast straight down towards the bottom). The vertical dimension represents the righting moment, whether that is expressed as the length of the righting arm or as a force in, say, foot pounds. On the positive side of the horizontal axis the area contained by the curve is a measure of the energy required to capsize the yacht in calm water. The area contained on the negative side is conversely, a measure of the energy required to right the yacht from a totally inverted condition. The point at which the curve crosses the axis, the point at which the righting moment is zero, is known as the point of vanishing stability.

In less scientific terms we could say that if a yacht has vanishing stability at, say, 137° then if she heeled to 136°, she would stagger back up again. However, if she heeled to 138° she would continue until she settled totally inverted. To be fair, these are hydrostatic analyses and the water is going to be far from static in survival conditions. However we have already seen that the report is looking for a correlation between the hydrostatic figures (which can be calculated) and the practicalities of sailing in breaking waves. Since the report of the 1979 Fastnet Inquiry we have known that the two yachts whose hydrostatic curves were highlighted, the Contessa 32 and an anonymous Half Tonner, had vanishing stability at 157° and 117° respectively. This indicated an alarmingly high arc of inverted stability for the Half Tonner, and the ITC recommended some rule changes to encourage lower centres of gravity.

The Southampton University report contains some historical consideration before the contemporary research, and highlights the fact that between 1960 and 1980 yachts have tended towards smaller maximum righting moments, smaller angles of zero stability, smaller positive areas under the righting moment curve and larger negative areas. There are those who would say that this is a shocking indictment of the way that design standards have reduced, but in defence of designers one can claim that he who pays the piper calls the tune. Most of our paymasters are concerned with winning races, or in securing large orders at boat shows – and none of the characteristics listed have necessarily had much influence in those spheres.

The real meat of the latest report is in the result of the testing carried

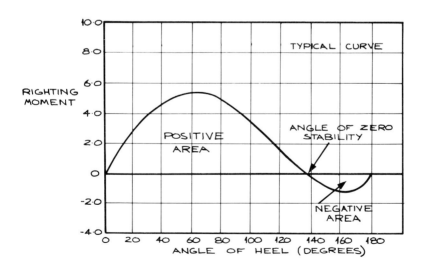

This typical stability curve shows a yacht with zero stability at 137°.

out in the towing tank on the nine models, based on the two parent models.

This selection enabled the team to study the effects of beam over the full spectrum, and to gain valuable data on the effects of the high freeboard which is a significant feature of contemporary design. They were also able to run tests at varying displacement and with the height of the vertical centre of gravity varied as well.

The models were tested in a 60m long towing tank, which, after considerable research, had been equipped with a computer-controlled wave generator. This enable a single breaker up to 0.5m (1ft 7in) high to be produced in a train of waves, and to be reproduced reliably for each of the tests. As the $\frac{1}{13}$th scale models were around 0.76m (2ft 6in) overall the waves were of very significant proportions

The first tests were made with the models free-running under power and with radio control. This enabled them to approach the breaking crests in a variety of attitudes and although not sufficiently consistent to produce soundly-based analytical data did permit rapid learning.

These tests found that no matter how steep the wave, capsizing only occurred when the wave actually broke, and also that if beam-on to the breaking wave all the models capsized. Depending upon their characteristics some of the models then returned to an upright condition while others completed the roll, and others floated upside down. Interestingly it was found that if the models approached the crest bows-on it was possible to pass right through the crest – although with a tendency to become airborne on the other side. This technique is markedly similar to the active technique practised by some crews and described in more detail later. That there is a fine line between success and failure with this survival method is indicated by the fact that an oblique approach was not so effective, resulting in the model being swept beam-on and then behaving accordingly. Finally, experiments were carried out with stern-on encounters, in which the model either surfed happily or broached beam-on. The long keel parent model trimmed to its original designed displacement seemed to come out of this part of the test with high marks, even when turned downwind. It does not take a great deal of imagination to guess from the drawings that this model was of the Nicholson 32 with its original superstructure. If we suppose that this is correct, the results form a useful yardstick because this design is well-proven in terms of heavy weather capability. The report does refer to the very full bow sections of the long keel model and this is entirely in character. It does however highlight the value of these sections because in the downwind experiments the wide beam fin keel model, which had fine bow sections, was evidently very much more difficult to control.

Within the fin keel variations the narrow version showed a noticeably greater reluctance to capsize or roll than the wide fin keel model which was easily knocked down and often rolled completely.

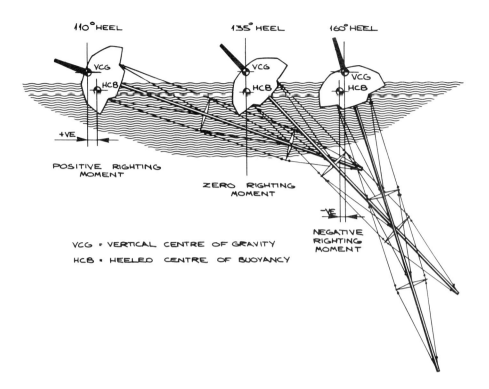

110° HEEL   135° HEEL   160° HEEL

VCG
HCB
+VE

POSITIVE RIGHTING
MOMENT

ZERO RIGHTING
MOMENT

-VE

NEGATIVE
RIGHTING
MOMENT

VCG = VERTICAL CENTRE OF GRAVITY
HCB = HEELED CENTRE OF BUOYANCY

A typical IOR yacht at 110°, 135° and 160° – vanishing or zero stability is demonstrated at 135°. The weight of the whole yacht acts through the vertical centre of gravity (VCG) which is constant in position. The heeled centre of buoyancy (HCB) varies its position and is influenced by the volume of the superstructure, cockpits etc.

To overcome the variables of the radio controlled tests a catapult launch system was devised, which when linked to the wave-making computer enabled an identical encounter with the breaking crest to be arranged for each test.

The results of this final stage were really the nitty-gritty of the whole exercise and each model was launched, at a full scale speed of some 5½ knots, with three different sizes of wave: equivalent to 5.5m (18ft), 4.5m (14ft 9in) and 4m (13ft) full size. In the smaller waves the launches were restricted to crosswave (parallel to the crest) situations. For the largest waves the models were also launched downwave (at right angles to the crest) and 20° off the downwave situation (as in a quartering sea). Each run was recorded on video and the analysis made from a frame-by-frame study.

The full scope of the tests are set out in the report, but here we will restrict ourselves to consideration of the conclusions – which are, after all, the important aspects.

The two strongest influences on vulnerability to capsize were taken to be in the form of the yacht. The report states 'A narrow craft appears to have improved resistance to capsize when beam-on to the seas, and the full lateral plane and more balanced ends of the long keel design make it less liable to broach and capsize in the following seas.'

Displacement (more rather than less) and a low centre of gravity increased resistance to capsize, but none of the models was immune to a knockdown to 130°, if an appropriately timed encounter was made with the largest wave.

A particularly significant observation is that initial stability is no measure of ultimate stability. A yacht that feels stiff when sailing at normal angles has not necessarily a sustained stiffness at extreme angles of heel. The report makes it clear that it is the righting moment between 100° and 130° which determines the resistance to capsize, and those with vanishing stability angles of less than 150° – 160° can be left floating upside down after a capsize.

The report also points out that no form or ballasting combination made any of the models proof against the highest waves, although it says that 'a wave which capsizes a model when lying beam-on can be survived either by approaching it head on, or by surfing ahead of it. Both these approaches require active rudder control and some skill to carry out' – another confirmation of techniques already practised by strong, experienced crews.

Within the report the significance of the coachroof-and-modest-freeboard option, when compared with high-freeboard-and-flush-deck, is covered both in the hydrostatic calculations and in the tank tests. The hydrostatic curve for a yacht with a coachroof shows a beneficial bump on the positive side of the righting moment curve, and this effectively moves the point of vanishing stability up to a higher angle by pushing the whole curve sideways.

The flush deck yacht which, when inverted is rather like a flat bottomed barge, has a substantial area inside the negative part of the curve. The tank tests showed that high or low freeboard as such made no difference to the propensity to capsize, but the high freeboard version remained inverted on more occasions.

One might suppose that the whole issue can be considered in terms of probabilities, and who is to say what those figures are for each situation. If one is designing for genuine deep water, offshore sailing then surely the only really honest approach is to accept that the probability of an encounter with the ultimate wave is likely and to consider the consequences.

Moving away from the Southampton University report itself we can consider some general design features in the light of its findings and experience at sea.

It goes without saying that if a yacht is going to be inverted, the less time that she spends in that condition the better. Water is bound to enter through hatches and ventilators, and however good the stowage many items, and crew members, are going to find their way on to the deckhead.

Inverted stability is governed by the immersed form and the position of the vertical centre of gravity. We have seen that superstructures give a benefit in that they represent buoyancy pressed into the water. The least desirable concept must be the beamy, flush deck types which, when inverted, are unhealthily stable.

Yacht design is always a compromise and a designer considering a design for survival in extreme conditions must attempt to strike a sensible mean. Resistance to knockdown should be a prime consideration but not to the extent of creating a half tide rock that will be pounded unmercifully by the impact of the sea. Within the analysis of the concept it should be recognised that ultimately a knockdown may well be met and a study of inverted stability must be considered.

The damage sustained in a knockdown is generally associated with the leeward side of the deck, assuming some impact as a boat lands in the trough, and quite likely within the rig. Internal damage entirely depends on the efficiency with which heavy items such as the engine, batteries, cooker and ballast have been secured.

In the writer's opinion the single most vulnerable part of the rig, assuming all the sails have been lowered, is the main boom and the stresses transmitted, through the gooseneck to the root of the mast at deck level. One cannot help feeling that one of the greatest contributors to overturning is the heeling moment generated by a badly furled mainsail absorbing the impact of a breaking crest. The actual damage to the boom and the sail is not fundamental, for if the only item severely damaged is the main boom one has good reason to be thankful for small mercies. It is however the consequential damage that is more serious. At least one yacht with a broken boom during the '79 Fastnet was afterwards found to have a crumpled mast section in way of the deck, and it may well have been that this was a matter of cause and effect.

It is impossible to draw conclusions that categorically support specific design features without first considering the techniques that will be adopted by the crew to meet extreme conditions when they occur. Various reports, including the Southampton one, have recognised that active rather than passive tactics can be successful. The Australians, in particular, strongly advocate active techniques; downunder they have a greater likelihood of severe conditions and a much greater reservoir of experience to draw on. Broadly speaking the idea is to keep as much sail on the yacht as can be reasonably managed and to maintain plenty of speed. By skilful and concentrated effort on the part of the helmsman, the bows of the boat are turned hard into the crest, with an equally rapid bear away on the back of the wave. The impact of the breaking water is taken on the sharp end of the yacht, which is surely best suited to withstand it. The speed and momentum of the yacht drive her through the crest so that the time in which the forces of the water can generate a roll are minimal. The models in the wave-testing at Southampton confirmed that yachts could survive waves in this way which would have capsized a beam-on yacht.

However to use this technique successfully for a sustained period a number of essentials must be satisfied. First this is a technique for a strong and experienced crew with a rota of capable helmsmen, and it pre-supposes at least a minimum team on deck capable of supporting the helmsman. In this respect it is vitally important, having adopted the techniques, to ensure that it succeeds. No-one should rule out the possibility of a 360° roll in extreme conditions and the best preparation is surely to have the minimum or better still no crew members on deck. Wedged in a bunk below the chances of survival are very high. On deck, a 360° is a horrifying experience.

The second essential to the bull-at-a-gate approach is a storm rig that is properly balanced with the centre of effort well aft. The storm jib tacked down in the stemhead may be small, but its leverage as the bow rises is very large, and a substantial amount of mainsail area is needed to counter that action. If there is any means of bringing the jib inboard then the difference is tremendous.

Thirdly, and this applies to all techniques, nothing must go wrong. Re-reading all the accounts of the '79 Fastnet the factor which comes across strongly is that disaster invariably followed a chapter of events. The hardest cross to bear was for those who had abandoned their chosen course of action because, having sighted flares, they naturally felt obliged to stand by others. In doing so they suffered severe damage, or a knockdown with crew members on deck, which might not have occurred if they had been alone in the ocean.

However, there are many occasions when exceptional conditions may be met and where passive rather than active tactics must be adopted due to the limitations of the crew. In singlehanded or two-man racing, or equally cruising, it is seldom practical to maintain human steering in such conditions.

It does seem that whichever technique is used the essential element for success is to avoid unnecessary time on the crest. If the yacht is allowed to forereach or lie a-hull parallel to the seas then the crest takes longer to pass, and the risk of a knockdown is probably at its greatest. In this respect it is valuable to keep some sail set aft of the mast.

It must be accepted that the modern, beamy, shallow-hulled yacht with small appendages does not lie a-hull very well. The heeled buoyancy of some designs is alarmingly high so that when pressed down by the wind, the yacht is riding very high in the water. In that condition she can be very vulnerable to the effects of the breaking crest. Nothing seems to serve better in critical conditions than moderation in all respects. Moderate beam, moderate displacement, moderate keel area and righting moment all contribute to that 'in the water feeling', that is particularly reassuring in really dirty weather. So much better to have a grip on the more stable water below the surface than, in the case of very light designs, to be entirely at the mercy of the surface confusion that exists in storm conditions.

It is only when an owner is contemplating long ocean passages in exposed waters that suitability for survival in extreme conditions becomes a purchasing priority. The most rugged designs are neither going to be race winners round the buoys nor, on the other hand, are they going to have the most commodious interior for their size or length. However ambitions may grow and exceptional conditions may be met in unexpected places. To this end any one of us may some day meet more than we bargained for and have to adopt a course of action best suited for survival.

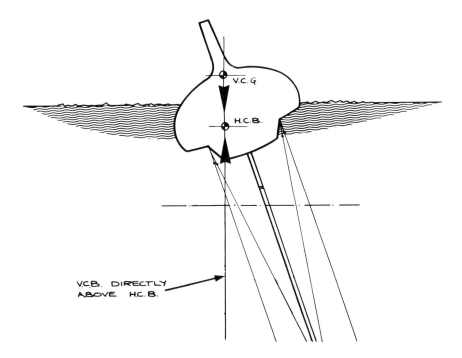

An illustration of a more conventional moderate design with less beam than a typical IOR design which can have positive stability up to 160°.

PART FIVE

THE RATING OF YACHTS

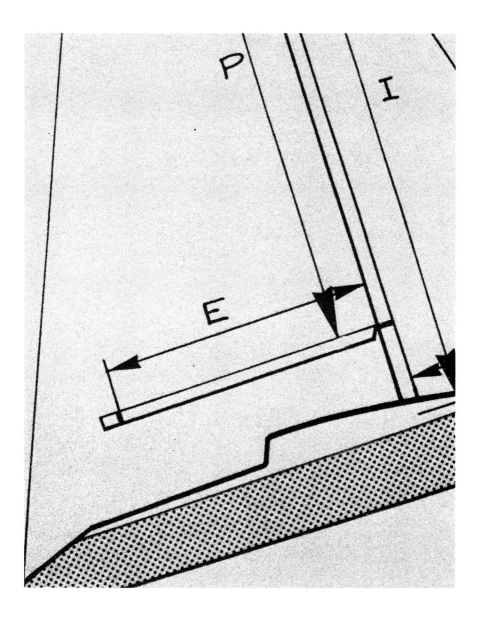

20

Elementary IOR

The history of the IOR is one of a long series of assaults by the designers and repairs of the defences by the rulemakers. For years designers have vied with one another to exploit the loopholes available, to the greatest advantage of their designs.

Gradually the weaknesses of the rule became apparent and each potential opening was plugged by a further complicated condition which effectively sealed each loophole in turn. There have been many recriminations along the way, as each designer considered that he had been singled out for victimisation. In the end I believe that the final outcome is quite fair. The guiding principle behind the policy of development would seem to have been that if a designer introduced some unconventional feature the purpose of which was purely to exploit the rule then, if the choice was between amending the rule or forcing all others to copy that feature, there had to be an amendment.

By 1982 a very considerable degree of stability had been achieved and few designers believed any longer in the existence of unfound openings for exploitation.

Since 1982 there have been further developments in the application of IOR MkIIIA. These have included the extension of the provisions to include new construction on the basis that sensible cruiser racer designs incorporated many of the characteristics of the earlier designs which were enjoying benefits.

There were some significant changes for 1985 in the CGF formula allowing either greater stability or a narrower Beam Water Line. This has been the outcome of several lines of research following the 1979 Fastnet and one hopes the effects will be a benefit to the breed. References to the CGF formula have been amended to take account of the revised calculations.

Fundamentals

To understand the workings of the IOR – the International Offshore Rule – it is necessary to explain how the rule has been constructed to reach its present form. Fundamentally, the rule requires measurement of the yacht's hull, rig, auxiliary installation and stability characteristics. From these measurements, formulas are used to compare the speed characteristics with the drag characteristics. The end result of these calculations is expressed as a notional length, or rating, from which a handicap can be calculated. The fundamentals are covered by a series of relatively easily understood formulas which are the first and most essential items to understand.

As time has gone by, the fundamentals have had to be surrounded by a mass of conditional requirements designed to catch up with the very natural efforts of the world's designers to identify their own private loopholes in the original rule and then exploit them thoroughly. These techniques can best be described as camouflaging speed characteristics and exaggerating drag factors to achieve the lowest rating in relation to the true potential speed of the yacht.

In parallel with these efforts to find ways round the rule the technology available to the boatbuilder has advanced very considerably and the rule has necessarily to cater for designs which were unheard of at the time of its inception. Thus the rule has gone through several revisions and we are now using IOR Mark 111.

There is a third element within the rule which is directly related to the advance in technology and this is the – less well understood – Mk -111A. This caters for the older style of boats and attempts to equate them on more equal terms with the latest breed.

The most straightforward beginning is therefore to try and identify the fundamentals of Mk 111 and leave the conditionals until later.

There are four principal values which are the main ingredients of the rating formula. They are Rated Length (L) and Sail Area (SC), these are the speed components, and Rated Beam (B) and Rated Depth (D), which are the drag components. It is no surprise therefore to see that L and SC are multipliers and additions, and B and D are divisors in the Measured Rating Formula:-

$$MR = \left[\frac{0.13L \times SC}{\sqrt{B \times D}} + 0.25L + 0.2SC + DC + FC \right] \times DLF$$

If we are concentrating on the fundamentals then it is better to ignore DC, FC and DLF for the time being. Just notice how L and SC are on the top of the formula, increasing the rating, and B and D are on the bottom, making it smaller.

These four components, L, SC, B and D, are best described in the order in which they are measured.

Rated Beam comes first and is an essential factor in the measurement

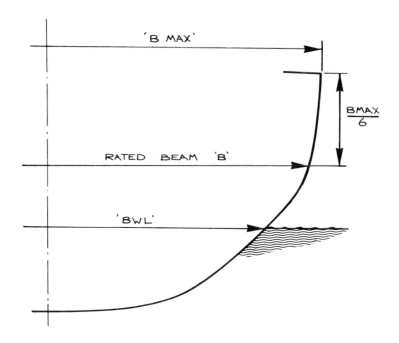

The B Max station showing the measurement points for B, BWL and BMAX.

of L and D which follow. The Rated Beam (B) is measured in the same fore and aft section as the Maximum Beam (BMAX), known as the BMAX station. This position is found by measurement. B is measured at a point one sixth of BMAX below the sheerline (see above). Beam Waterline (BWL) is measured on the same station.

Rated Length (L) is calculated from a whole series of measurements taken at the bow and stern. The process is intended to identify an effective sailing length which is self-adjusting each time new values for fore and aft trim are obtained. In principle, what the calculations do is to define two sloping lines, one under the bow – called the FOC line – and the other – the AOCC line – under the stern. By relating these lines to the freeboards, obtained when the yacht is measured afloat, it is possible to arrive at the horizontal distance between the points at which these two sloping lines cut the surface of the water. This horizontal distance is the Rated Length (L), (opposite).

This concept of an imaginary line drawn under the boat is probably the most difficult thing for the layman to grasp, particularly the less mathematically minded. It is not easy to see that a whole row of figures in a book of rules actually mean something and have not been arbitrarily put together at the whim of the rulemakers. Once this understanding has been acquired the designer, amateur or professional, can concentrate on manoeuvring these imaginary lines rather than

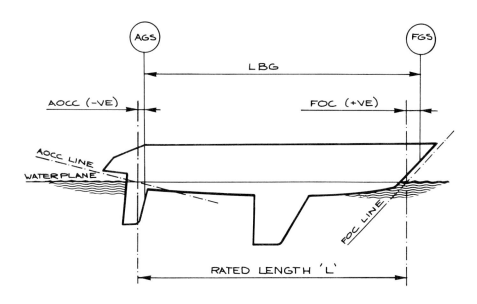

This shows the relationship between L and LBG, FOC and AOCC.

treating each measurement point as a separate entity, to be experimented with individually.

The mechanics of the measurement of L are to define the Forward Girth Station (FGS) and the Aft Girth Station (AGS) and measure the distance Length Between Girths (LBG) between the two. All the other measurements then go towards calculating the overhang components, which are the horizontal distances between the girth stations and the points at which the sloping lines cut the surface of the water. The Rated Length is quite simply:-

$$L = LBG - FOC - AOCC$$

FOC (Forward Overhang Component) is, in the writer's experience, always positive, whereas AOCC (Aft Overhang Component Corrected) is very frequently negative. A negative component establishes that the sloping line is cutting the water beyond the girth station and so it becomes an addition to LBG, and L may well be longer than LBG. The diagram above illustrates the process involved. It shows an example of a negative AOCC and a positive FOC.

Rated length is the most interesting element of the entire rule because there are so many options open to the designer. To be more specific the Aft Overhang Component is the interesting part because, with a few

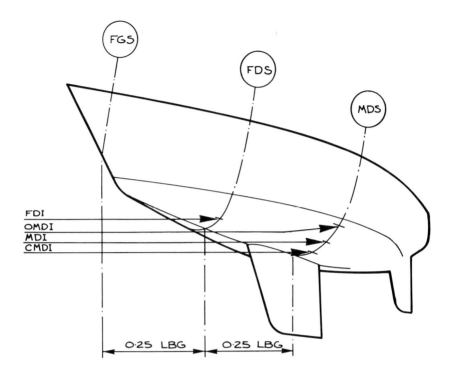

FGS

FDS

MDS

FDI
OMDI
MDI
CMDI

0·25 LBG   0·25 LBG

Rated depth is calculated from only four measurements of immersed depth on each side of the yacht.

isolated exceptions, designers tend to accept that there is no room to be enterprising at the bow and their whole efforts towards controlling L are concentrated on manipulation of the stern sections.

Rated Depth (D) is calculated from only four measurements of immersed depth, (above). The Forward Depth immersed (FDI) is measured at a point one tenth of B from the centreline in the Forward Depth Station (FDS), which is a quarter of LBG aft from FGS. The other three depths are measured at one eighth B, one quarter B and three-eighths B from the centreline in the Mid Depth Station (MDS), which is at the mid point of LBG, generally a short distance forward of BMAX. The three depths on MDS are Centre Mid Depth Immersed (CMDI), Mid Depth Immersed (MDI), and Outer Mid Depth Immersed (OMDI) respectively. The calculations are so arranged that these measurements have a varying influence on the total value of measured depth. CMDI and FDI are the largest contributors and OMDI is the smallest. MDI has acquired much more significance than used to be the case as it is now involved in many of the conditionals.

The fourth main element is the Sail Area Value (SC) which, in simple terms, is the square root of the Total Rated Sail Area (RSAT). In a single-masted yacht RSAT is the sum of the Rated Area of the Mainsail (RSAM) and the Rated Area of the Foretriangle (RSAF), plus a correction factor which places more emphasis on foretriangle than mainsail area. In effect RSAT = 1.1 RSAF + 0.857 RSAM. This intentional bias towards the mainsail is one reason why a fractional rig has physically more sail area than the masthead rig for the same rated area. Within the calculations of both the mainsail and the foretriangle are adjustors that penalise aspect ratio so that a tall narrow sail is more highly rated than a short squat one. There is also a Sail Correction Factor (SCF) that penalises exceptionally large sail plans.

The essential items that contribute to the calculations of RSAT are the luff of the mainsail (P), the foot of the mainsail (E), the height of the mast (I), and the foot of the foretriangle (J) (below). P and E are measured on the spars between black bands. I is, nowadays, the result of an involved calculation which is intended to represent the vertical height between the intersection of the forestay and the forward face of the mast and a point 4% of B above the sheerline. J is the horizontal distance between the forward face of the mast and the intersection of the forestay and the deck. All the permitted spinnaker dimensions are related to I and J and where the permitted amounts are exceeded the rule allows for I corrected (IC) or J corrected (JC) to be greater than I and J as

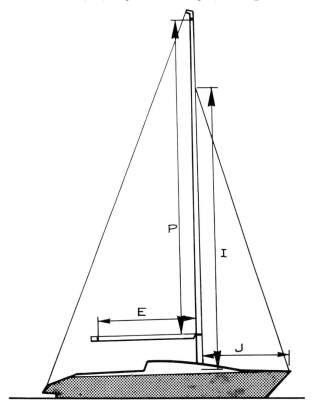

The four main dimensions that are derived from the rig – 'P', 'E', 'I' and 'J'.

measured, to accommodate the excess. For instance the Spinnaker Maximum Width (SMW) is 1.8 × J. If, on measurement, the largest spinnaker has a width exceeding 1.8J then JC = SMW ÷ 1.8. In the case of genoa overlap 1.5 × J is permitted and if this is exceeded then there is a penalty but it is small and does not affect JC.

Now that we have looked at the four most important elements of the rating, L,B,D and SC, we can look at DC and FC and DLF which complete the calculation of Measured Rating (MR). DC stands for Draft Correction and is a penalty or a reward for a deeper or shallower draft than the expected amount for the size of yacht. This amount is called Base Draft (DB) and is very simply L × .146 + 2ft. When the Draft Measured (DM) is greater than DB the correction is positive and vice versa. In recent years designers have grown to recognise the value of increased draft, particularly for close quarters windward racing, and a positive DC of anything up to 0.3ft has become usual.

Freeboard Correction (FC) operates on much the same basis. Base Freeboard (FB) is .57L + 1.2ft and any excess in Freeboard Measured (FM) is rewarded by a negative FC. FM is calculated as being

$$\frac{1.2FF \text{ (Freeboard Forward)} + .8 \text{ FA (Freeboard Aft)}}{2}$$

The majority of modern designs have a negative, in other words beneficial, Freeboard Correction.

Displacement Length Factor (DLF) is the final multiplier in the calculation of MR. It is intended to penalise those yachts whose displacement is less than a prescribed amount in relation to their length and to do so increasingly severely as the displacement gets smaller. The calculation of the Base Displacement Ratio (BDR) is not a pretty sight unless you have the benefit of a reasonably good calculator.

$$BDR = \frac{(2.165L^{0.525} - 5.85)^{0.375}}{(L \times B \times MDIA)^{0.125}}$$

The only one of these items that has not been mentioned in this chapter is MDIA which is the Mid Depth Immersed Adjusted. It is in fact a stepping stone in the calculation of Rated Depth (D). It is a value based on the three immersed depths of the Mid Section only. For the purpose of calculating DLF the value of BDR is never taken as less than 1.0.

By comparison with BDR, the DLF formula looks relatively harmless.

$$DLF = 1 + 5.7 (BDR - 1.0)^{1.75}$$

from which it can be seen that, if BDR is 1.0, DLF will be 1.0 also and the MR will be unaffected. The value of DLF is not to be taken as greater than 1.1. It should be said that at that value it would be a bitter pill to swallow for any yacht.

The Measured Rating (MR) is not quite the end of the rating process because there is still one more calculation required to arrive at the Rating (R).

$$R = MR \times EPF \times CGF \times MAF \times SMF \times LRP \times CBF \times TPF \times CSF$$

The last six factors are all intended as penalties for unusual features and as far as this article is concerned they are best forgotten. Suffice to say that their full titles are Movable Appendage Factor (MAF), Spar Material Factor (SMF), Low Rigging Penalty (LRP), Centre Board Factor (CBF), Trim Penalty Factor (TPF) and Crew Stability Factor (CSF). None of these six is ever less than 1.0 so they can never be turned to advantage. If your yacht has no trim tab, no carbon fibre in the mast, no more than three sets of crosstrees, and the centreboard, if any, comes out of a stub keel, then the four factors can probably be ignored. TPF is a new factor introduced to penalise those boats which have been measured on shore at an angle of fore and aft trim that is widely different to that found afloat. Because of the increasing emphasis on placing crew weight as far outboard as possible and keeping them there perpetually whilst racing, the ITC has introduced a new factor to apply to yachts measured after January 1986. This is a Crew Stability Factor (CSF) and applies a penalty to low freeboard, ultra wide, flared hulls that are coupled to light displacement. This places a limitation on BMAX and Beam at the Aft Inner Girth Station.

The other two factors, CGF and EPF, are much more important and have a very powerful influence on the final rating.

The Centre of Gravity Factor (CGF) is related to the Tenderness Ratio (TR) and is intended to measure the sail carrying power of the yacht. Some will say it rewards tenderness, others that it penalises stiffness. It depends on your viewpoint. It is a very controversial part of measurement and rating. It is not the intention of this article to take sides or express opinion, so let us concentrate on the mechanics and arithmetic involved.

The measurer obtains a Righting Moment (RMC) by physical experiment afloat. This is done by hanging cans of water on the end of a spinnaker pole rigged off the topsides at right angles to the centreline and measuring the changes of angle of heel. The formula for TR (Tenderness Ratio) is:

$$TR = \frac{0.97L \times (BWL)^3}{RMC}$$

Noting that the Beam Waterline is cubed, it will be realised what a significant factor it is in the calculation.

Having arrived at a value for TR there are then a variety of calculations for the establishment of CGF. If the yacht has an age date not earlier than 11/1984 and if TR is less than 35 then there is a formula that is related to Rated Length for the calculation of CGF. The calculation is so arranged that a TR of just less than 32 will give a minimum CGF of 0.9680 for a maxi rater, while a mini-tonner will have the same CGF for a TR of a little over 28.0.

If the age date is before 11/1984 then a different formula gives a notable benefit and allows a smaller minimum CGF depending on L.

If the TR is 35.0 or over an increasingly penal calculation of CGF applies, which is to be avoided if at all possible.

The Engine and Propeller Factor (EPF) is a straightforward compensation for the disadvantages of carrying the weight of the auxiliary engine and the drag of a propeller while racing. EPF is calculated from the Engine Moment Factor (EMF) and the Drag Factor (DF), and is never taken as less than .9600.

$$EPF = 1 - (EMF + DF)$$

EMF is the product of the Engine Weight (EW) and its distance away, forward or aft, from the Mid Depth Station. It is rightly argued that carrying the engine towards the ends of the boat is more detrimental to performance than carrying it centrally close to the fore and aft centre of pitching rotation. EMF will be applied to an outboard motor in its stowed position although in this case DF will be zero. The EMF is also related to L, B and D so that the factor is proportional to size. A 20hp diesel in a Half Tonner will receive a generous allowance compared with the same engine installed in an Admiral's Cup Yacht. Drag Factor (DF) is calculated on the diameter and type of the propeller and the depth of its installation below the water. Whether this depth significance is properly weighted is a moot point. The writer has not yet seen any convincing evidence that, once a propeller is fully submerged below the hull, the drag is increased so directly in relation to its depth. Allowance for propeller diameter is limited to 5% of L and the factor is multiplied by the Propeller Factor (PF), which is specified according to type. The smallest PF is 0.35 and applies to a folding propeller not on an exposed shaft and the highest, and therefore most rewarding, is 2.05 which applies to a fixed propeller on an exposed shaft. To qualify as an exposed shaft installation, several requirements concerning the length of shaft exposed and the dimension of the strut, or P bracket, supporting it, must be satisfied. For serious racing most designers favour a maximum diameter folding propeller on an exposed shaft which, with the average layout, will probably give an EPF between .9700 and .9750.

The study of these principal ingredients in the IOR mixture is necessarily an over simplification of the subject. There is not a lot more to be said about Rated Beam, Rated Depth and Rated Sail Area, except to study the small print and the arithmetic in more depth and identify the design features that will produce the best values.

21

Advanced IOR

In the previous chapter we studied the framework of the IOR as being the application of the four main elements – Rated Length (L), Rated Beam (B), Rated Depth (D) and Rated Sail Area (SC). Of these four, Rated Length is far and away the most contentious. It is also the one element that is still open to manipulation, with a variety of options available to the designer. It is this variety of approach to the problem of balancing speed characteristics with rating penalties that accounts for the obvious difference in the shape of the yachts in the racing fleets.

This chapter is therefore devoted to the subject of Rated Length and, as this is an absolute rabbit warren of algebraic formulas, there is no way that the subject can be dealt with without some fairly complicated descriptions.

We saw in the last chapter that L is obtained by taking the Length Between Girths (LBG) and subtracting from it the Forward Overhang Component (FOC) and the Aft Overhang Component Corrected (AOCC). The latter is not infrequently negative in which case its subtraction is really an addition.

Let us deal with FOC first, because compared with AOCC, it is relatively simple. Please note the word relatively.

The measurements for the calculation of FOC are taken in the Forward Girth Station (FGS) and the Forward Inner Girth Station (FIGS). FGS is at the point where the girth is 0.5B and FIGS at the point where the girth is 0.75B. Girths are measured in the vertical plane from the sheerline down to the centreline and back up to the sheerline on the other side. The beam on deck is measured in each station and is called Beam Forward (BF) and Beam Forward Inner (BFI). Finally the freeboard is measured in each station, Forward Freeboard (FF) and Forward Freeboard Inner (FFI). Girth Station Difference Forward (GSDF) is the fore and aft distance between FGS and FIGS, (opposite).

The intention of the rule is to establish an imaginary line below the

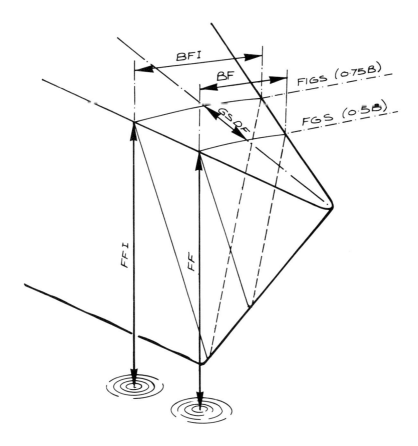

The elements of FOC (Forward Overhang Component) and the measurements required to compute it before it is subtracted from LBG (Length between Girths).

bows which cuts the water plane. This line passes through points in each station that are half the girth at that station plus 5% of B, less 15% of the local beam, below the sheerline (page 230). In the formulas the amounts are expressed as heights above the water, hence the expression FF – 0.3B + 0.15B. which describes the height of the line above the water at FGS. The 0.3B is half the girth,0.25B,plus 0.05B. The height above the water in FIGS is FFI – 0.425B + 0.15BFI and this quantity is quite likely to be negative because the point is often below the water in practice. To find the difference in height between the two points the rule subtracts the height at FIGS from that at FGS thus:

(FF – .3B + .15BF) – (FFI –.425B +.15BFI)

which simplifies to

.125B + FF – FFI – .15 (BFI – BF)

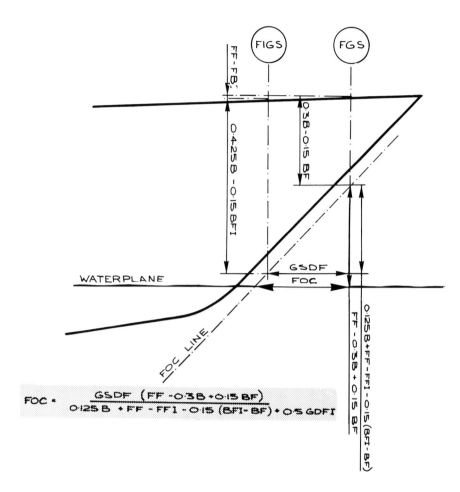

An illustration of the components of the FOC formula, FOC is the horizontal distance between FGS (Forward Girth Station) and the point at which the FOC line cuts the waterplane.

The rule then divides this amount into GSDF and, applying the law of similar triangles, multiplies by the height at FGS to obtain FOC. FOC is the horizontal distance between FGS and the point at which the FOC line cuts the water plane. The formula looks like this

$$FOC = \frac{GDSF(FF - .3B + .15B)}{.125B + FF - .15(BFI - BF)}$$

The diagram above gives a graphical illustration of the whole process at work. It should be noted that FOC has been drawn longer than GSDF. In practice the FOC point on FIGS is likely to be immersed in which case .125B + FF – FFI – .15 (BFI–BF) will be larger than FF – .3B + .15BF.

The important thing to remember is that the FOC line is fixed in relation to the profile of the yacht. In a contemporary IOR design it will be found that alterations to the sheerline resulting in increased freeboard will not affect the FOC line. Increased Freeboard results in increased girth so the two girth stations move forward thus increasing LBG. However if the proportions of the bow are simple, the FOC line will merely be extended through the revised girth stations and will continue to cut the water plane in the same place. LBG and FOC will be increased by equal amounts and L will be unchanged.

There is, in fact when you read the rule book, one further item called Girth Difference Forward Inner (GDFI) which occurs only when there is a hollow in the profile in which the normal position of FGS would occur. For these purposes it is best ignored. There is also a provision that effectively prevents FOC from exceeding 1.5GSDF.

Experience shows that the whole concept of FOC is in general very fair. Very few new designs have any fullness in the bow sections so that the strongest influence on FOC is the flare of the bows, represented by the Beams in relation to the half girths, which between them represents three sides of a triangle. In the writer's opinion there is no worthwhile means of gaining any rule advantage in the bow. You get what you pay for and a fast bow will cost more in rated length than a slow one.

Before diving into the ramifications of AOCC it would be as well to reflect for a moment on the importance of the 'ends' in the design of a successful racing boat. Forward one wants a fine entry, straight water lines, and a happy balance between a destroyer bow, which will not dampen pitching sufficiently, and a very flared bow, which will absorb too much energy when pitching.

At the aft end of the yacht, a steep rise is fine at low boat speeds, but self defeating at high speeds. In general, with the modern high performance light displacement types a slack profile suitable for high speeds off the wind is the most sought after condition. In addition, the designer generally wants to retain a reasonable degree of fullness in the stern so that, at high relative hull speeds, there is an ample reserve of buoyancy in the stern, to support the yacht, as the trough amidships tends to rob the hull of its original support in static trim. It is these two features, slackness of profile and fullness of section, that the rule aims to measure, as speed characteristics, in determining the aft end of Rated Length (L); by the application of the Aft Overhang Component Corrected (AOCC).

AOCC is a combination of two separate but interrelated overhang components. When the rule originated, it measured the Aft Overhang Component Girth (AOCG) and the Aft Overhang Component Profile (AOCP), took the average, and that was AOC. Unfortunately it became obvious that great gains could be made by playing one component off against the other.

The two components, AOCG and AOCP, are found, in the same way as FOC, by drawing imaginary lines below the profile. In the case of the stern, the slopes of the lines are measured first and called Aft Girth Slope (AGSL) and the Aft Profile Slope (APSL). Both of these can be found listed on an up to date rating certificate. The slopes are expressed as co tangents, of the angles between the AOCG and AOCP lines and the waterplane. They are, in fact, gradients and a large number is a more gentle slope than a small one.

AGSL refers to the 'imaginary AOCG line' that passes through the two girth stations at a point below the hull equal to half the girth minus 20% of the beam in that station. To arrive at this we need to look at the definition of the two girth stations. The Aft Girth Station is, in practice, nearly always at the point where the sheerline ends and the transom begins. The Half Girth Length Aft (HGLA) is made up of half of 75% of B plus half of the excess which is called Girth Difference (GD). If the full girth at this point is less than 75% B, AGS moves forward along the sheerline until the girth becomes 75% B and GD is then entered as zero. This is not the description in the Rule Book, which was written when a GD of zero was normal. It is the description that more accurately relates to the current designs. The diagram (below) shows the meaning of HGLA = 0.5 (.75B + GD).

The Aft Inner Girth Station (AIGS) used to be at the point where the girth amounted to 0.875B + GD. Nowadays that is the case only if the Girth Station Difference Aft (GSDA) is greater than 0.1 (B + GD). When GSDA would be less than this amount then AIGS is re-located at the exact point 0.1(B + GD) forward of AGS and the Girth is measured at that point and becomes the Girth Length Aft Inner (GLAI). For the purpose of the calculation the Half Girth Length Inner (HGLI) is

This drawing illustrates the composition of the total girth in AGS (Aft Girth Station). GD may be zero.

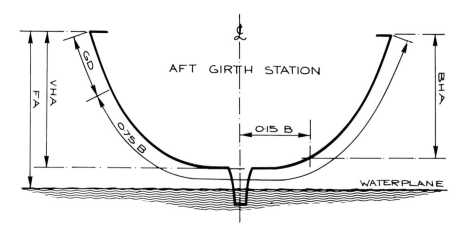

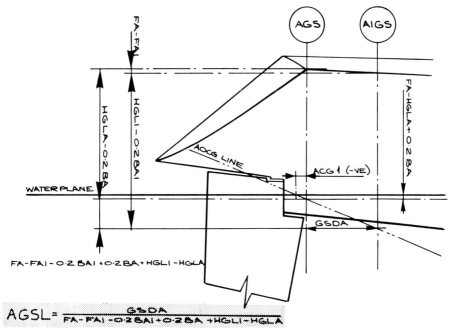

Illustrates the way in which AGSL (Aft Girth Slope) is obtained.

either 0.5 (0.875B + GD) or 0.5GLAI whichever is the greater. In fact GLAI will only occur if it is greater. The Freeboards at AGS and AIGS are FA and FAI respectively.

It is now possible to draw a diagram, (above) showing the construction of AGSL. The point at which the imaginary AOCG line passes through AGS is at a distance below the sheer of HGLA – 0.2BA. BA is Beam Aft measured across the deck on AGS and BAI is its equivalent on AIGS. The point at which the line passes through AIGS is HGLI – 0.2BAI below the sheer. The difference in the two heights is divided into GSDA to arrive at the co-tangent of the angle between the sloping line and the water, thus

$$AGSL = \frac{GSDA}{FA - FAI - 0.2BAI + 0.2BA + HGLI - HGLA}$$

APSL is the slope of the line that is 1.8% of the Length Between Girths Corrected (LBGC) below the profile of the yacht. LBGC is an adjustment to LBG to approximate to the length that should exist if the hull was extended until GD was zero. If GD is zero then LBGC = LBG. In order to draw the imaginary AOCP line we need to look at the way in which the profile mentioned above is measured. Two measurements, Vertical Height Aft (VHA) And Vertical Height Aft Inner (VHAI), are considered to represent the vertical dimension between the sheerline and the profile in each station. In simplified terms VHA is measured as the lowest point on the hull in AGS (see below) except that if, as is likely, there is a skeg in way of the girth station then it is measured at a point 4% of B away from the centre, the angle of the hull surface is measured at that point, and the theoretical height on the centre line is obtained by calculation. On a hull with no skeg and no hollow in the profile aft of AIGS, VHAI is measured on the centreline. This is, nowadays, a fairly rare condition and the alternative is to draw a buttock line (parallel to the centre) at 15% of B away from the centre, and to measure the difference in height as it passes AGS and AIGS. This difference is then added to VHA to establish VHAI. The slope of the profile line is therefore quite simply.

$$ \text{APSL} = \frac{\text{GSDA}}{\text{VHAI} - \text{VHA} + \text{FA} - \text{FAI}} $$

The fact that the line is 0.018 LBGC below the profile is not at this stage important (below).

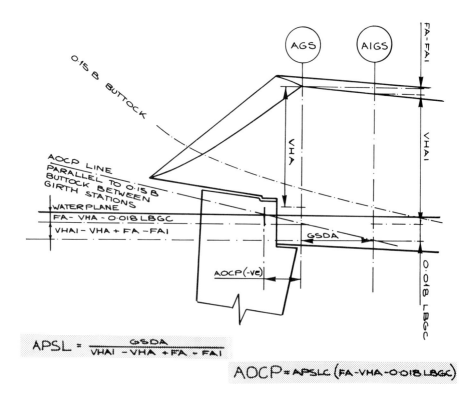

Illustrates APSL (Aft Profile Slope).

Due to the success of one or two designers, notably Laurie Davidson in New Zealand, in drawing yachts with almost completely flat profiles which nonetheless appeared reasonably steep when measured, the ITC had to invent yet another sloping line called Base Aft Profile Slope (BAPSL) to be compared with APSL. The greater of the two is then adopted as Aft Profile Slope Corrected (APSLC). The formula for BAPSL is

$$BAPSL = \frac{0.4\,(0.9LBG + GD + Y)}{CMDI + MDI + 2(FA + VHA - 2BHA)}$$

if GD, and for that matter BHA, is zero then BAPSL is taken as zero and ignored, the reasoning being that if either of these conditions existed there could be no question of APSL having an unduly artificial value. CMDI and MDI are the two depths immersed measured at one eigth B and one quarter B from the centreline on the Mid Section. Y is the length of the yacht aft of the AGS and BHA is the distance below the sheerline that the 15% buttock passes through AGS. To understand the construction of the BAPSL formula we should look at the expression 0.5 (CMDI + MDI +2(FA + VHA – 2BHA)).

If this expression is examined carefully it will be seen to represent the vertical height between the average of CMDI and MDI and the BHA measurement point (page 232), plus the amount that VHA is below BHA. The rulemakers have then divided this amount into half of a length of 90% LBG, plus GD, plus Y; so that the overhang is involved. Because there is in effect 0.5 on the top and the bottom of the fraction it cancels out. The rulemakers have then by observation of existing boats introduced a factor of 0.4 to indicate the approved angle. In other words, taking into account the depth of the mid section and length of the yacht, they consider that any APSL that is smaller, and therefore steeper, than BAPSL must be unacceptably artificial. As this sort of situation is only likely to occur with a negative AOCP the crafty designers were gaining an advantage by being able to show an artificially steep APSL. The AOCP is then calculated thus
AOCP = APSLC (FA – VHA – 0.018LBGC).

The next condition which the rule examines requires a comparison between AGSL and APSLC. This provision arose to combat the tendency led by Bruce Farr, again from New Zealand, to draw a stern in which a very slack APSL could be offset by a steep AGSL. If AGSL is equal to or greater than 80% APSLC (an acceptable situation), then the measurement of AOCG is a straightforward multiplication of the height of the imaginary AOCG line above the water at AGS multiplied by AGSL. This arrives at the distance forward or aft, depending on whether the answer is positive or negative that the AOCG line cuts the water in relation to AGS (see p 233 again). For the time being the amount is defined by ACGl = AGSL(FA – HGLA + 0.2BA)

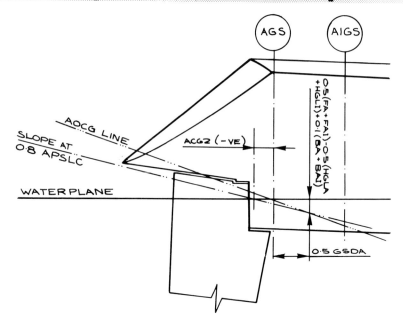

$$ACG2 = 0.8 \, APSLC \left[0.5 (FA - FAI) - 0.5(HGLA + HGLI) + 0.1 (BA + BAI) \right] + 0.5 \, GSDA$$

AGS

AIGS

AOCG LINE

SLOPE AT
0.8 APSLC

ACG2 (-VE)

0.5(FA+FAI)-0.5(HGLA
+HGLI)+0.1(BA+BAI)

WATER PLANE

0.5 GSDA

Illustrates the formula used to obtain ACG 2.

If AGSL is less than .8 APSLC then the rule says that

ACG2 = 0.8APSLC (0.5(FA + FAI) – 0.5(HGLA + HGLI) +
0.1(BA + BAI)) + 0.5GSDA

This looks fearfully complicated but what has in fact been done is that a sloping line at 80% of the profile angle has been drawn through the imaginary AOCG line midway between AGS and AIGS, and a distance measured to the intersection of the water plane. The value of half GSDA has been added back again so that ACG2 is once again measured to AGS (above).

ACG1 and ACG2 are then compared and the lesser of the two is taken as AOCG. It should be remembered that if one or both of these values is negative the lesser of the two may well be numerically greater; in other words, longer if drawn graphically.

In the good old days AOC was quite simply 0.5 (AOCP + AOCG) in other words, the average of the two. Nowadays things are no longer simple and AOC = (0.5(AOCP + AOCG) or (0.05LBG + 0.95AOCP) or (0.05LBG + 0.95AOCG) whichever is the smallest) + YCOR.

The reason for the two alternatives to the original formula is yet another effort to close up a loophole, this time attributable to our very own Stephen Jones. In yachts with positive values of AOC, a very large positive AOCP was being traded against a small negative AOCG.

YCOR is introduced so that, basically, an unacceptable penalty is placed on any yacht with a Y larger than 15% LBG. When it was introduced in November 1980 this rule resulted in the immediate application of a sharp saw across the stern of several yachts, particularly among the French level raters.

Having established AOC the end has still not quite been reached until AOCC has been established. If AOC is positive it must not exceed 1.25GDSA, if it does AOCC = 1. 25GSDA. If AOC is negative and Y is small so that AOC + Y is still negative (the J24 for instance) then AOCC is negative with its absolute value the greater of the absolute values of 0.6 AOC or Y. In all other circumstances AOCC = AOC.

Within the calculations of AOCC are a number of limitations which the writer has chosen to ignore until now, because they would only heap confusion upon confusion. They can now be listed separately.

If APSL is negative it shall be taken as 6.0 positive.

APSLC shall not be taken as greater than 7.0.

If (FA – VHA – 0.018LBGC) is negative APSLC

shall not be taken as greater than 6.0.

If (FA – VHA – 0.018LBGC) is positive.

APSLC shall not be taken as   greater than 4.0.

Now that FOC and AOCC have been established we should remember that Rated Length is L = LBG – FOC – AOCC and this shows that a high positive value of FOC or AOCC is very desirable. However desirable it may be, high positive values are usually associated with a long LBG.

The point that should now be made is that the designer controls the placing of AGS by the angle and curvature of the transom. He can place it well aft and hope to achieve a high positive value for AOCC, or he can place it well forward and hope to keep the resulting negative AOCC as small as possible.

Looking back over the formulas it is not difficult to identify the important features. For the calculation of AOCG, it is obvious that a large GD is an expensive feature, but designers have long since given up trying to pinch the stern to reduce L. The value of girth aft in light displacement yachts is now undisputed. That same girth must be offset if possible by a large BA, which is why the typical IOR section is so flared in the upper half of the topsides. As far as AOCP is concerned the most critical dimension of them all is VHA. All IOR-conscious designers make some effort to reduce VHA, if at all possible. To be more specific it is the height between the VHA point and the water (the value of FA – VHA) which is really important. This accounts for the very common appearance of a hull that appears to have been booted very hard just under the aft end of the deck. It also accounts for the preoccupation with presenting a light stern at the time of measurement in order to achieve the maximum value for FA.

Anyone who can fight his way through all of this rigmarole and find a new loophole will undoubtedly have his name in lights for a while. If the loophole is too good then a further complication to the rule will undoubtedly be invented, and that name will be added to those of Farr, Davidson and Jones for whom special clauses have been written to prevent their success being too long enjoyed.

The days were when L could be tackled on a simple calculator. Nowadays AOCC alone requires at least 340 programme steps on a Hewlett Packard and is much better understood if it can be studied on a more sophisticated mini computer.

To return to a final and more serious note of warning; this has been written with the object of making the relevant clauses in the rule book more intelligible. Whether it succeeds or not, it is the book that counts and some of the small print has necessarily been glossed over. If there is any intention to apply the rule to a specific design then acquire the book and make sure that you read the small print very carefully.

22

Old IOR

IOR MARK IIIA was introduced in 1976 as an alternative formula to be applied to yachts of 1972 or earlier. For several years the age date moved on each year, so that an owner could expect his yacht to qualify when she became four years old or so. However, this process was too simple to be safe, and it soon became apparent that there were going to be yachts gaining benefits that would nullify the advantage that their earlier counterparts has been intended to enjoy.

Up to around 1973/4 the general trend of design under IOR Mk III was to draw larger and larger yachts for a given rating. Generous displacement and fine ends contributed to quite subtstantial yachts for each rating band. This was the heyday of Sparkman and Stephens and Dick Carter, and a (27.5ft rating) One Tonner might displace as much as 17,000lb. Then along came Doug Peterson with 'Ganbare' and 'Gumboots' and Ron Holland with 'Golden Apple' and suddenly the big boats were out-of-date overnight. Displacement dropped by about 30% and little boats were running rings round big ones. Since then we have, of course, seen the 12,000lb One Tonner become outdated as the dinghy influence has crept up the fleet, and higher potential speeds have become more commonplace.

The rulemakers had to make a more accurate analysis on an historical basis and abandon the simple idea of moving dates on each year. As will be seen later, three separate divisions have been defined. The mathematics have, however, been designed to identify the types that the rule has no inclination to assist, and reduce their benefits progressively, so that, in many cases, they are back to square one and their Mk III rating applies.

All rating certificates have printed on them the age date and series date of the yacht. The series date applies to production yachts and refers to the date of the launching of the first of the type. Mk IIIA is related to the hull date which is the same as the age date, unless an earlier series date exists, which will then apply; except that, if a hull has been modified, the modified hull date applies. This, in effect, means that a new Contessa 32 will have a 1971 hull date, with all the benefits that go with it, because the original Contessa 32 was launched in 1971.

There are several points relating to the IOR Mk IIIA which are worth stating at the very outset. The first is that MK IIIA is never taken as being greater than 100%, nor less than 85% of Mk III for yachts earlier than 1982 and 96.8% for those with hull dates of January 1982 or later. The second factor, is that there are no additional measurements required and L, B and D are determined by exactly the same process.

The changes occur in the measurement of sail area and in the use of a different formula for Measured Rating.

It will help the reader if it is made clear that Mk IIIA values are identified by adding an A. Thus R is Mk III Rating, RA is the Mk IIIA Rating. In the same way Mk IIIA involves fresh values for MR, SC, DLF, CGF, and CBF, which become MRA, SCA, DLFA, CGFA and CBFA.

Mk IIIA is applied to some extent to all yachts. There are in fact three divisions by age and the benefits are potentially greatest for the oldest division. The picture looks like this ...

Division 1	Division 2	Division 3
1972 and	1973, 1974	1976 and
earlier	and 1975	later

All three divisions have their Measured Rating (MRA) calculated by the same formula which is the lesser of

$$\text{MRA} = \left(\frac{0.13L \times SCA}{\sqrt{B \times D}} + 0.25L + 0.2SCA + DC + FC \right) \times DLFA$$

which is the same as for MR except for the use of SCA and DLFA in place of SC and DLF.

$$\text{or MRA} = [SCA \left(\frac{0.0777SCA}{\sqrt{B \times D}} + 0.2216 \right)$$

$$+L \left(\frac{0.0659L}{\sqrt[3]{L \times B \times MDIA}} + 0.1738 \right)$$

$$+ DC + FC] \times DLFA$$

It is this second option which is of real benefit to the type of yacht that Mk IIIA was intended to favour when it was first invented. Although it looks pretty complicated on paper, its construction is simply one of taking a figure for the sail area, which has been qualified by relating it to the Beam and Depth, and adding it to another figure for the Length, qualified by relating it to a theoretical displacement represented in part by the expression L × B × MDIA. Remember that, MDIA (Mid Depth Immersed Adjusted) is a product of the Mid Section only. The effect is a benefit for yachts with small sail areas in relation to their beam and depth and with high displacement/length ratios. Both of these tend to be characteristics of the yachts of yesteryear. In particular it favours a yacht with a low prismatic coefficient, which is not conducive to fast off the wind speeds.

MRA is converted to RA by the formula ...

$$RA = MRA \times EPF \times MAF \times SMF \times LRP \times CGFA \times CBFA \times CSF$$

The difference from the ordinary Mk III formula is the change of values to CGFA and CBFA of which we will see more in due course.

There are thus four items of variable benefit, depending on age, the Displacement Length Factor (DLFA), the Centre of Gravity Factor (CGFA), the Centreboard Factor (CBFA) and the Sail Area Value (SCA).

The two clever factors are the first and the last of these four because they are so arranged that they identify the Division 3 yachts which might gain undeserved benefit from Mk IIIA. They identify the light boats with large sail areas and factor the ratings upwards to nullify the gains that have perhaps been obtained from the MRA formula contrary to the intention of the Rule.

DLFA for a Division I yacht is 0.98. This is a straight reduction for all yachts prior to 1973. For Division 2 and 3 DLFA is calculated from the formula:-

$$DLFA = 0.98 + 5.54 \times (BDR - 0.94)^{1.92}$$

In Division 2 DLFA shall not be taken as greater than $0.5 \times (1 + DLF)$. As DLF is never less than 1.0 this effectively halves a penal DLF.

In Division 3 DLFA shall not exceed 1.1

In Division 2 and 3 DLFA shall not be taken as less than 0.98. If it has been noted that DLF is never less than 1.0 this relaxation in terms of DLFA is one more way of giving benefit to the heavier designs irrespective of age.

CGFA for Division 1 yachts is the average of the CGF and CGFM (CGF Minimum). For Divisions 2 and 3 there is a much more complicated calculation involving a Centre of Gravity Factor Corrected (CGFC). The greater the Rated Beam in relation to the sum of the immersed depths on the mid section, the larger the figure for CGFC. The larger the value of CGFC the larger the value of CGFA. So within Mk IIIA this is a penalty for being broad and shallow, which is not the type that the rule is trying to help. By instituting a minimum CGFC value of 0.5 and a maximum of 1.0, the rule ensures that the yachts in Divisions 2 and 3 receive varying benefits within the limits.

For yachts in Division 3 Centre Board Factor CBFA = CBF, so there are no benefits allowed. For yachts in Divisions 1 and 2 there are just two possible situations. If, under Mk III, CBF was calculated as being less than 1.0 then CBFA is 0.99. If CBF was equal to, or greater than, 1.0 then CBFA is 1.0. This means that for those yachts with centreboards in which the Measured Draft (MD), plus the lowest measurement point on the hull CMDI, is greater than 13% of L there is a 1% reduction in rating. For all those that suffered a CBF penalty under Mk III there is an amnesty under Mk IIIA and the penalty is forgotten.

The most complicated element of Mk IIIA is the rating of the Sail Area. The final answer that it is necessary to determine is the Mk IIIA Sail Value (SCA). In order to arrive at this we need to determine the square root of the Sail Area, which may be either SA or S depending on the rig date. We also need the Sail Area Correction Factor (SCFA), which is the Mk IIIA version of SCF under Mk III. The Sail Value (SCA) which goes into the MRA formula is either SA × SCFA or S × SCFA depending on the rig date.

To achieve an SA a yacht must have a rig date of November 1975 or earlier, a hull date of 1972 or earlier and the rig dimensions must not have been altered beyond certain limits set out in Rule 1104. If these requirements are satisfied then SATCA will vary from SATC.

Whereas, under Mk III, a single masted yacht has a Total Rated Sail Area (RSAT) which is effectively 1.1RSAF + .857RSAM, Under Mk IIIA the equivalent is 1.3RSAF + .34RSAM, except that the total cannot be less than .75RSAF + RSAM which would occur when RSAM was 83% of RSAF or greater. In other words the benefits cease to grow when the rig is unusually fractional.

Those yachts that do not qualify for SA revert to the Mk III measurement of S with no change in total correction SATC.

When we considered IOR Mk III in the first of these articles Sail Correction Factor SCF was mentioned very briefly as only having any effect on yachts with very large sail plans. Under Mk IIIA SCFA, on the other hand, is much more critical, with the exception of the yachts in Division 2 for whom SCFA = SCF. For Division 1 yachts there is a calculation for SCFA which gives a further benefit for small sail plans. In Division 3 the calculation works in such a way as to increase SCFA above 1.0 for yachts with relatively large sail plans.

Once the application of SCFA is critical the complications of calculation become much more involved. Because SCFA varies with L and B and MDIA it is no longer possible to use a constant figure for sail area when experimenting with trim. Every time the freeboards change, L, and D change and in Mk IIIA sail area changes with them. It can be very time consuming if you have limited computing facilities.

Finally, readers should remember that Mk IIIA and age allowance are separate things and should not be confused. Age allowance is a percentage reduction in TMF related to the year of build without reference to the series date.

23

Time scales and age allowance

There are a great many misconceptions and false hopes centred on the handicap element of IOR racing. From time to time it is necessary to put the matter into perspective and explain the relative factors that govern the eventual handicap each yacht receives and evaluate the significance of this handicap on the water.

When the great enthusiasm for One Design racing broke upon the scene some years ago there were one or two who shook their heads wisely and pointed out the weaknesses of the system. If you fail to win in a One Design, they agreed, you can only blame yourself. If your boats are the same and the other chap is faster, then you and your crew must be the weak link.

To put this another way is to say that in handicap racing you have at least one, or even two, alternative scapegoats to cover any lack of success. Firstly, the conditions did not suit your particular boat on that day and, secondly, either your rating is far too high or the boat that beat you is enjoying a rating which is much too low. Either way your ego is allowed a little less condemnation than if you had suffered a similar defeat in apparently identical yachts.

It is a great pity that the concept of horses for courses is not better understood, particularly when it comes to major events such as the RORC races. The object of a handicap race is to give a fair chance of winning to the best yacht, which necessarily means the best comb-ination of yacht and crew. If a race could be sailed in absolutely uniform conditions of wind and tidal stream for an entire fleet, then, for the handicap to be a success, a well sailed Maxi should finish level with an equally well sailed Mini tonner on corrected time. In reality, after only three hours, the Maxi yacht will be anything up to 20 miles ahead of the Mini tonner and from then on their respective weather and tidal conditions are unlikely to correspond. Particularly in UK waters, the phenomenon of the tidal gates is bound to occur. If the big boats get past a headland before the tide turns against the smaller boats, then they are effectively separated and no handicap system can correct the injustice. By the law of averages there should be an equal number of races where the big boats are held back by a foul tide, which miraculously turns fair as the smallest boat reaches the turning mark. In just the same way, a fast race that finishes slowly in a dying wind will favour the big boats and a slow race that finishes fast will favour the smaller fry.

There are some, particularly the national press, who are so dazzled by the bru ha ha surrounding the competitors in Class I, particularly in an Admiral's Cup year, that they will only very grudgingly give credit to an overall winner if the yacht concerned comes from a smaller class.

Ocean racing is intended as a sport for the enjoyment of all those taking part and it is, in many ways, the fact that a modest entry, say in Class V, can carry off a major trophy that stimulates entries and cultivates hope at all levels.

It should not be thought that the winner of a major ocean race is just the lucky holder of the winning sweepstake ticket. Even if the Gods are for once on your side, there are always the rest of your own class to contend with. The trophy will always go to a yacht that has put in a very high performance in relation to her rating. The dedication and concentration necessary to win Class V is every bit as demanding, often in much less pleasant conditions, as those needed to win Class I.

This then is the principle that governs the concept of the overall prize winners and Class winners. There is an element of luck in winning the overall prize, but it is a means of spreading the glory in a way that is not influenced purely by size and expense. In order to compensate for this fleets are divided into classes in order to narrow the band of competition and so that, irrespective of the overall winner, it can be seen which was the best big boat and best small boat and so on.

There are two main systems of handicap racing; they are Time on Distance and Time on Time.

To operate a Time on Distance handicapping system each yacht is given a Seconds per Mile figure based on her rating and related to an estimated performance in average conditions. The advantage of the system is that everyone knows, in advance, exactly how much time they give or receive as soon as the length of the course is known. The disadvantages are that conditions, particularly on short races in British waters, are seldom average. A fast race will favour a small boat and a slow race a larger boat. The most famous race to operate on a Time on Distance handicapping system is the Whitbread Round the World race. With such very long legs it is supposed that conditions must average out and with the media interest so widespread, the system does offer more intelligble situations on a day to day basis.

In UK waters Time on Time is most universally used. Its application is governed by the policies of the RORC; not by any mandate but purely by setting an example that most other organisations have chosen to follow.

Measurement under the International Offshore Rule (IOR) results in a yacht receiving a rating expressed as a length in feet, if necessary converted from metres. This rating is shown on the yacht's rating certificate to four places of decimals but is finally rounded up or down to one place.

It will be seen in the section dealing with the IOR that the age of the yacht, or in the case of production yachts, the age of the original design, is taken into account in the calculation of the yacht's rating. This is not to be confused with age allowance which we will come to very shortly.

All that the IOR does is provide the rating. As performance is always taken to be related to length, this is expressed as a relative length from which a handicap can be calculated. In UK the RORC has adopted a calculation for the TMF (Time Multiplying Factor) based on the yacht's rating. It so happens that all other clubs in the country follow the RORC and use their formula for TMF. If any club or organisation felt it could invent a better formula it would be at liberty to do so. The fact of the matter is that the IOR finishes with the Rating in feet and each race committee adopts the calculation for corrected time that it considers most suitable. It so happens that no club in UK, known to the writer, does anything but accept the RORC formula as being the best available.

The RORC formula is based on the square root of the rating on the principle that speed is directly related to the square root of the waterline length. The RORC formula in 1986 was as follows:

Rating below 23.0ft TMF =

$$\frac{0.4039}{(I/\sqrt{R}) + 0.2337}$$

Rating between 23.0ft – 30.0ft TMF =

$$\frac{0.2424}{(I/\sqrt{R}) + 0.0567}$$

Rating above 30.0ft TMF =

$$\frac{R^{0.48} + 2}{7.0249}$$

There are two significant features that it should be realised are entirely premeditated in the choice of values. Firstly the TMF of a yacht with a rating of 29.0ft is 1.0000. This is the chosen scratch boat around which the calculations centre. There is, in theory, somewhere a yacht rating 29ft whose elapsed time is exactly the same as her corrected time, because her multiplying factor is 1.0. Bigger boats have TMFs in excess of 1.0, their corrected times are greater than their elapsed times and the smaller boats TMFs will be less than 1.0 and their corrected times will be reduced from their elapsed. If our 29.0ft rating yacht sails round the course in 10 hours, a Maxi yacht rating 70ft, with a TMF of 1.3787, will have to sail round in less than 7 hours, 15 minutes, 12 seconds to do better. The mini tonner, rating 16.5ft with a TMF of 0.8417, must complete the course in less than 11 hours, 52 minutes, 52 seconds. To establish the correct amount of time one yacht will receive from another, follow this procedure on a pocket calculator. Enter 60 (minutes), multiply by the TMF of Yacht A and divide by the TMF of Yacht B. Subtract 60 from the answer and that is the amount of time allowance in decimal minutes between the yachts in one hour's sailing. If there is any doubt which yacht is the beneficiary then a positive answer means that Yacht A is giving B the amount of time shown and vice versa if the answer is negative.

A very simple and approximate rule of thumb is to consider that one tenth of a foot of rating is worth 4 seconds an hour or 1.5ft of rating is worth 1 minute an hour. This applies reasonably accurately to yachts of 20 to 30ft rating but at the smaller end of the scale the difference is around 50 seconds a foot of rating and about 20 seconds at 60ft rating.

This brings us to the second feature of the calculations and that is the changes in the formula at Ratings of 23.0ft and 30.0ft. If a graph of TMF against Rating is drawn there will be two kinks in the line corresponding with the changes in formula. The object is to compensate the larger boats for the planing capabilities of the smaller boats with more racing dinghy characteristics. The new formula for Ratings of 30.0ft and above has been introduced for the 1986 season and is intended to counter the concentration of boats at the lower limit of the Admirals Cup band.

Now we come to the question of Age Allowance, which it has already been said is nothing to do with the IOR. In exactly the same way as TMF, age allowance is entirely at the discretion of the organising club. Once again this means in fact that the RORC have a formula for Age Allowance and this is followed by most other clubs in UK. The current calculation is as follows:-   A deduction of 0.15% of TMF per year to a maximum of 4.35% using the formula given below may be allowed to any yacht launched before 31st December 1981.

$$0.15 \ (1982 - \text{year of launch}) = \text{age allowance}.$$

So the yacht launched in 1981 gets 0.15% from her TMF and the yacht launched in 1953 or earlier gets the maximum reduction of 4.35%. To the unmathematical it should be explained that a multiplying factor of 0.9038 (Half ton rating 22.0ft) is the same thing as 90.38%. Thus a 1981

Half Tonner with a deduction of 0.15% has a corrected time of 90.23% of elapsed time or a TMF of 0.9203.

The justice or injustice, depending on your viewpoint, of age allowance is a thorny issue. The fact of the matter is that there are good age allowance yachts which, if well sailed, will be very hard to beat in certain weather. There are those who consider that this is grossly unfair on the owners of brand new expensive designs who should be allowed a proper return for their investment. There are others, the writer included, who take wholly the opposite view. Success should depend on a good boat being sailed well and one of the biggest disincentives to IOR racing is the feeling that there are those that can afford new boats every year and they will mop up all the prizes.

One of the vital factors in winning races is the state of the gear particularly the sails. Age allowance is not prejudiced by re-equipment and a number of older boats have remained competitive through the regular use of funds to keep the rig and sail wardrobe in line with new developments. The provision of age allowances maintains second hand values of older boats and can only be a healthy arrangement.

When one considers a production yacht, Age Allowance is applied in relation to the individual launch date of each yacht, whereas the IOR rating is calculated on the date of the first hull launched.

So, if you buy a new Contessa 32, launched in 1986, you will obtain all the benefits of Mk IIIA and your rating will be based on the same hull measurements as the earliest boats built in 1971. Your new boat will not however get the age allowance. Whereas your rating might be identical with the original boat, that boat will have $11 \times 0.15\%$ deducted from her TMF and your new boat will not. The time allowance between the newest and the oldest boats works out at roughly 50 seconds an hour. The Contessa 32 is an exceptional case because it is something of an evergreen and has had a longer life span in production than most others. The fact remains that the owner of the original boat can buy a brand new suit of Grand Prix sails and replace any worn out gear and may come to the starting line in better shape than the new boat owner who may have had to buy his sails from a more modest supplier in less exotic materials.

What does all this amount to on the water? Owners worry a great deal about ratings, particularly when another owner of a similar boat is 0.1ft or so better off than them. Obviously if there is an anomaly on your rating certificate it should be corrected if possible and the benefits gained. However, small differences are far less serious than is sometimes thought to be the case.

If two yachts rate 20.9 and 21.0 their TMFs will be .8927 and .8937 respectively. The difference is 0.1% or 3.6 seconds an hour. Four knots is the equivalent of 6.75ft per second so that 3.6 seconds represents just under 25ft or less than one length. It follows that the yacht rating 20.1ft must be one length ahead for every hour sailed in order to win. If two boats are so closely matched that they regularly finish this close then attacking the rating has got to be approached with the utmost caution. To save 0.1ft of rating without making 0.1% reduction of performance is not easy if sails have to be re-cut or trim altered. In the past many nice boats have been spoiled in search of rating improvements. Piling lead into the bows can have a magic effect on rating in certain designs. It can, however, have a far from magic effect on handling and performance in a seaway.

There are many ways of looking at handicaps and deciding how important they are. In a short race, for instance, lasting two hours, a good start that puts your boat two lengths ahead of your opponent the first time you cross tacks, is worth a tenth of a foot of rating. Two seconds saved each time you tack is worth a tenth after only four tacks. A slick spinnaker hoist at the weather mark that gives you an immediate build up to full speed can be worth another four seconds, or yet another tenth on a twice round course. At the leeward mark a late drop, but a clean one, can double that gain. What the writer is trying to encourage is the thought that the time to worry about a tenth of a foot of rating improvement is when all other aspects of your racing are within 99.9% of the best you can hope for, then if you still need 0.1% improvement, start work on your rating by all means.

As a passing thought, take the results of a recent J 24 race off Lymington racing level as One Designs. The winning boat had an elapsed time of 2 hours, 41 minutes, 32 seconds, the boat that was tenth out of 18 starters had a time of 2 hours, 47 minutes, 20 seconds, nearly six minutes behind. This is a performance of 96.5% of the winner. If the boats had been equally well sailed the difference in performance corrected into equivalent ratings would have been over 3ft. In other words, if the winner had been sailing to a rating of 21.7ft, the boat coming tenth, in the middle of the fleet, would have needed a rating of 18.5ft to compensate for the difference in performance on the water.

Index